MICHAEL
REAGAN

ZEBRA BOOKS

are published by

Kensington Publishing Corp.
475 Park Avenue South
New York, NY 10016

First printing: April, 1988

Printed in the United States of America

MICHAEL REAGAN

ON THE OUTSIDE LOOKING IN

WITH
JOE HYAMS

ZEBRA BOOKS
KENSINGTON PUBLISHING CORP.

To my wife Colleen,
who has really been my strength.
To Cameron and to Ashley,
whom I love dearly.

Prologue

I am the adopted son of Ronald Reagan and Jane Wyman. My adoptive parents were actors, skilled in the art of communication. But when I look back on my life the episodes I remember most vividly have to do with a failure to communicate.

I was born forty-two years ago, the result of a romantic liaison between a twenty-eight-year-old Kentucky farm girl—one of ten children—and a married Army Air Force cadet. The odds against an adoptee ending up as a child of the President of the United States are staggering. But then, so are the odds against a movie actor becoming president.

I grew up convinced that my birth mother gave me away because she didn't love me and I was bad. It is a terrible thing to go through life thinking that you have been chosen to feel the wrath of God. But that was my childhood lament.

At the age of seven I was sexually molested by a camp counsellor. I told no one. Jane and Ronald were divorced by then, and I suffered alone and in silence as I have all the other traumas of my life. It is only in the light of recent discovery that I have come to realize that my memory has been selfishly selective. My parents—birth as well as adoptive—were not villains, and I hobbled through my early years on the crutches of adoption and sexual abuse.

In March, 1987 I decided to tell Jane about the molestation incident before she read it in this book which I was then writing. I called her at home one afternoon before she left for the studio where she is the star of *Falcon Crest,* a successful television series. When she said "Hello," I pictured her in her book-lined study overlooking the Pacific, impatiently tapping her fingers on the desk at the sound of my voice.

"I was just leaving for the studio," she said.

"I have to talk with you, Mom," I said.

"Michael, we're working overtime because a directors' strike is imminent. I'm just too busy to talk with you. Tell me whatever it is that you want to say on the phone."

I recognized the wearied, forced patience in her voice. I had demanded her attention too many times in the past for her to take me seriously now. But this was different. For the first time I wasn't conning her. "I have to see you face to face," I said.

"I don't have the time," Mom replied firmly.

I couldn't tell her on the phone, and so I hung up.

To a large extent that's the story of my life with Mom. When I was a child, she was so busy with her film career that following established practice among many Hollywood families, she farmed me out to boarding schools. Now in her seventies, her career has been resurrected but time stands still. She is still too busy for me.

Meanwhile, the news magazines reported that my book would

be a "Daddy Dearest." They also claimed it would be a devastating account of my life with the First Family.

Nancy telephoned me at home. "Your Dad doesn't need another book written by a family member," she said, referring to their daughter Patti's recent novel about a fictional first family.

"I'm not writing a 'Daddy Dearest,'" I said defensively. "I want to write a book about my life, not Dad's."

"We've read the publicity in *Newsweek,* and your father is upset."

"Put him on the phone, please."

Dad came on the telephone.

"If anything my book is a 'Michael Dearest,'" I said. "When it's written, I'll send the manuscript to you before publication, so you won't be surprised by anything that's in it. If you have any questions or problems then, we can talk them over."

Dad seemed mollified. "The press is probably playing off of Patti's novel," he said. "I hope yours will be different."

"It will be," I promised.

When I spoke with Mom later in the week, she said tartly, "I've read about your book. When are you going to stop living off your father's name? I can't believe you have anything to say at this time in your life that's worth reading." I still couldn't bring myself to tell her on the phone about the shame I had lived with for so long.

Nevertheless, I knew I had to tell Dad about the molestation incident before he read it in the manuscript. I owed it to him.

It was about this time that he and Nancy invited my wife Colleen and our children to celebrate Palm Sunday and my daughter Ashley's fourth birthday at the Santa Barbara ranch. I'd had a stormy relationship with the First Family for the past few years, and it was to be the first birthday either Ashley or eight-year-old Cameron would spend with Grandma and Grandpa Reagan. It would be the first time that we would be alone together as one family.

That afternoon at the ranch I was uncomfortable and tense as we all gathered around Ashley and a big cake set up on the dining-room table. Everyone chatted amiably and smiled as my petite daughter blew out the candles—a moment recorded for posterity by the ubiquitous White House photographer.

After Ashley opened her birthday presents, Nancy suggested that Colleen take the kids for a walk around the pond. "We have something to talk about with Michael," she said. Nancy had picked up on something in my behavior that alerted her to my inner turmoil. More than the rest of the family, Nancy often perceives what is going on beneath the surface when others, including Dad, are completely oblivious. It's one of the things that makes her a remarkable person; it can also make her dangerous to those with something to hide. I have always been intimidated by Nancy because I feel she can see right through me.

Colleen, who knew what I intended to tell my parents, squeezed my hand encouragingly and cupped my face for a kiss.

Nancy, Dad and I found a spot to ourselves. Dad gazed into the distance. He has always deferred to the women in his life, and this occasion was no exception. He let Nancy take the lead.

"Now, Michael," Nancy said, her eyes pinning mine, "will you please give your father and me some idea about what's in the book you are writing. What's in it that we are not supposed to know?"

The moment of truth was at hand, but I did not know how to begin. Where had the trouble started? When had what should have been an idyllic childhood as the pampered son of Ronald Reagan and Jane Wyman turned into a daily nightmare? Did it begin when I was seven years old, or had it started long before then? Or was the real tragedy how I was affected in later life, as an adult still groping for acceptance, still hiding my shame from the increasingly prying eyes of the world?

I thought back, and, haltingly, I began to tell Dad and Nancy my story.

Chapter I

"You're not special . . ."

It is Easter Sunday, 1987, and I am in pew fifty-four of St. John's Church, which is known as "The President's Church" in Washington, D.C. The *prie-dieux* in front of each member of my family have the names of former presidents lettered on the petit point thus joining us with history. This is the first time I have been in the President's Pew, although I have been in the church before with my father, President Ronald Reagan, and his wife Nancy. But on this morning I am accompanied by my wife Colleen, eight-year-old Cameron and my four-year-old daughter Ashley. It is memorable for me because it is the first time that I have not felt like an imposter here. So much of what has happened between my father, Nancy, and me has finally been resolved, and yet I was unable to sleep last night, tormented by a familiar nightmare.

As the pastor delivers his message, my thoughts return to that nightmare. In it, my wife and children are walking hand in hand with me through clouds to the gates of heaven where God is standing. The gates open, and I step aside to let my family precede me. Suddenly God steps in front of me, placing His burning hand on my chest. My son Cameron turns around. "Come on, Daddy," he says impatiently and starts toward me. But God is still halting my progress. He turns his back to me and takes out my Book of Life from deep within his white robes. He opens the book and shows my family a page. His voice booms in my ears. "Michael Reagan is not allowed into heaven because he is illegitimate and he once committed a homosexual act." My wife, who knows this, starts to protest: "Michael has changed. He is a good man." God holds up his hand to quiet her. My children begin to cry as God closes the book. The gates of heaven start to shut, and I am left standing alone outside the gates, watching my loved ones disappear from sight.

When I awoke from the nightmare, my side of the bed was soaked with perspiration. I lay quietly so as not to disturb Colleen and waited until it was time to rise. But that nightmare still plagues me, and I wonder when it will end. When will I be free of the past? When will I be worthy of the name Reagan which is not really mine but which I was given at birth? And when will I have my own identity?

It's hard to learn about your parents' courtship. What I found out about mine was gleaned from snippets of stories I have read. Ronald Reagan and Jane Wyman met on the Warner Brothers Studio lot in 1937. Dad had just been signed by the studio as a contract player after a stint as a radio announcer in the Midwest. He was twenty-six years old, tall, handsome, muscular, and unmarried. Mom was reportedly smitten with him at first glance. There was only one hitch: Mom was separated from Myron Futterman, a clothing manufacturer from New Orleans whom she had been married to for only a year.

Dad and Mom were teamed together romantically in *Brother Rat*. I have seen the picture, the sixth Mom made in that year, and it's obvious that they really were attracted to each other. Knowing my old-fashioned father, however, I am certain he did not begin to get serious about Jane until she was divorced in 1939.

Years ago I came across an article co-written by Mom in *Motion Picture*, a fan magazine. Here is her description of Dad's proposal: "We were both working on a picture and were about to be called for a take," she wrote. "Ronnie simply turned to me as if the idea were brand new and had just hit him and said, 'Jane, why don't we get married?' I couldn't think of any reason why we shouldn't. I'd been wondering for a whole year—since I first saw him—why he hadn't asked me. I was just about to say a definite yes when we were called before the cameras. I managed to muff a few lines and toss in a whispered yes after the director said, 'cut.'"

They were married a month later, on January 27, 1940, at the Wee Kirk o' the Heather Church at Forest Lawn, which is more famous as a cemetery than as a place for weddings. Mom was twenty-three years old and Dad was twenty-nine.

After Maureen was born on January 4, 1941, Mom apologized to Dad for not giving him the son she knew he wanted.

It was my sister Maureen who was responsible for my becoming a Reagan. As the story goes, when she was a child, she wished for two things most in the world: a brother and a red scooter. Her parents told her she would have to save her allowance money for whatever she wanted. One day when Maureen was four years old, she went with her father to the toy department at Saks Fifth Avenue in Beverly Hills. To his surprise and mild chagrin she dumped the contents of her piggy bank on the counter and asked for a brother.

A few weeks later, her parents said they had a surprise for her. Since Maureen's hopes for a brother had been recently dashed, she expected the red scooter. Instead she saw an infant boy. Maureen really wanted an older brother, probably because she was at boarding school most of the time and she wanted a playmate. But a deal is a deal in the Reagan family, so she ran to her room and retrieved her piggy bank. She gave the lady from the adoption agency ninety-seven cents.

The story is undoubtedly apocryphal. What I am certain of, however, is that friends of my parents, Betty and Arthur Kaplan, handled the specifics of the adoption. They went to court in Los Angeles to pick me up. Arthur was a lawyer, and my parents wanted to be certain everything was completely legal. The fact that I was adopted was probably going to be withheld from me as long as possible in keeping with the custom of the time. Little did my adoptive parents know how much pain the fact that I was adopted would soon cause me.

I've often wondered why my parents added to their family by adopting a child. Although touted in the fan magazines as one of Hollywood's happiest all-American couples, there were problems with their marriage.

Mom had been making movies for ten years and was well established. She had made the transition from playing cute chorines and the leading lady's best friend to starring dramatic roles. While Dad was still in the Armed Services, she blossomed into a major star as a result of her role as Ray Milland's fiancée in *The Lost Weekend*. Dad, who had just returned from the Army, had played romantic leads in some fifty films and was considered

14

King of the B Movies—this, despite what many critics consider his best acting role in *King's Row*. In one scene which still brings tears to my eyes when I see it, he awakens in a hospital room to find his legs have been needlessly amputated. Although he was the bobbysoxer's hero, the Michael J. Fox of his day, his career was at a standstill, and Mom was the principal wage earner of the family. Also, Dad was beginning to get involved in politics through his involvement with the Screen Actors' Guild. I know my mother was as bored with politics then as she is today. I suspect that like many young couples at the time they thought another child might help their worsening relationship.

After Maureen was born the doctor told Mom she could not have any more children; Maureen's birth had been too difficult. Apparently, she and Dad wanted a son just as Maureen wanted a brother, though perhaps not an infant who would be doted on and who would steal love and attention from her.

I was three days old when I was adopted. Around four years ago, I received in the mail from Dad's former business manager a hundred dollar War Bond accompanied by a letter that said the bond was "in celebration of your coming home." The bond was bought on April 4, 1945 by Ronald Reagan for Michael Edward Reagan. Receiving that bond took me back forty years in time. I realized that my dad must have loved me dearly, if only I had known it during my childhood.

My adoption was treated as a celebration. Tommy, the head waiter at Chasen's, my parents' favorite restaurant, still tells me, "I was there the day you came home." Lew Wasserman, Dad's film agent, once told me he was also at the house. (Lew is now Chairman of the Board and Chief Executive Officer of MCA, which operates Universal Studios; but at that time he was an agent, and Dad was his first client.)

Unfortunately, there was a lot of mention in the fan magazines about the Reagans' new adopted son. I was very soon to become aware of the fact that in the eyes of many people, there is a stigma to being adopted.

From time to time I have tried to learn about the background of my adoptive parents. For forty-one years Mom has led me to believe that she was found on a doorstep in Missouri and grew up in a variety of foster homes, but I have recently read differently. While writing this book, I asked her for some answers. "Look them up in an encyclopedia," she snapped. My mother has consistently refused to talk with me about my book, believing that it was going to be a "Mommie Dearest," but then she refused to talk to any writers for years.

I know her given name is Sarah Jane Fulks, and I once saw a picture of people who I thought were her parents; but she has always refused to discuss them. I have always suspected that she is hiding some dark secret, because her mouth snaps shut like a mousetrap whenever I ask about the past. If you ask her what happened yesterday, she'll say, "I don't know. What's happening tomorrow?" She combines a positive outlook for tomorrow with a negative recall of her childhood.

I do remember that back in the early sixties, she told me she was invited to St. Joseph, Missouri, where she had been raised, for the opening of The Jane Wyman Theater. According to her, she refused and suggested to the sponsors that they name the theater after another important person who had come from St. Joe—the bank robber Jesse James.

It has been almost as difficult to find out about the Reagan side of my family. I am glad Dad ran for public office because, of the few things I know about the Reagans, most were culled from books and articles written as a result of Dad's success in politics.

Dad has an older brother Neil, nicknamed Moon (because he parted his hair in the middle like the comic strip character, Moon Mullins). From stories I have heard, I know they had a ball as kids growing up in Tampico, Illinois, a little country town just twenty-seven miles from the Mississippi River, where Dad was born on February 6, 1911 above a bank converted from a bar. He had come screaming from the womb, all ten pounds of him, and his father described him as a "little bit of a fat Dutchman." Ever since birth, Dad's nickname has been Dutch.

Dad once said in a speech that his father, John Edward Reagan, who everyone called Jack, was a first generation black-Irishman and that he was an alcoholic, which is probably why Dad rarely drinks anything alcoholic today except for an occasional glass of wine. In that speech he recalled the special delivery letter his father received on Christmas Eve, 1932. The family thought it was a Christmas bonus check. Instead, it was a notice that Jack was fired from his job as a shoe salesman. When I heard that speech, I was in tears because Mom always told me how much she loved her father-in-law who, despite his drinking, was a great guy. Only recently did I read that Jack was orphaned at the age of six and shuttled among relatives.

I believe that my father remembers his childhood, but he rarely discusses it. For instance, I was forty years old before I discovered that there was somebody else in the family with my name. In a magazine article published in 1985, Moon mentioned that his grandfather's name was Michael Edward Reagan. Until then I had always been led to believe that my name was chosen because my mother wanted me to be called Michael while Dad opted for Edward. I like the story better the way Mom tells it.

In every story the family tells about Dad, he always emerges heroic. I have never heard of him doing anything wrong. There was no way a child of his, especially one who was adopted, could live up to the image of the man who never made a mistake.

I recall very little about my infancy and earliest years. We lived in a secluded residential area off Sunset Boulevard, now known as

Truesdale Estates. The house was big, with a swimming pool in the backyard. Dad had been a lifeguard for seven summers, starting when he was a teenager in Illinois, and had saved seventy-seven people from drowning in the Rock River, a tributary of the Mississippi. He was determined that I learn to swim. When I was about three years old, I was given a life jacket and some lessons. One day Dad announced to my mother that I didn't need the jacket anymore. "You're out of your mind," Mom said. Dad picked me up, took off the jacket and dropped me into the deep end of the pool. For forty years I have jokingly asked him what he expected me to do. He invariably answers, "You swam, didn't you?"

I had a nanny who was responsible for my care and feeding, and we had two Scottish terriers, Scotch and Soda, who were my first playmates. When my parents were home, they doted on me, which probably made Maureen jealous.

Since my parents worked six days a week when they were filming, Mom wanted time alone with Dad and often arranged golf and lunch for them at the California Country Club where they were members. On those weekends, Dad, who hadn't seen much of Maureen and me during the week and didn't want us to be raised by nannies and maids, would drive us over to his mother's house to spend the day.

As so often happens after a couple adopts a child, Mom got pregnant. A daughter, Christina, was prematurely born in June, 1947 and died three days later. I don't remember Mom being pregnant, nor do I recall anything about the funeral. Dad was in the hospital with pneumonia when Christina died, and perhaps Mom faulted him for that in some way. In any event, the loss of a daughter must have hit Mom very hard. Even today—forty years later—Christina is still mentioned in her will.

I don't think it was a coincidence that my parents were divorced a year after Christina's death; many families seem to divorce after losing an infant child. I have read that Dad took Maureen, who was then seven, and me out to his car where he tried to explain the divorce to us, but I have no recollection of it. I only remember that suddenly he was gone from the house. Mom got custody of Maureen and me and kept the two-story colonial-style house they had recently bought on the edge of Beverly Hills. Dad moved into an apartment in Hollywood and became a weekend father with visitation rights.

I looked forward to Saturday mornings when I would go outside at ten o'clock and sit on the curb with anticipation, looking for Dad's red station wagon. When I saw it, I would yell to Maureen or whichever friend was going with us to hurry because Dad was there to take us to his ranch in Northridge, California, an hour's ride from Beverly Hills on a single-lane highway. It wasn't a ranch like the Ponderosa of television fame. There was only a one-room shack on Dad's acreage where he and his foreman, Nino Peppetone, raised thoroughbred horses.

When we were in the station wagon, I usually sat between Dad and Maureen, and we played car games like Beaver. In those days many station wagons had paneled sides of wood like Dad's; today they are called "woodies." One of us shouted "Beaver" every time he or she saw a wagon. The one who saw the most by the time we arrived at the ranch was supposed to win the game, but Dad was the referee. No matter who won, he tried to make it a tie, just as I do today for Cameron and Ashley.

Dad sometimes tweaked my ear or patted me on the knee and called me his "little schmuck." I used to tell the kids at school that that was my Dad's nickname for me. I didn't find out what the Yiddish word meant till I was in high school.

We really had a great time being with him on those Saturdays. Most of the time we played in the farmyard with the chickens and goats and watched Nino train the thoroughbreds. Dad usually brought a picnic lunch along, and we would sit on the grass and eat while he drank his near beer.

Some Saturday nights, Dad took us to his mother's house where we spent the night. Nelle Wilson Reagan was a wonderful and loving woman with auburn hair and black eyes. She was Scots-English and Protestant as opposed to my grandfather who was Catholic. (Moon is Catholic and my Dad is Protestant.) Nelle, who had been a poetess and playwright as well as an amateur preacher, was the one who instilled a Christian attitude in the entire family. She drove Maureen and me to Sunday school in her old Studebaker, and then we'd go back to her house and have brunch. Dad would pick us up by mid-afternoon and bring us back home.

During this period, Mom's career was in full swing. She had been nominated for an Academy Award for her performance in *The Yearling* the previous year. Every day she was up at five-thirty A.M. and off to Warner Brothers Studio where she was under contract. At the time, she was starring in *Johnny Belinda,* her fifty-fifth film, in which she played a deaf-mute rape victim who has to go to court to get custody of her child. Mom gets into and stays in character for her roles. During the time she was in the film, she rarely spoke, preferring instead to use sign language. Maureen learned to sign a little, and they were able to communicate. Mom earned an Academy Award as Best Actress in 1948 for her superb performance.

I don't remember the award ceremony, but I do recall the gold statuette suddenly appearing on one of the shelves in the library. Mom has moved almost a dozen times since then, yet the statuette is always placed in the library of her home. I have seen that Oscar all through my life and, as a child, used to pick it up and admire it. Mom and I have talked about that Oscar for years. When she announces to Maureen and me that she is making out a new will and asks what we want, Maureen always opts for Mom's beautiful antique game table, but I have told her the only thing I really want is that Oscar.

When I recently repeated my request, Mom retorted, "Wouldn't you rather just have my money?" Although she doesn't seem to be particularly proud of her Oscar, in my view it is a root to the past, something I can hold on to that will become a family heirloom for my children and grandchildren. It is something that money can't buy as well as a symbol of Mom's perfection.

Maureen boarded at Chadwick School in Palos Verdes, California, and I went by bus every day to the prekindergarten class at Buckley, an exclusive school in North Hollywood. I still recall one weird moment at Buckley. I was in my jeans in the classroom, and I raised my hand and told the teacher that I had to go to the bathroom. She said, "If you have to go that bad and you can't wait, why don't you go in your pants." And that's just what I did. All over myself. She made me stay in the classroom the rest of the day in wet jeans. I learned to go to the bathroom before class.

I learned that I was adopted when I was four years old. Somehow or other I found out what Maureen was getting for her Christmas-birthday present (she was born on January 4th, so the two celebrations were often combined). Although we were at the same boarding school, we saw very little of each other during the week, and I really didn't know her. With the hope of trying to make conversation, I went into Maureen's bedroom and found her standing in front of her mirror, brushing her blond hair.

"I know a secret," I said, anticipating that she would say something like "That's real neat" and then try to worm the secret out of me.

"Don't tell me," Maureen said, "I don't want to know."

"You're getting a blue dress for your present," I said anyway.

21

I thought I was doing her a big favor, but Maureen started to cry because I had ruined her surprise. "I know a secret, too," she snapped. "You're adopted."

I didn't know what adopted meant, but the way she said it made me think it was bad, so I ran to my mother and asked what Maureen was talking about.

Mom's eyes got big and round. She didn't say anything to me, but I knew that something was wrong because she dashed out to find Maureen. I don't know what transpired between them, but later that night or the next day Mom sat me down opposite her in the living room. She explained to me that my parents couldn't give me a nice home, and they wanted the best for me, so they put me up for adoption. Then she said, "Your father and I chose you because you were just what we wanted." I was the chosen member of the family and therefore special, which back in the forties was what you were expected to tell an adopted child. It was generally assumed in those days that it was enough to give a child a roof over his head, clothes on his back and an education, thus fulfilling all the obligations of adoptive parents. I didn't really understand what Mom was talking about, but I picked up on the fact that I was chosen. I didn't make the connection that she wasn't my real mother, although there was something about her attitude that made me uneasy. Mom is not the kind of person you can get into a discussion she doesn't want to have, so I let the matter drop.

One day at school I got into an argument with a kid who claimed his daddy was better than my daddy, typical kid stuff. At some point I bragged, "I'm better than you are. I'm special because I was chosen."

"What do you mean, you were chosen?"

"I was adopted," I said proudly.

He had no more idea of what adopted meant than I did, but he must have gone home and asked his parents because, not long after that, he told me sneeringly, "You're not special; you're a bastard. Your mother didn't want you, so she gave you away."

Pretty soon the other kids were giving me little digs like: "Didn't your first parents like you?" "Is that why they gave you away?"; "Were your parents married?"; "Are you a bastard?" I didn't know the answers to the questions, and I had no idea what a bastard was until one of the other kids explained it to me. From then on I began to wonder if I was illegitimate, a word that scared me even then. It is true that many adopted kids are born out of wedlock as I now know; but I didn't realize it then, and there was no one I could ask. I knew intuitively that Mom didn't want any further discussion. I was afraid to ask my father for fear of upsetting him because I wasn't living with him and I didn't know why he had left home. I was afraid that maybe it was my fault he left because he had found out I was illegitimate. Dad and Mom were apple pie a la mode, and I was certain that if they knew I was a bastard they would never have adopted me in the first place. Also I was seeing Dad only two days a month, and I didn't want to spoil any of the time I had with him.

I never felt "special" again. For the first time, I began to feel different from the rest of the family. No matter that my mother had said I was chosen, I was insecure about my status because I didn't know whether adoptive families kept you forever or if they were able to give you back if you caused problems, as they would give a maid or nanny back. Mom went through a lot of nannies and maids at that time. As an adopted child I felt I had to earn my way into the family, but I didn't know what I had to do.

From then on I never talked about my parents to my classmates. Instead, I talked with the other kids about *their* families. I wanted to know who their parents were and what they did together as a family during the week and on weekends. I tried to learn whether my family fit into the mold of other families. Most often they didn't, so I thought maybe it was my fault. I also began to wonder who my real mother was and why she gave me away. Was it because there was something wrong with me? I worried about that a lot.

When I was six, Mom sent me to join Maureen as a boarder at Chadwick where I went to first grade. Chadwick was co-ed with separate dormitories for the boys and girls. Many of the students were day students which meant they got to go home after school. I envied the day students and cried myself to sleep at night wishing I could be home with Mom. But I knew Mom was busy; she had just completed *The Glass Menagerie,* an adaptation of the Tennessee Williams play.

Sunday mornings at Chadwick were special to me, however, because the boarders got toast served to them in bed. The toast was often burned because it was the type of toaster that opened from the sides. To this day, I like burned toast. My wife knows if she burns the toast I'm the one member of the family who will eat it. In fact, I got so accustomed to burned toast during my Chadwick days that I still love anything that is crispy and burned on the bottom, especially chocolate chip cookies.

At that time I wasn't really aware of what my parents did for a living. I knew they were famous, but I didn't know why. In those days it was very "in" to have initialled towels. Mom's towels had JWR on them. Sometimes we would drive into Beverly Hills to go shopping at JW Robinson's department store. The store had only JWR in the front, and when we went shopping there, I thought Mom owned it because everybody gave her special treatment.

It was at Chadwick that I first realized how famous my parents really were because I started getting teased by some of the other kids. I remember well a day when I was outside the dormitory playing baseball and one of the older kids picked up a baseball and said, "If your parents are so good, let's see you catch this baseball.'' He threw it at me hard and fast. My heart stopped beating as I saw the ball coming at me. I had just started to learn how to catch a ball with a glove, and, somehow or other, I got my glove up and caught it. He walked away. My hand stung for days afterward. That was the first time that I realized some people would like me or dislike me just because of who my parents were. Years later I would discover that many people would like me *only* because of my parents.

Although I was only a child, I understood that the older boy was probably jealous of me, and I felt sorry for him. After all, my parents were not only famous, but Mom was beautiful and Dad was tall, handsome, and athletic. Everybody always told me how lucky I was to have such famous parents while I always thought the other kids were the lucky ones because they got to go home to families with mothers and fathers and they went on family outings and vacations together. My parents were so well known, however, that whenever they went anywhere a crowd invariably gathered, so they rarely ever took us to ball games or any other public place. I always held that against Dad, although he did take us to the ranch, which made me the envy of some of the other kids, especially when I told them about the good times we had riding horseback there.

Maureen and I grew up very close. She was pretty, blond and had a pert nose like Mom's. She was the one person I could turn to when I had a problem, although I couldn't talk to her about my being adopted. Nevertheless, I felt that by getting on her side during occasional family arguments I would make a friend of her and I needed that. If she was angry with someone, I was angry with that person, too. Maureen was not only my older sister, but she started taking the place of my mother. I admired and emulated Maureen and followed wherever she led.

Like so many children of busy parents we missed having a normal relationship with ours because we saw each of them only a couple of days a month. Speaking for myself, I never really found out who they were, and I don't think they ever really knew me. It wasn't their fault, however. Dad was a typical weekend father who had to fit his children into a tight schedule. Mom had all the problems of a typical single parent. She not only had a full-time job but she had a big house to support and kids to raise.

I do have warm memories of some occasions with Mom, however: the time I had measles and she sat on the edge of my bed rubbing calamine lotion on my back until I fell asleep; a summer vacation in New Jersey with her friends Sonny and Lea Werblin, owners of the New York Islanders and Madison Square Garden; Maureen, Mom and I flying to New York—it was my first ride in an airplane.

That vacation was the most memorable time of my life. We stayed at a plush hotel in Manhattan where I discovered room service: A hamburger and chocolate shake were mine for the asking anytime of the day or night. We did all the tourist things, including an excursion to the top of the Empire State Building. Mom pointed out the Statue of Liberty in the distance and the next day took us there on a ferry. Merm (my nickname for Maureen) and I scrambled up the stairs to the statue's crown, leaving Mom to follow, breathless but smiling and infected with our excitement.

We went by taxi to Pennsylvania Station where we boarded the train for New Jersey. Across the aisle from us was a very nice man who introduced himself as the proprietor of F.A.O. Schwarz, the famous toy store where we had spent almost an entire day gaping and playing. The man had a load of toys brought to us from the baggage car: teddy bears, tin soldiers, Tinker Toys, ski ropes. All the gifts were for us because he admired Mom and we were her children.

Near the Werblins' home there was a boys' camp, a sprawling complex with wood-framed buildings surrounding an outdoor boxing ring. I went there for a visit with Sonny's son Hubbard. At the end of the day, someone proposed that the younger boys pair up and box. I'd never boxed before, but I relished the feel of the eight-ounce gloves as they were tied on my hands. I was matched against another boy, a little older and smaller than me. When someone shouted "Now," I shuffled into the ring unprepared to defend myself. The other boy started throwing punches. One to my nose drew blood. I got angry and threw a wild haymaker which landed flush in his stomach. He doubled up, grabbed me and started to moan. I hit him in the head and heard someone shout, "Finish him off, Mike."

The boy dropped to his knees, gloved hands clasped over his head. "Please don't hit me again," he whimpered. "Please."

I knew that he was hurt and helpless, and I ran out of the ring. That was my first and last fight, and I have never forgotten it, and in the years since I have thought of that boy as me.

When we flew back home, Mom laid my head on her lap and covered me with a blanket. She stroked my hair and rubbed my back until I fell asleep. I remember lying there and thinking how much I needed her and loved her. That day she was the best mom anyone ever had and I didn't want it to end.

Chapter II

"Meet your new father."

It is August, 1986. The crickets are competing for attention with the voices of eighty guests wearing Western garb who are gathered at the ranch for a BBQ in honor of Nancy's birthday, which is being celebrated a month late this year. The White House photographer poses Nancy, Dad and my family in a grouping. Nancy leans over me as the picture is being taken and whispers in my ear: "What do the children call your mother?"

I am taken aback. "They call her grandma."

Nancy frowns. "They'll have to call me something else."

Puzzled, I ask, "What's wrong with grandma? The kids call Colleen's dad Grandpa Ed and Dad is Grandpa."

"I don't want them to think of me the same way that they think of your mother. How about their calling me Nanny?"

I laugh. "I've had nannies and you don't remind me of one. And Cameron has been calling you grandma for eight years."

"We'll just have to think of something," Nancy says and smiles for the cameraman.

For thirty-five years I feel as if I have been in the middle of a battle between Mom and Nancy, beginning on the day I was about six years old and Dad introduced Maureen and me to a smiling and beautiful brunette lady. "This is Nancy Davis," he said. "She's an actress."

Years later I learned that Nancy and Dad had met by accident. There were several actresses named Nancy Davis in films during the late forties and early fifties. At that time congressional committees were searching out so-called Communist sympathizers in Hollywood. One of the Nancy Davises was apparently a Communist. Nancy, who was an established actress with eleven films to her credit, told director Mervyn LeRoy that she feared she would be blacklisted because of her name. What could she do?

LeRoy promised to talk with Ronald Reagan, who was then president of the Screen Actors' Guild. Dad checked her out. At LeRoy's insistence, he called Nancy and reported that she had nothing to fear. If there ever was a problem, the Guild would defend her. That conversation led to a dinner date. When Dad's divorce from Mom became final, he and Nancy began dating steadily.

It was obvious to us kids that Dad and Nancy were very much in love. They held hands, and when they didn't think we were looking, they sneaked kisses. Dad asked if we objected to Nancy going with us to his new ranch in Malibu, a much more elegant spread than the one in Northridge. It was the kind of ranch I had seen before only in movies. White fences bordered a long, tree-shaded drive where horses gamboled or watched our car as we proceeded on the road which stretched almost a mile from the highway. The ranch, which Dad called Yearling Row, was set in four hundred acres of mountain wilderness. It was here that he raised young thoroughbreds for sale. Huge eucalyptus trees stood in the center of the courtyard where there was usually a dog or two barking welcome. Houses for the family and foreman sparkled white in the sun. A swimming pool on the hill behind the house was enclosed by huge oak trees. From the barn, I could see acres of rolling hills where cows and a Texas Long Horn grazed. The ranch was heaven for a father and son, and I loved every minute we were there. However, it seemed that every time there was a fire in the area it spread across Dad's land. The fire department often used the back half of the ranch as a fire break. I don't recall how many fires Dad, Nancy, Maureen and I fought there. During one of the first fires which destroyed most of the ranch, Dad was out of town on a trip for General Electric. Nancy drove out to the ranch to help fight the fire. While the firemen hosed down the houses, Nancy struggled through the smoke and soot and splashed buckets of water on the white fence posts which Dad had made and painted himself. I didn't think much of it then, but even today, whether there are family problems or flash fires at the White House such as Donald Regan and the Iran-Contra affair, Nancy is on hand to douse the flames and help protect what Dad has built.

Maureen and I saw very little of each other at Chadwick because she was four grades ahead of me, but we came home together every other weekend. Some nights Mom took us to my favorite restaurant, the Brown Derby in Beverly Hills, where I always had an avocado cocktail with Thousand Island dressing. If Mom was

31

working, as was often the case, Dad and Nancy picked us up in his green Cadillac convertible (a present from Mom on his thirty-seventh birthday, which arrived with a card reading, "Love, Michael and Maureen"). On the weekends when Maureen and I could not go home, Dad and Nancy would drive up to Chadwick to visit with us. I loved those weekends together, and when they left, my heart went with them.

I remember one Memorial Day when I appeared in a school play at Chadwick. I had to wear a monkey suit. Dad and Nancy picked me up afterward. It was hot, and when I sat down in the back of Dad's convertible, I got sick. I threw up in the area behind the seat where the top was stored, but I never said a word about it. He must have had to put the top down at some point and discovered the mess, although, to this day, he has never mentioned it.

That's just the kind of father he was. He never raised his hand to us, and it took a lot to get him to raise his voice. Whenever I did something wrong, he just gave me that Ronald Reagan look, and I felt guilty. I always listened to him, but I never told him my problems because I thought that would be a sign of weakness and it might be a reason for him not to like me. Also, the family was set up so that we went to our mother with problems and she then reported back to Dad.

After visiting with us, Dad would take us back to Mom's house and drop us off. Most nights Carrie, our cook, would make dinner for us, and then we would watch television. Carrie was a wonderful black lady who I thought of as my surrogate mother. Carrie was always there when I had problems and was a constant source of comfort to me. Carrie sometimes brought her son Horace to the house to play with me. That was the first time I became aware of prejudice; the other kids would make fun of me because my friend was black. In those days a black in Beverly Hills was someone who did not socialize there but only worked there.

One thing I clearly remember about Mom's house was that it had a full basement with a laundry chute that dropped from the second floor down to the washer and dryer. When Maureen and I had little fights, we used to try to shove each other or our friends down the chute. Fortunately we were smart enough to lock the bottom end and put sheets in to cushion any hard spills so that no one got hurt. It was a great hiding spot for games like Hide and Seek. When Mom would call us for lunch or dinner, she would hear a muffled "help." She forbade us to play that game, and when she caught us at it I knew we were in big trouble. I'd be sent to my room for an hour, which was my usual punishment.

During my punishment periods, I soon discovered that if I locked my bedroom and bathroom doors from the inside I could go out the bathroom window and climb down a tree to the ground. I would then sneak over to visit Connie and Mickey Freiberg, my best friends, who lived behind us. I would play there until it was time to go home. I never knew that my mother was aware of what I was doing until recently. I thought I was being sneaky, but as always I hadn't fooled her one bit!

Like most kids of that age, I was mischievous and could be a nuisance from time to time. In retrospect, I suppose many of the things I did that I knew would make Mom angry were probably my way of getting attention. My childhood was spent seeking affection, trying to get my parents to put their arms around me and say, "I love you." That was something neither parent could do. Mom tried in her way, but when Dad was raised, men didn't hug other men. Dad has a hard time doing that even today. He can give his heart to the country but he just finds it difficult to hug his own children.

When I really got out of hand and talked back to Mom or took something from her purse, she used a riding crop to discipline me. I could tell by the look on her face what was coming, and I would shiver and ask her, "Do you want me in the 'libary' or upstairs?"

She would lead me into the library or take me up to my room and bend me over my bed, giving me ten whacks on the calf of each leg, hard, with the leather loop of the crop. She sometimes yelled at or ridiculed me in public, but to her credit, when she hit me she did it in private.

To this day, that riding crop still sits inside the door of her condominium in Santa Monica, California. In Mom's eyes, I've never grown up, and even today she offers that riding crop to my wife suggesting she use it to keep me on the straight and narrow.

I also learned discipline from the teachers at Chadwick, who did not hesitate to bend a ruler over our knuckles or over our bottoms. I sometimes acted up, knowing the punishment but seeking it so I could get attention—any attention, good or bad—from an adult.

I was miserable about being away from home, so I cried almost every night. The other kids teased me for being a crybaby, but I kept sobbing until the dorm mother came in to rub my back to put me to sleep. I missed my Mom and felt that she didn't love me or she would have let me live at home with her. I missed my father, too, and couldn't understand why I saw so little of him. I was becoming very confused.

I lived for the Saturdays when Dad would take me with him to the ranch. Nino Peppetone, who had been foreman of the Northridge ranch, became the trainer for Dad's thoroughbreds, and the new foreman was a man named Ray Jackin. Ray was a short stocky man with thin hair and a paunch belly from having too many beers. He rarely wore a shirt, but boy, could he cook chili!

Dad taught Maureen and me how to ride by leading us around the corral. He was a pussycat as a teacher, always calm and patient. When he didn't busy himself with us, I would watch him doing chores: cutting trees, painting fences, making roofs for the sheds and training his jumpers. I was in total awe of him. He was a man's man and everyone loved him. I wanted to be just like him.

I particularly liked those Saturdays at the ranch because when Nancy came along she sat in the front seat of the car and I would sit on her lap. She would massage or tickle my back. As far as I was concerned, I was number one. Thinking back on that period now, I feel sorry for what my sister must have been going through. Not only was there a new woman taking her Daddy away from her so she wouldn't be Daddy's girl anymore, but her brother was even in the front seat having his back scratched.

Those back rubs were bonding me to Nancy so much that, although I wanted to be with Dad at the ranch, I looked forward most of all to being in the front seat of the car and having Nancy love me. I never told her that, however, because I didn't want to be disloyal to my mom.

Maureen and I talked about Dad and Nancy, and we both agreed it would be wonderful if they got married because then we would have another mother. Most of all, I hoped that if they got married they would have me move in with them. I would have a Mom and Dad and a normal house like many of my friends and I wouldn't have to board at school.

I enjoyed being with Dad and Nancy more than with Mom because they were a family. Nancy represented to me all the motherly attributes I was seeing on television in shows like *Father Knows Best* and *The Stu Erwin Show*. She was always cheerful, unlike Mom who had constant mood shifts. She was affectionate, whereas the only time Mom seemed to show real concern for me was when I was sick. Nancy also had parents she talked about with love while Mom never spoke about her parents or the past. Unlike Mom, Nancy had a background and roots. But most important she also had my father, something I blamed my mother for.

I started to build a barrier between me and Mom. Nancy didn't like Mom any better then than she does today. When she said something derogatory about Mom, I would agree with her. I wanted to be her friend and to have her think of me as hers.

On the other hand, Mom didn't like giving me up to Dad and Nancy on Saturday, I guess because it reminded her of a marriage that had ended. When I would come home from being with them and talk glowingly about the good time I'd had, omitting my feelings of joy about having my back rubbed by Nancy, I'm sure she was jealous. She always spoke badly of Nancy, who she considered "that other woman." Since I didn't want to upset her, it became a game with me to agree with her. I realized that if I wanted to get along with Mom it was a good idea not to speak highly of Nancy.

I was very confused and getting mixed signals from both my parents. I didn't know who I was supposed to be with, and I remember trying to please them both. It soon became a game on my part to put Mom down to Nancy and Nancy down to Mom. When I spoke badly of Nancy Mom was pleased, and that gave us something in common to talk about. It appeared that the only time we communicated was when we talked derogatorily about Dad and Nancy.

I knew the two women disliked each other, and I really didn't know what to do. Until recently, I was behaving the same way, still seeking acceptance from my mom and Nancy.

Nancy and Dad were married without fanfare or publicity on March 4, 1952 at the Little Brown Church in the Valley. I recall them talking about getting married, but the actual wedding was a surprise. They called Maureen and me at Chadwick with the news. Looking back, the fact that my sister Maureen and I were not present at the wedding was a portent of things to come.

When Nancy became pregnant, she would let me touch her stomach and feel the baby kicking, which I thought was neat. There finally came a point when Nancy was too big for me to sit on her lap in the front seat of the car. I was relegated to the back seat. I was in second place again: My biological mother had pushed me out of her life, Mom had sent me away to school, and now I was being pushed into the backseat by an unborn infant. Again, I felt rejected. Patti was born on October 22, 1952. Nancy would act in only two more films: *Donovan's Brain* in 1953, and *Hellcats of the Navy* with Dad four years later. She was willing to give up her career to become a housewife and mother—something Mom would never have done.

Meanwhile, Mom had met a musician-composer named Fred Karger whom she was dating and whom I had met a couple of times. On Halloween night—less than a week after Patti's birth—Fred came by the house with his daughter Terry, a pretty brunette. She was to join Maureen and me trick-or-treating. Mom invited us all into the den. "Fred is going to be your new father," she said. That was her way of telling us that she planned to get married. I was stunned. I didn't know how to react. What did she mean by "new father"? What about Dad? Was he no longer going to be my father? I knew Mom didn't like Dad, and since I lived with her I put on a happy face.

The following day, Carrie gave Maureen and me a handful of rice. "What's this for?" I asked.

"When the front door opens, throw it on your mother and Fred," Carrie said.

Mom and Fred had eloped to Santa Barbara.

The next morning when Fred came down to breakfast, he asked me where the toothache medicine was.

"What's toothache medicine?" I asked.

"The booze," he said.

I knew where the booze was because I had seen my mother drink, so I brought him into the den and showed him the bar area. Whenever I saw Fred after that, he always wanted the toothache medicine, and I would bring it to him.

I wanted to please Fred because he was now my new father, but then Dad started to come by again to take me to the ranch on Saturdays. I knew that didn't make Mom happy, so I was tentative about going, although I wanted to because those were always my happiest times. Also, I didn't want to be disloyal to Fred. Mom. Nancy. Fred. Dad. Was I mixed up! I didn't know what to do or who to turn to. Dad must have been aware of my confusion, and one day he invited Fred to the ranch so that I could see both of my fathers getting along together. We hiked and rode horses, and Dad took Fred on a tour of the ranch. Although I was with them both together, my stomach was in knots with confusion.

Afterward, Fred told me, "Let's not tell your mother what we did at the ranch today. It will only upset her." He was intimidated by Mom, too. So we never talked about the fun we all had that day.

Since I lived with Mom and Fred, I looked forward to being part of a family. But Mom was busy most of the time at the studio, and Fred never had time for us kids. During the day he worked as a composer. Every night he and his band played at the Starlight Room at the Beverly Hilton Hotel. He was not a father I could relate to, a man who would play games with me and take me places as did the fathers of most of my friends.

Although I have only a few memories of Fred, one stands out clearly. He had planned a birthday party for Mom. Maureen and I went shopping in Beverly Hills to buy her a gift. That was the year that serving trays with the original calendar nude photo of Marilyn Monroe in *Playboy* were popular. I thought the tray would be a great gift, but Maureen talked me out of it. Instead we bought Mom a sugar bowl.

The night of the party I wore my new suit because my job was to welcome guests at the door. At one point the doorbell rang. There, standing in front of me, was Marilyn Monroe! I was so excited I almost shut the door on her. Later, I found out that Marilyn was a friend of Fred's.

Dad and Nancy had become a family unto themselves after Patti was born. Until then, Nancy had treated Maureen and me like her own kids. It soon became apparent that we were becoming less and less important in her life and Dad's.

Maureen and I boarded at Chadwick for the remainder of the school year. The next September, I was to be enrolled in Warner Avenue School, a local day school. I really looked forward to that because it meant that I would finally be living at home with Mom. I hoped that all the things I had wanted were going to come true: I would at last be part of a family.

Mom enrolled me in an after-school gymnastics camp, which was fine with me because I would be home at night, but my excitement about being part of a normal family like those I had seen on television was short-lived. I had no way of knowing then that a tragic and traumatic event which would forever change my life was about to take place.

Chapter III

"Let's make this our game."

August, 1983. The local newspapers carry daily headlines about the alleged sexual molestation and abuse of dozens of children at the McMartin preschool in Manhattan Beach, California. Soon after the first disclosure, Mom is on the line. She rarely calls me unless I have done something wrong. As usual, I am intimidated just by the sound of her voice. "Have you read about all those kids being sexually abused?" she asks.

"I've read about it," I say, relieved that I am not going to be on the carpet for some reason or other.

"Nothing like that ever happened to you, did it, Mike?"

She is giving me the perfect opening to finally confide in her. I put the telephone down for a moment while I think about my reply. I almost tell her and then think better of it because I don't want to hurt her. "No, Mom," I say, "that never happened to me."

"Am I glad to hear that."

The McMartin story is the main topic of conversation among our friends, most of whom are also the parents of young children. They are outraged over the victimization of the children and concerned about the effect it will later have on their lives. Everyone wonders how such a terrible thing can happen.

I know the answers because I, too, was sexually abused when I was eight years old. But it was not until the McMartin story became news that I realized that my experience, a secret I have never shared with anyone until recently, was not unique. One of every eight boys and one of every four girls today is sexually abused or molested.

The words *abuse* and *molested* alone fail to convey the torment experienced by child victims who are emotionally and physically manipulated. Something so monstrous does not take place in a vacuum, however, so let me set the stage.

The counsellor at the day camp where I had been enrolled to occupy me after school was about thirty years old. He soon became my idol and father image. I tried to do everything I could to get his attention and praise. There was nobody better in the day camp than I at trampolining, somersaulting, doing back and front flips and throwing a baseball or football. I worked triple hard to impress him, and because of him I became a good all-around athlete. I felt that if I impressed him, I could also impress Dad.

He constantly told me how proud he was of me and that I was the best student at the camp. He gave me all the compliments I so much wanted to hear from my father. Dad had been an athlete all of his life and loved and respected the sports heroes of his youth who he always talked about. I wanted desperately to be like him so he would accept me as his son.

The counsellor saw this and capitalized on my need for love and praise by making me feel that the world revolved around me. He recognized my need to win even if it meant cheating. During a football throwing competition, my hand was sweating from nervousness. The ball slipped from my grasp as I threw it. Although only one throw was allowed, he let me throw again, and I won the prize. During a yo-yo contest, I placed third, but no one was good enough to win the Champion patch. I cried because I couldn't admit to my parents that I had placed third; as a Reagan, I felt I had to win—anything less wasn't good enough. The counsellor talked the man in charge of the contest into giving him the Champion patch, which he then gave to me. I was triumphant when I showed the patch to Mom and saw how proud she was, as was Dad the following Saturday. What I hadn't counted on was that Mom would frame the patch and hang it in my room alongside my blue ribbons from swimming meets. It would remain a constant reminder of my big lie. Years later Dad would hang it over my bed at the ranch.

When camp was over each day the counsellor always let me sit next to him in the car—just like Dad—while he drove the other kids home. Invariably he took me home last. When we were alone, he would drive slowly, his arm across my shoulder, and tell me how great I was as he tousled my hair.

Without my knowing it, he had gently manipulated me by stages into a relationship in which I was beholden to him. It began one day as he was driving me home he asked me if I wanted to make him feel good. He had done so much for me I said yes, not knowing what he would ask next. He then unzipped his pants and took out his genitals and asked me to touch them. It didn't seem right but he had been so good to me I didn't want to disappoint him.

It wasn't long before he began doing the same to me, while always confiding in me that this was our game and I couldn't tell anyone, not even Mom.

43

He seemed to want to touch me every time we went anywhere alone together, or in a group, like at the movies. He would lead me to a seat away from the others and would then put a coat over our laps. During this time I never understood the meaning of what we were doing. I thought of him as my best friend and an adult who was giving me the affection and praise I so much yearned for.

Then one day he took a group of campers for a weekend hike in the Santa Monica Mountains where he organized a game of Hide and Seek. He told the others he would be my partner. The plan was for us to hide and they would try and find us.

He led me by the hand up the mountain until we reached a small cave near the top—a perfect hiding place. "Let me take a picture of you here," he said, taking out his camera. I posed leaning against a rock.

He snapped a few pictures and then said, "Let's take some of you undressed."

I told him I was afraid that the other kids might see me naked, and that would be embarrassing, but he reassured me, saying he would listen for them. I also thought he might be disappointed if I refused, and I wouldn't be number one anymore. He had just taken the last picture when I heard the other kids coming toward us. I quickly dressed. For the first time I really felt something was wrong but I didn't know what. All I know is I felt guilty.

When he dropped me off that night, he asked Mom if he could take me to a movie and dinner later in the week after camp. Mom was agreeable.

Instead of taking me to the movies, however, he brought me to his apartment. He put some TV dinners in the oven and then took me on a tour of his small apartment. I'll never forget that all the walls were painted green. He led me into his bathroom, which had been converted into a makeshift darkroom with negatives hanging from a clothesline over the bathtub and an enlarger on the wash basin. He mixed some solutions in trays on the floor and showed me how to develop photos. His face—he had a day's growth of beard—scratched my cheek and left a mark as he bent over and developed a scenic photo.

"How would you like to develop some pictures?" he asked. I was delighted at the prospect and eagerly took a pair of tongs that he gave me. He put an exposed paper in the developing solution. With his hand on my arm, we moved the print from tray to tray. As the print became clear, I couldn't believe what I was seeing. It was one of the nude pictures he had taken of me.

"Do you want to take the pictures home to show your mother?" he asked me.

I didn't know whether to run or hide. I only knew that something was terribly wrong, and I stood in stunned silence, aware that if Mom saw that picture she'd break the riding crop on my backside at best. I was scared out of my wits. All I knew was I couldn't let her ever find out.

At this point he took me by the hand and led me out of the makeshift darkroom into the living room. He had me stand in front of a chair. I was almost catatonic as he unzipped and took down my pants. What happened then made me worry for the rest of my life that I was or would be thought of as a homosexual. It was so dirty that to me it would have been easier to die than to re-live it. All I know is that my stomach was in knots and I wanted to vomit. Thirty-five years later, while telling my father, I did.

That was the last time I remember seeing that man because my memory is blank from that episode on.

Later that night when Mom asked me why my cheek had a red mark on it, I said that I had scratched it on the trampoline. I didn't dare confide in her, not only because I didn't know how to go about it or what to tell her—other than that something had happened that frightened me and that I thought was bad—but also because I was afraid she would think I had made up the story to get attention. Besides, the counsellor was an adult, and I had been taught to obey adults. In my child's mind, adults didn't do bad things to children. Somehow, whatever happened that troubled me so much had to be *my* fault and that was the real reason I never told. As years went by, I became angry with Mom because I felt if she had been a real mother and not sent me away or had picked me up at school instead of sending me to the camp, this thing would not have happened. It was easier to blame her than accept responsibility myself.

I was confused about who to turn to. I spent more time with the counsellor each day than with any other adult, so he was my only real adult confidant. I didn't tell my father because I was scared I would lose him. He was busy with Nancy and Patti, and I didn't know how he would react. I had no intention of spoiling what little time we were able to spend together.

I couldn't talk to my stepfather Fred because I never saw him. He, like Mom, was always at a studio working during the day, and he was busy every night playing with his band in a local hotel. I couldn't tell Maureen because the last time I had told her a secret she had told me about my being adopted. I didn't want to tell Nancy because she still treated me lovingly. She might have been disappointed with me and never rubbed my back again.

As years went by, I even became angry with my biological mother who had rejected me and had given me away to what everybody described as the most perfect family in the world. I felt ashamed, guilty, confused, afraid and dirty. As much as I bathed, as much soap as I used, it was never enough to get rid of that feeling of being dirty. I believed that I was bad, that there was something wrong with me that provoked the relationship. Then there were other residual effects: From then on I was suspicious of all male adults. And, very soon after I saw the photos, I began to have a nightmare that tormented me for years. In it, I am standing atop a mountain or a high building, being chased by a nameless, faceless person or thing. No matter what it is, I can't run fast enough to escape it because my feet are mired in deep sand. My heart is pounding and my gut is churning. My only choices are to turn around, fight the thing and kill it or to jump off into space. I have always jumped. I wake up in a cold sweat as I am hurtling toward the ground. And upon waking, I feel as though I have died.

It started with the lie about the yo-yo patch, which grew to entangle my life in a network of lies and deceit. I started to build barriers between myself and others to protect myself as well as my family from what I then considered to be an awful secret. I was filled with the anger of confusion and frustration, made even greater because there was no one to vent the anger on. I was only aware that the man who I thought was so good had somehow done something terrible to me, although I was unable to put what happened between us into words. Concepts such as child abuse, sexual molestation and child pornography were not part of the public consciousness or vocabulary in those days. I didn't feel like a victim then; however, I considered myself a party to whatever had happened. At that time I was not aware that all of my feelings, including my anger, bewilderment and frustration were typical emotions felt by most sexually molested children. I did not know I had been molested.

I also had another reaction that is common with molested children: I became confused about my sexual identity and preoccupied with sex and sex play. I felt I needed to have a girlfriend, so I often went to play with Connie Freiberg whose family lived on the street behind our house. I knew that Connie liked me. I tried to set scenes in front of the other neighborhood kids in which Connie and I practiced kissing. We'd press our mouths together and try to hold our breath until one of us started to turn blue. I wanted to prove to myself as well as to them that I was a normal boy. The other kids didn't know there was a game going on in my mind that set me up as the actor and them as my audience. I was role playing, taking on a persona that was not mine, a deceit that would continue for most of my life.

To many people, those photos would seem harmless enough, but to me, at that time and even now, they were not. For the past thirty-five years I have blackmailed myself with the knowledge that they exist. My family has an image of being good Christians, and I was horrified that I would be responsible for destroying that image. As an adult, I lived in fear that at some point in one of my father's political campaigns those photos would surface and I would have to explain them. I was afraid that I would be labeled or perceived as homosexual because that is what I came to consider my experience.

Not until the McMartin case became public decades later did I realize that I was a victim of a male predator, that I had been sexually abused. By that time I had built up so many walls to hide behind that only therapy would help me tear them down and convince me that I was not unique, homosexual or evil.

Chapter IV

"The work of Satan."

It is Father's Day, 1985. I feel the pastor's firm hand on my head as he asks me if I accept Christ as my Lord and Saviour. I have just time enough to answer "Yes" before he puts a handkerchief over my face and gently pushes me down into the tank of cold water. I take a deep breath before being submerged. Although I am only under the water for the blink of an eye, memories race through my mind: the times in my life when I had cursed God for putting me on this earth as an illegitimate child, thereby causing me untold suffering as I lived out my mother's sin; the three times I have prayed to Him and my prayers have been answered but I have never given Him either credit or thanks.

As the pastor releases his pressure on my head, I stand erect. The ceremony is over, and I am now committed to Christ. Water from the baptismal tank drips from my hair and clothes. The pastor hands me a cloth to dry my eyes. I hear a murmur of approbation from the congregation and look at my wife Colleen, holding our infant daughter in her arms, standing next to our son Cameron who is in his Sunday-best suit. My family's eyes shine with pride. Colleen nods her head and smiles with approval. My thoughts stray again. This is the first time in my life that I have made a conscious decision to go against my mother's will, and I feel anxious, aware that she will be angry with me. Although I am now an adult, I still want her approval in everything I do, but I seem never to get it.

I flash back in memory to the first time I ever became aware of religion.

When Fred and Mom were married in church, it was outside the railing because Mom was not a Catholic. That always bothered Mom, who decided that if she were Catholic God would bless their marriage. So she decided to convert herself and her children to Catholicism. We all went to church every Sunday, which made Mom happy. But I was miserable in church because for the first time I learned that sex between men meant damnation and exclusion from heaven, proof that I was doomed. My worst fears were reinforced.

Although neither Maureen nor I liked Catholicism, we wanted to please Mom, so we were baptized with her on December 8, 1954, the day of the Feast of the Immaculate Conception.

The next morning, Mom awakened me while it was still dark. "Get up," she said. "We're going to mass."

"What time is it?" I asked sleepily.

"It's four o'clock, and since we are new Catholics, I want to be at the first communion."

"Why don't you go, and Maureen and I will go to later services?"

"No," Mom said. "Get out of bed. We're going as a family."

Mom wanted me to fit in with her new friends, many of whom were also Catholic, including her oldest and best friend Loretta Young Lewis, who brought her to Catholicism. I remember visiting Loretta and her children in Ojai—a rural town about one hundred miles northwest of Los Angeles—where we children spent the day riding our bicycles, horseback riding and swimming. Years later I learned that Loretta's sister, Sally Foster, was my godmother, although I only remember seeing her once in my life.

I was sent to Good Shepherd School in Beverly Hills for the fourth grade, where Mom hoped that I would learn discipline and would learn to become a good Catholic. Little did she know that her son wasn't going to heaven no matter how good a Catholic he pretended to be.

Mom also arranged for me to go to summer camp in Prescott, Arizona, thus starting a routine that was to last until I was seventeen years old. The ranch was run by Art Reichle and his family, and I soon looked on them as my surrogate family during those summers.

Saturdays at the ranch with Dad, with or without Nancy and the rest of the family, were great. He was wonderful to be around. He was a big, handsome, patient man. I loved him and was proud to have him as my father.

Dad is a marksman with either a rifle or pistol. He does everything right-handed except shoot a gun. I was ecstatic when he bought me a .22 caliber Remington single-shot rifle and gave me lessons in safety and how to shoot it.

During our time together, I listened carefully to Dad and watched his every move. I tried to imitate him because everybody liked him. Dad was the only adult male I ever trusted. I felt safe with Dad, but I never told him about my problems because I saw him only on Saturdays. He was always upbeat, and I didn't want to upset him. I wanted him to think I was a man and perfect just like him. Our relationship was also good because he never lifted a hand to discipline me. He expected Mom to handle any disciplinary problems just as his mother Nelle had ruled his family. If Dad knew I was having difficulties at home with Mom, he never mentioned them, and at the time, Mom thought she and I were getting along fine because I was in Catholic school being a good boy.

I loved horseback riding, and everyone knew it. I will never forget the Saturday when we arrived at the ranch and I saw a palomino in the corral. He was a beautiful golden quarter horse with a white stripe down his face. Dad had already taught me to ride Babe, a big sixteen-hand thoroughbred that was his horse. As a special treat, Dad put me up on the palomino and led me with a lanyard around the corral while asking questions: "Do you like riding?"; "Do you like the horse?"; "Would you ever want to have a horse of your own?" The truth was that I wanted that horse more than anything, and all my answers were strongly affirmative because I knew that was what he wanted and expected to hear. Dad told me it was too bad that I liked the palomino so much because it belonged to another man and his young son and we were only training him for them. He also asked me if I could think of a good name for the horse. At that time, *Rebel Without a Cause* was a hit film starring James Dean so I answered, "Rebel."

The following Saturday Dad asked me if I would want to take Rebel away from the other youngster. "No," I said biting my tongue because I knew that was the answer he expected of me. "Good," Dad answered. He told me that when I wasn't at the ranch the other boy rode Rebel, which made me jealous of him.

On the day before Christmas, 1954, we went to the ranch. Dad told me that this would be my last day to ride Rebel because the other boy was going to get him as a Christmas present. My worst fears were realized, and I was heartbroken as I raced out to the stall to say good-bye to the horse I had come to love so much. When I opened the top part of the stall, Rebel stuck his head out. He had just been washed and was shiny gold. Around his neck was a big red bow with a note: *Merry Christmas, Michael. Love, Nancy and Dad.* I was so excited I jumped up and down and then ran and gave them a hug. I couldn't wait to ride him. What a gift! It was the first thing I could remember Dad giving me. I felt as though he had finally accepted and welcomed me into his life. It was significant to me that he had a horse and now I had one so we could ride together. I also had something I could really show off to my friends, something my father had given me. I even had a horse of my own to take to summer camp that year. It was, up to that point, the happiest moment of my life.

When I got home and told Mom about my gift, she seemed cold, almost hostile, which put a bit of a damper on my joy. I wasn't aware of it then, but Mom and Dad had made a deal that Christmas: Dad would give me Rebel and Mom would give me a saddle and bridle. Perhaps even though she had agreed to the arrangement, she now felt that her part of the gift would inevitably be eclipsed by Dad's. But a child has no insight into such matters. I went to bed and couldn't sleep, worrying there would be no toys under the tree because I had displeased my mother. Yet—maybe Santa Claus had slipped in after all and left a few presents. Certainly he wouldn't have forgotten Maureen. She was good. And then I had a horrible thought. Santa knew everything. He knew about me and the counsellor. He knew I'd been bad. If there weren't any presents, maybe Mom would figure out why! I began to panic. I crept out of my room and headed for Maureen's room to see if she was still awake. As I came down the hallway Mom was just walking out of her bedroom lugging the saddle and bridle. When she saw me she was furious. Dropping the tack with a thud on the floor, she said, "Here's my Merry Christmas present to you, Michael. You can go down and put it under the tree yourself!"

Downstairs, gently laying the saddle and bridle behind a pile of holiday-wrapped gifts, I peeked at the card attached to the stirrup. She had written: *These are for Rebel. Ride him well. With all my love, Mom.*

One Saturday soon after that Dad was unable to take me to the ranch. I was miserable because I wanted to spend the day with him and Rebel. I went to the park near our house to play football with some friends. Someone threw the football over my head, and when I went to get it, I saw Dad driving by. I yelled to him. Dad stopped and got out of the car. He took off his jacket and joined my team— we were playing two on two—which made me proud because I could show him off to my friends. I wanted desperately to impress him, to get his approval, and I felt I could only do that by winning. I thought myself a good player, and I was the leader of our team. I was certain that with him on my side we would win. But we lost. It was the first time I had ever lost in a game; everyone had always let me win because of my parents. So I threw a tantrum. In my mind I had failed even with my father by my side. As I think back, in all likelihood Dad was just being gracious when he played so the other kids would feel good. He had no way of knowing how it would disappoint me.

*   *   *

54

Not long afterward, Mom got a starring role in a television show named for her, *The Jane Wyman Theater,* and began working long hours every day. It became a big hit on television and was one of the most satisfying projects she had ever undertaken. I was happy because she was happy. For my tenth birthday she gave a party for me on the film set. I was so proud and happy. It was the first time I had been on the set, and she introduced me to her co-workers: the actors and director, the producer of the show, stagehands and the makeup people.

Once again I felt I had the best mother in the world.

But she had her problems which I was not privy to: Her marriage to Fred Karger was coming to an end.

Since Mom was unable to devote time to us, Maureen was sent to Marymount Girls' School in West Los Angeles. Mom told me that she had enrolled me in St. John's Military Academy, a Catholic boys' school in downtown Los Angeles. I didn't realize it was a boarding school until Mom filled out some papers at the desk and then turned around to me and said, "I'll see you on Saturday." I was dead scared when she left me alone with one of the sisters. And then I started to cry. I couldn't understand why she had sent me away from her again.

Being at St. John's was hell for me. I was frightened because the students were all boys, and I had never been to an all-boys school before and was concerned that I might be a homosexual. I lived in a dormitory and did everything I could to avoid going nude into the community showers with the others because I was concerned they might perceive me as queer. I quickly slipped in and out of the shower trying not to expose myself.

I had to repeat the fifth grade because I was told the Academy was more advanced scholastically than Good Shepherd. One of my teachers was Sister Mary Cyprian, who wore a nun's habit and had a leather cast with a reinforced metal bar on her hand, the result of a fall she had taken before the semester started. The school didn't have air conditioning, but then, to the best of my knowledge, no Catholic school ever does.

During the warmer days, we'd always start to doze off after lunch. Sister Mary Cyprian would choose her moment to sneak up behind us and hit us right behind the shoulders with her leather-and-metal cast to jolt us awake. I thought we wore ties because they looked "proper," but on many occasions the nuns would use those ties, grabbing them and tugging on them to get our attention; and then I understood the real reason we had to wear them. We were all intimidated by the nuns.

It was about this time that I began to wear glasses. At Good Shepherd I had trouble reading the blackboard. When I complained to Mom that I couldn't see well enough to read, she scoffed and told me I was just giving her an excuse for my bad grades. But my problem became acute at St. John's. I was given an eye test, and glasses were prescribed for me. When Mom heard about that, she seemed surprised until she remembered how near I had to sit to the TV set.

School was only a half-hour from home. I couldn't understand why Mom didn't want me to live with her, intensifying my feeling of isolation. Being away at school also kept me from seeing my father, because boarders weren't allowed to leave the campus until four-thirty Saturday afternoon and had to be back by seven P.M. Sunday night. This rule meant that I could see him at the ranch only during holidays or before or after summer camp. I really missed him and Rebel.

I hated boarding at St. John's so much that it got to the point that on one Sunday afternoon, when Mom was ready to take me back to school, she couldn't find me. I was hiding on the roof of our house. She finally located me, but there was no way Mom could talk me into coming down. I cried, yelled and screamed that I wasn't going back to school; I wanted to stay home. Carrie finally was able to talk me off the roof. I trusted Carrie.

I was so angry about being kept away at school that one day when Mom shouted, "Mr. Reagan, you get ready for school," I rebelled again. She was standing just outside the den of our house with her hands on her hips like Mr. Clean when I came running down the stairs. I charged at her like a bull and tried to hit her. She grabbed my arm and flipped me over her back. I crashed to the floor. She knelt over me with one knee on my chest and asked, "What would you like to try next, little man?" I gasped and said, "Nothing."

I was still having nightmares, and worse, I started to wet my bed. I got up before the others in the morning so I could change my sheets surreptitiously, remake my bed and get back into it before the other boys in the dormitory awakened. Invariably, the first thing one of the boys would jeeringly ask in the morning was, "O.K., who wet his bed?" When another boy admitted his failure to stay dry, I'd just smile. We'd all laugh and tease him; I always jeered the loudest.

I hated being teased, so I soon hit on the idea of attending six o'clock mass, although it meant I had to be up at five A.M. This gave me an excuse for rising early. It also gave me the opportunity to shower alone. The nuns began to consider me a great kid, one of the few who attended mass regularly. Although I hated church, it was better than being teased by the other boys. I was rewarded for my diligence by being promoted to a corporal and the next year sergeant. The nuns told Mom I was so good that I should become an altar boy, which pleased her immensely. I had become quite expert at deception!

I went out for the school football team. All of Dad's boyhood heroes were football players, and I wanted to prove to myself and him that I was a real boy. Ironically, thanks to the counsellor, I had become a good athlete. On the day of the tryouts for the team, it came down to one position left open as center. The coach told me if I could stop his number one halfback, I would be on the

57

team. The halfback was a giant in size compared to me. The coach blew his whistle, and I charged in. I hit the halfback so hard that I knocked myself out. When I came to three minutes later, the coach said I was on the team.

I began my school football career playing center on the Academy's C football squad. The next year I was moved to halfback. The big game that year was to be held during Father and Son's Day. Dad and Mom were coming to see me play for the first time. The coach, who had become my friend devised a play which, if it worked, would allow me to make a touchdown and become a hero in my parents' eyes. We practiced that play for two weeks before the game, and it worked like a charm.

As luck would have it, I fell during practice and strained the cartilage in my right knee. It swelled to twice its size. I showed my injury to the other kids, hoping they would be impressed that I was playing with such a handicap and would praise me for my courage. I asked them not to tell the coach. In my imagination I was Jim Thorpe, the Gipper and Red Grange—all my father's heroes—in one package. I was living for the moment when everyone would stand up in the stands and applaud me as I made the first touchdown.

Before the game I told Mom about my injury, but in her view, men played hurt, and those who aren't men don't play at all. I limped onto the field. The play called for John Thomas, the quarterback, to fake the ball to me. I was to run through the opposition, and he would then actually throw the ball to me. If the play worked, I was to try for a touchdown. I caught the ball ten yards past the last defender and hobbled on one leg for forty-five yards till I was finally nailed on the five-yard line.

After the play, the coach took me out of the game. Dr. Joe Morreale, a schoolmate's dad, examined me and went into the stands were he reported to my parents that I really was hurt. Dr. Morreale taped the knee. I pleaded in vain with the coach to allow me to go back into the game because I wanted to prove to my father and my mother that I was willing to kill myself if necessary. We won the game, and I thought, "Wow, with me playing hurt and us winning the game, everyone is going to say, 'Yeah, Mike Reagan!'" But no one, except Dr. Morreale, seemed to care.

Later Mom decided I should take piano lessons because one of the nuns told her that I had long fingers. She probably thought it was safer than football. I rebelled because I thought only queers played the piano, and I quit almost immediately.

My grades were good during my first two years at St. John's. Heck, after sitting through the fifth grade twice, even a dummy's grades would be good. I made two friends during my second year: Bruce Daniels, the son of Singer Billy Daniels—the vocalist who popularized the song, "That Old Black Magic"—and Richard Morreale, the doctor's son. Rich, who spent what seemed like hours combing his hair in front of the mirror before breakfast, and Bruce were the class clowns, and I started to imitate them. I even combed my hair the same way they did. Everyone laughed at them when they ridiculed the other students and instructors, but because of that they were always in trouble.

One day Major Scanlon, who ran the school, caught the three of us goofing around in back of the latrine by the armory. Major Scanlon was a paunchy, gray-haired martinet who attended all the celebrity events in the hope of getting more students. Our punishment was to stand at parade rest with our noses against the latrine wall for ten minutes. After a few minutes we started laughing. After all, what could be funnier than standing with your nose against a latrine wall? That incident cemented our friendship.

After Mom and Fred decided to end their marriage, Mom got itchy feet and began to move; between the end of sixth grade and

59

the beginning of the eighth grade we moved three times. Whenever Mom moved, it seemed she would have a cab pick me up at school. It got so that every time I heard there was a cab waiting for me, I knew we had moved again. And each time we moved, I lost all my friends.

Moving made me miserable, so by the seventh grade I started acting up in class to get attention. Also, I figured that if I messed up badly enough, maybe I would be kicked out of school and Mom would let me live at home and send me to a day school.

Once, a nun caught me acting up in class. My behavior, she said, was "the work of Satan." To help cleanse Satan from me, she sent me to the holy water by the classroom door, saying that if I dipped my fingers in it and made the sign of the cross I would feel better. I went to the bowl of holy water, put my fingers on each side of my head like a devil, dipped each finger into the holy water and crossed myself. The other kids started to laugh. The nun turned around and saw me. By the look on her face, I thought she was going to have a cardiac arrest. She took me by the ear out of the classroom to Major Scanlon's office. He stripped me of my stripes. There was talk of expelling me from St. John's, but Mom bought an entire set of the Encyclopedia Britannica, not an inexpensive gift, and donated it to the seventh grade class. I was given another chance. I began to learn that one way to get Mom's attention was to get in trouble. I also learned that when I got in trouble, Mom would bail me out.

Unfortunately, like so many children of famous or rich parents, I was not being held accountable for my actions. The school had no intention of letting me fail, because it was a black mark on them. They were able to use the fact that Jane Wyman's son was a student in their sales pitches to other film community parents. I stored away the knowledge that no matter what I did I could get away with it because the school and my parents would clean up the mess after me.

Chapter V

"I've had it with you, Miss Wyman."

Soon after Mom's divorce from Fred Karger was final in 1955, we moved to a new house in Beverly Hills, and a new man came into our lives. His name was Gail Smith, and he was an executive with Procter & Gamble, the big soap firm which sponsored Mom's TV show.

A handsome man, I thought Gail looked like Perry Como, the singer who was then the big rage on television. Like Como, Gail was gentlemanly, personable and easy going. He was also generous. I once admired his gold watch, and he took it off his wrist and gave it to me. He played games and spent time talking with me. Maureen and I pumped ourselves up into hoping that he would marry Mom because we wanted to have him as a stepfather. When he was around, the house was an oasis of calm. Even Mom seemed happy. Gail had two daughters about my age, and I looked forward to having two more sisters.

I couldn't see Dad on the weekends because of my school schedule, but I didn't miss him so much because I looked forward to seeing Gail. But, within a year, Gail disappeared from Mom's life. Later, I learned that he had refused to convert to Catholicism. I felt alone and depressed when he left. Every time I got close to a man who I thought would be a father to me, he left. I was afraid that, somehow, their leaving was my fault. Maybe they had found out I was a bastard.

Along with the homosexuality issue, at Catholic school I was also being taught that sex outside of marriage was a mortal sin and that children from those encounters were doomed to purgatory—neither heaven nor hell—and only through the Virgin Mary, on her trips to purgatory, could you hope to be lucky enough to hide in her robes as she snuck back into heaven.

That fear occupied my thoughts so much that one night while I was alone at home I picked up Mom's Bible. I idly scanned the concordance looking for bastards or illegitimacy. It directed me to Deuteronomy 23:2 where I read, "No one born of a forbidden marriage, no illegitimate child nor any of his descendants may enter into the assembly of the LORD, even down to the tenth generation." I was stunned. What I had learned in school was right; I could not enter heaven. So it really didn't matter what I did; I was a lost soul. I was the one person in a Catholic household who was going to hell, and I was afraid and determined never to allow anyone to get close to me again. The end result was that I didn't open a Bible again till December of 1983.

There was no way I could find out whether I was illegitimate. I was too scared to ask Mom or Dad because I might learn the truth and all those bad thoughts in my mind would be substantiated, or worse, they would throw me out of the family. I prayed that I wasn't illegitimate, but deep down I knew I was.

I was so miserable that I considered suicide. The only reason I didn't follow through was because I had learned in church that if you commit suicide, like Judas Iscariot, you go to hell. I thought, however, that suicide would get the burden off me and my family; if I went to hell it would be for that rather than for being illegitimate or for *those* pictures. But I didn't want God to tell me that all the bad things I thought about myself were true. So I decided against suicide.

I thought that the only way I could spare Mom the pain of discovering all those bad things I thought about myself was to get out of the house. The way to do that was to mess up so badly at school that this time they would have to kick me out. Then I could figure out a way to go and live with Dad and Nancy who were a family. Maybe they would send me to a day school.

My behavior at St. John's usually resulted in my receiving demerits. If I didn't get too many during the week, I was allowed to play on Saturday before being picked up, but if I had demerits, I was forced to sit in a room with my arms folded, looking at the wall. Actually, I didn't mind the detention. I felt it was better to be in detention than to get into my heavy brown cord uniform and play in the downtown Los Angeles smog.

On Saturday nights and Sunday, I had the house pretty much to myself. Mom was usually busy either with work or friends, so we had very little time together. Her favorite pastime was playing cards, and since I wanted to spend time alone with her, I asked her to teach me how to play gin rummy and hearts. After I learned to play, it became important for me to win. I thought if I played on her level she would then accept me. I soon learned that the only way I could beat her was by cheating. Mom knew what I was

63

doing, but little did I know that from then until today, even if I won without cheating, she would be convinced in her mind that I was a con man.

I spent much of my time watching television. I grew up with shows like *Father Knows Best*, the Erwins and *Leave it to Beaver*, family fare with idealized families. My favorite show, however, was *Have Gun, Will Travel* starring Richard Boone as a hero named Paladin. It was the first TV series I remember which had a hero doing good and helping people. Richard Boone always had a woman on his arm and other women chasing him. I used to watch him and think, "Now there's a real man." The other part of that equation was that girls liked him, too, because he was a real man.

Even though I wanted to get away from my mother, I still adored her. I couldn't understand why she didn't seem to like me and why I couldn't seem to do anything right in her view. When I was home, I desperately wanted to please her. One Christmas Eve morning, I went downstairs to the dining room to light the candles on the table so it would be festive for our breakfast. Carrie had made a centerpiece display with little Santa Clauses and reindeer resting on some angel hair. Somehow or other I accidentally knocked over one of the burning candles, which landed on the angel hair. The display burst into flames. I was frightened out of my wits. My heart was in my throat, so I was unable to utter a sound. I panicked and ran out the front door crying. Luckily Carrie came in, saw the fire and called the fire station, which was just three blocks from the house. Carrie later found me hiding in the bushes by the fire station, sobbing uncontrollably as I visualized the house burning down. And, it was all my fault! I berated myself: I couldn't even light the Christmas candles without screwing up. Everything I did came out wrong. Now Mom would hate me because it was her favorite table and never let me come home. Carrie put her arms around me and told me everything was all right. The fire department had put out the blaze, and there was only a little damage to the table. After calming me down, Carrie brought me home. If Mom was aware that I had started the fire, she never said a word about it, at least not then. In recent years, however, she has often told the story about "the Christmas Michael almost burned down the house."

The highlights of my life and the few times I felt good about myself were when Dad took me with him to the Malibu ranch, usually on holidays. To be with him I learned to cut firewood and paint fences, but my favorite time was when we'd hunt ground squirrels together, Dad with his semi-automatic rifle with scope and me with my single-shot rifle. Dad had bought Nancy a black .22 caliber Ruger six-gun so that she would have protection at home when he was out of town. He tried to teach her how to shoot, but Nancy hated guns. She would aim the pistol, shut her eyes and pull the trigger. Even the barn was too small a target for her. Dad let me use the gun with a black holster, and I taught myself how to quick-draw just like Paladin. I was a fine shot. Years later when Dad became Governor of California, his security people had an informal shooting contest at the ranch, and I was asked to join in. Even though we were using .38s I outshot everyone on the detail.

My only conflict with Dad came about because he rode horseback English style, wearing jodhpurs and boots. He wanted me to dress and ride the same way; but I thought his outfit looked sissy, so I refused and learned to ride Western style. Following an afternoon of riding we all would wind up at the pool for a game of tag or just a refreshing dip to cool off after a hot day. I usually challenged Dad to race against me, thinking that if I could beat him I would win his acceptance and everyone else's. I behaved badly when I lost—just as I had during the football game. At such times Dad thought I was a spoiled brat. He couldn't understand why it was so important to me to win. To this day I have never beaten Dad, but then no one else has either.

Before leaving the ranch Maureen or I would flip a coin to

decide whether we would return home via the road alongside the Pacific Ocean or take the highway through the San Fernando Valley.

In those days, there were orange groves, apple orchards and farms lining the Valley, and the air was clear and pungent with the aroma of the fruit. If we took the valley route home, we would stop on Ventura Boulevard at a fresh apple cider stand. If we returned on the Pacific Coast Highway, we would stop at Foster's Freeze by the Malibu pier for an ice cream cone and a last whiff of the clean salt air. If Dad was in a hurry to get back to town and didn't stop at either place, I would give him a hard time so he would have to stop the next time.

Meanwhile, Mom and I were at each other. She had a habit of cutting me and everyone else to the quick when we didn't measure up—and I felt I never could. However, one day I asked her to get me a new ten-speed bicycle so I could join my friends, all of whom had new bikes. Ten speeds were the rage. She looked me up and down and said, "Even though I can afford to buy you anything you want, the important thing is for you to go out and earn the money for it. You'll appreciate it more, and people will respect you more. If you earn things by yourself, when you grow up you won't be a forty-year-old child, you'll be a forty-year-old man. I build men; I don't build little boys."

However, she did buy the bike with the stipulation that I earn the money to pay her back. That worked out well for me. I arranged to sell the Sunday newspaper in front of Good Shepherd Church. I told Mom that I was going to church on Sundays, even though I never actually entered the sanctuary. Instead, I played with friends. But I did make it a habit to look at the Daily Missal which included the gospel of the day as well as the wardrobe the priests would be wearing. When Mom quizzed me later, I told her accurately what had transpired.

Thanks to my convincing Mom that I was going to church on a

regular basis, we started to get along better. Then she decided to move again, this time to a house in the heart of Beverly Hills. On the night I arrived at the new home, Mom said she had a surprise for me. She handed me a dog leash and took me outside. She had bought me a standard size poodle which she had named Stuffy. She had even had him sent to obedience school. Just like me at St. John's. Mom demonstrated all the commands he had learned and told me that he was now my dog and my responsibility. Mom had always had miniature poodles. Her favorite had been Suzette, who would come running when she whistled. I heard that whistle so often that it is the one I use for my dogs. Although I soon came to love Stuffy, I had a bit of a problem because he was a poodle and, in my mind, only women had poodles, not men.

Every time I could, I complained to Mom that I wasn't seeing Dad often enough. But Mom and Dad were having problems. Mom didn't like Nancy, and I felt that she took it out on me by not allowing me to see Dad and by keeping me in that stupid school, St. John's Miniature Alcatraz, as we referred to it.

More than ever at this point, I resented being away at school all the time. I felt that I didn't belong anywhere, not at school and especially not with Mom. I envied kids with normal families. I needed some consistency in my life, and Mom had moved homes four times during five years. I'd no sooner have an address and phone number memorized when it was time to memorize another. I had no one to talk to, not even Maureen, who was going to school in Tarrytown, New York.

I constantly complained to Mom that because of our constant moving I couldn't keep friends. My complaints created friction between us. It seemed that we couldn't have a conversation about anything without it becoming a quarrel. Mom chose to believe that all our problems were caused by Dad, who, she was convinced, had poisoned my mind against her.

In 1958, after an especially bad argument, Mom told me, "You won't have any more problems because you're never going to see your father again. We are moving."

I started to cry. The row escalated. It ended with Mom grabbing the riding crop and whacking me on the legs. She finished with a swat in the middle of my back. That last blow shocked and hurt me so much that the anger in me boiled up and I could no longer control it. I turned around and shouted, "I've had it with you, Miss Wyman." To my shame, I slapped her on the cheek.

When Maureen found out about the row, she told me how hurt Mom was when I called her "Miss Wyman." She thought I was telling her that she wasn't my real mother, which is exactly what I meant at the time. I was using that anger to push her away from me. As a result of that argument, any bond that was left between us was broken. I don't believe our relationship has ever been the same since.

All the men who had come into Mom's life who I had thought were going to be fathers to me had disappeared. Added to that, she had told me that I was not going to see my dad again. I felt I had to fight back. I was mad.

A few weeks after that when it was time for Mom to pick me up at school for the weekend, I was buzzed in my dorm and told a taxi was waiting for me. I said good-bye to my friends and told them I would see them again on Sunday night, but when I went down to the taxi, the driver said he was taking me to Lido Isle in Newport Beach. Mom had moved after all.

The first thing I did when I got to the new house was ask the Russian cook who had taken Carrie's place where Stuffy was. She just stared at me blankly. Mom was not home, so I ran through each room of the house, calling for Stuffy. While I was upstairs searching, I looked out the window and saw Mom in the courtyard, but Stuffy wasn't with her. I ran outside. "Where's Stuffy?" I asked Mom.

"I didn't bring him," she said. "Dogs aren't allowed in Newport Beach, so I gave him to another family."

I was tired of crying, so that night I lay on my bed and stared at the ceiling, wondering why my mother didn't like me.

I never did see my friends at St. John's again because the next week I was enrolled as a day student in Horace Ensign School at Newport. To an extent, my plan had worked. I liked Newport and going to day school, but Mom wasn't home during the week; she had an apartment in Hollywood. So it was just me and the Russian cook whom Mom put in charge. Everything began to calm down between Mom and me for the next few months. I went to school during the week and she would come home Fridays for the weekend. I began to find friends to play with and just as I thought it was all coming together Mom announced that she was sending me to Loyola High in Los Angeles, another all-boys school, because it was one of the best Catholic schools in the area. I protested that it was a boarding school and I didn't want to board anymore. Mom insisted that that's where I was going. To be certain that I got in to Loyola she was going to get me a tutor during the summer. I went to bed angry and woke up even more furious. When I went into the garage to get my bike and go for a ride, I found that the chain had come off the sprocket. That was the last straw. All I could think of was that the bike was a gift from Mom and it didn't like me either. I went into the house and got a ball peen hammer. Then I returned to the garage and beat the bike until it was unrecognizable. With every smashing blow I thought of that bike as my mother, hoping if I somehow destroyed it I was also destroying her. Before, when I got angry, I had hit walls and doors. This kind of rage had never surfaced and when the cook heard the racket and came out to see what was going on, I raised the hammer and told her if she said anything she would be next. Her eyes got as big as silver dollars, and she discreetly

69

disappeared. When my rage was spent, I took the bike across the street and threw it off the dock into the bay. Later, when Mom asked me where my bike was, I told her it was stolen. Mom replaced the bike but I didn't care. I had given up on myself and the proof was in my final report card. My grades were all D's. Loyola wouldn't dare take me. But sure enough, when summer vacation began, here came my tutor.

Mom had to rent a white Plymouth Valiant for the tutor so he could commute to our house. He came to work with me every day. I hated being tutored. Learning was not the problem; *I* was the problem, and I fought with him constantly.

Although my last semesters—at St. John's and Horace Ensign—were bad, I was accepted at Loyola anyway. There should have been no way that a child with my bad grades could get in to Loyola, but my mother, as always, prevailed. I wasn't held accountable for those D's because I was the son of Jane Wyman. I wasn't even allowed to flunk out of school!

But Mom was despairing of ever being able to handle me, so instead of handling our problems herself, Mom turned to the church: She sent me to our priest for consultation. I never told him about the counsellor; he would have kicked me out of church. And, neither did I talk with him about my fear of being illegitimate. I knew the priest was a friend of Mom's. I was afraid he would tell her and she would never forgive me. If she found out about those pictures, I was certain she would send me away. Or, if she let me stay with her, she would throw it up in my face every chance she got. I knew how bad I was and I didn't need her, the priest or anyone else to tell me.

At one meeting with the priest I asked why I had to go through him and could not speak to God personally. Boy, did I catch him by surprise with that question. The priest had no answer and reported to Mom that there was nothing he could do for me.

Mom now thought my problems were beyond our priest's

scope, so she arranged for me to see a child psychiatrist in Beverly Hills. That frightened me because, in those days, the only people who went to see psychiatrists were thought to be crazy. At Mom's insistence, I met with him four or five times, answered his questions and responded to his ink-blot tests. But I thought he was a friend of Mom's, so I didn't trust him. I did tell him, however, that I wasn't getting along with Mom because she didn't want me to see my father and I wanted to be part of his family.

The psychiatrist told Mom that what I needed was a family environment, that it would be better all around if she and I had a break from each other and I went to live with Dad and Nancy. The next time I saw Dad, he asked me if I would like to move in with him and Nancy. "Great," I said. I thought that at last I would be living with a family unit just like a normal kid. Ron Jr., who was nicknamed Skipper by Dad at birth, had just been born, and Patti was around seven years old which meant that I would be the big brother to both of them. In my mind it all added up to respect, acceptance and protection against hurts and pains and bad things like my day camp experience. Once again my plan had worked. I was going to live with Dad and Nancy and would not have to go to Loyola as a boarder. After all, they loved me, and children who were loved are not sent away to school. I would have a new family and a new start. What I didn't realize was that Nancy was as strong or stronger than my mother.

That was in 1959, when I was fourteen years old. Again, I felt something positive was going to happen in my life and that I had finally worked my way up to number one.

Mom's only comment on the day that I moved out was, "Good luck and remember always that it was your choice to move."

Chapter VI

"You're not living up to the Reagan name or image."

Dad and Nancy lived on San Onofre Drive in the Pacific Palisades, a lovely residential community on a bluff overlooking the Pacific Ocean. Their white stucco house, called "The House of the Future," had every conceivable electronic device and had been built for them by General Electric because Dad's TV show was sponsored by the corporation. There was a swimming pool in front with a view of the Pacific Ocean and a small backyard with swings for the children.

Although the house was large, it was filled with people because Dad and Nancy were already a family. There was a big master bedroom for them. Ron and Patti had their own rooms off a playroom where the nurse slept on a day bed. The cook's room was behind the kitchen. There wasn't a bedroom for me, so I slept on one of the two couches in the living room, waiting until company left before I could go to sleep. I used the guest bathroom.

The first thing Nancy did when I moved in was send me to the dentist. I had worn braces to straighten out my teeth, but I had not been to the dentist in years. The dentist, whom we kids called Dr. Fuddlefingers, discovered I had almost a dozen cavities. Nancy was livid with Mom because my teeth had been let go for so long. She also took me shopping for new clothes, something Mom rarely had time for. My entire wardrobe seemed to consist of school uniforms. Such attention made me feel that at last I belonged.

Ron was a really cute baby and anyone could see that Nancy adored him. After all, he was the real heir apparent—a true Reagan—and I was a little jealous of him because he got the attention I wanted. I liked having a baby brother and sister because I felt they would look up to me.

Nancy had intercoms all over the house so she could hear everything that went on in the nursery or anywhere else. I looked forward to the times Nancy put Ron down for his nap and she and I could sit alone in the kitchen and talk while he slept. Together we listened to the sounds from his nursery on the speaker. Before going to sleep, Ron usually would sit in his crib and talk to himself about everything that had happened to him from the moment he got up. Then he would walk along the top of the crib railing, balancing himself against the wall.

Once while we were having lunch, Ron apparently decided to balance himself on the other side of the crib without using the wall for support. Nancy and I heard him crash to the floor. When we got to his room we saw he had landed on his face, sustaining a big lump on his mouth. I think that was the first time we knew

Ron was going to be a dancer; he already was working on his balance while still an infant!

Since there wasn't a bedroom for me in the house and I had already been accepted at Loyola, to my chagrin I was enrolled there as a boarder instead of as a day student despite the fact that I had done everything in my power to stay out of that school. I complained to Dad about being sent to a Catholic school. He shrugged. "I am abiding by your mother's wishes." I was tired of my mother's wishes, and I thought to myself, "What about *my* wishes?"

"Why can't Nancy drive me to school every morning and pick me up in the afternoon just like the other kids?" I asked. "It's only half an hour from home."

"She's too busy with Ron and Patti," he said. "Don't you think it's enough that she has opened up her house to you and invited you in?" I couldn't argue.

On my first day at Loyola, Father Palos, who was the religion teacher, addressed us: "All you boys who went to sissy schools like St. John's should know you are no longer in a sissy school. You are now being taught by Jesuits, so when Sister Mary Five Fingers gets a hangnail, you aren't going to get an extra day off; you're going to be in school."

I respected the priests but they frightened me because they had taken a vow of celibacy and the other kids giggled and made jokes about them. They suspected that some of them were queer and that worried me. So because of my past I never truly trusted any of my teachers and never could really get along, although in the beginning I tried. While I was no longer wetting my bed, it didn't take long before I fell into my old routine of going to early morning services in order to shower alone. I had become an altar boy at St. John's so I could get up early before everyone else, which meant I didn't have to shower with the others. It seemed the older I got the more insecure I became. I felt as though that whole incident back at day camp was my fault.

I didn't go out for any sports because I was afraid of failure, which I equated with being a sissy. I had also discovered that even when I did well in sports Dad or Mom weren't there to see me, and that's who I wanted to impress. But, to push my ego buttons a bit, I sometimes went onto the field during intramural events to prove to myself and to my schoolmates that I could throw a baseball more accurately or a football farther than most of them. In fact I still have a trophy from a baseball throw.

In the beginning my relationship with Nancy was guarded but good. I even considered calling her "Mom" but decided against it, knowing it would upset my mother. Instead I addressed Nancy by her first name. Like everyone else in the house, including Dad, I was a little intimidated by Nancy. She, like Mom, seemed to go through maids and cooks every month, and I was always worried that with one wrong move I might be the next to go.

I had very little contact with Dad. I was at school most of the time, and he was busy traveling on behalf of General Electric. When he was at home, I had to compete with Patti, Ron and Nancy for his time, and I resented that.

I was especially envious when Nancy or any of the kids was alone with him. At the same time, Nancy seemed to begrudge the time I spent with him alone, and she appeared to do everything in her power to keep me, and everyone else, from him. Ronald Reagan was hers, and in my eyes, even as a child, no one else seemed to matter to her as much, not even her children.

Even though I was living with him, nothing had changed. The only time I spent with Dad was on Saturdays and holidays when we went to the Malibu ranch. I was most happy when we went alone to the ranch, but I didn't dare talk with Dad about my feelings because he always seemed to be uncomfortable whenever he and I embarked on anything resembling a personal discussion. The only arguments he and I have ever had were over Nancy.

Once when we were at the ranch, I mentioned some grievance I had against her. Dad told me, "There is a wall building between you and Nancy, and it's up to you to tear it down. Nancy opened her house to bring in another child that was not hers and took care of you because your mother was not doing the job. You should be beholden to her."

"Why is it up to me to make peace with Nancy?"

"Because I'm married to her," he answered testily. End of conversation. As other people have discovered, you can go at Dad all you like but never make the mistake of attacking Nancy. And vice versa. Back then I didn't understand the relationship as I do today. I was upset because I wanted to be number one.

Although people often accuse Dad of being a warmonger, the truth is that he is, and has always been, caring, loving and compassionate. Ray Jackin, the foreman of Dad's ranch, once told me about the time one of the thoroughbreds was dying of cancer and had to be put out of its misery. Dad was heartbroken. The horse, named Bracing, was one of his favorite mares and had birthed Ronnie's Baby, the only one of his horses actually to win a race at Santa Anita.

Ray led Dad to the corral and handed him a 30-30 rifle. Then Ray nuzzled Bracing and drew a chalk line from the base of one ear to the opposite eye and from the other ear to the other eye, making a cross.

"You put a bullet right there where the X is, Mr. Reagan," Ray said. "She'll die instantly. There's nothing to worry about."

Dad stood for a long time with the rifle by his side, just looking at his horse. At last he raised the rifle to his shoulder, but then he lowered it. He couldn't bring himself to pull the trigger. Ray let go of the horse, walked over to Dad, took the rifle, aimed and fired. The horse dropped. "That's how you do it," Ray told Dad.

Dad shuddered, and Ray said he saw tears in his eyes.

When the kids were at the ranch, we all went riding. Although Nancy had a horse I never saw her ride one until Dad decided to run for president.

Actually, Nancy's horse was a monster. A wild gray mare, it had to be tied to a tree in order to put a bridle in its mouth. It was so unmanageable that Dad finally had to send it out to be retrained. Maureen named the horse Nancy D. because she said it reminded her of Nancy. (Many years later, however, when Maureen was trying to make points with Nancy, she would say, "But I named a horse after you because I loved you so much.")

There is one thing that scares Dad. Bees. After Dad and I came back to the corral after a ride, a bee began buzzing around him. Nancy was there and told him not to swat at it because it might sting him. Dad dropped his hands as the bee buzzed around. "Don't move," Nancy said. Dad sat like Stonewall Jackson as the bee landed on his forehead, but the bee stung him. Dad looked at Nancy and said, "Don't ever tell me to stand still for another bee." We all giggled.

Dad and I did a lot of things together when we were alone at the ranch. I didn't enjoy the chores like cleaning out the horse stalls and chicken coops, but I did anything he asked in order to please him. I also painted the fences white for part of my allowance.

Dad had agreed to pay me ten cents a foot for the fences and fifteen cents a post. We had a lot of fences to paint, so one day I made a deal with some friends who lived nearby and got them to paint the fences for seven and a half cents. When Dad came out to the ranch, he saw my friends painting, but I was nowhere in sight. When he learned that I had farmed out my chores, he was upset, but later, he admitted that I was showing signs of becoming a businessman.

Still, the most fun I can remember is when we hopped into his Jeep and shot ground squirrels. The ranch was overrun with the little rascals who dug holes in the ground. Dad didn't want one of his horses to step in a hole and break a leg.

Dad knew where the ground squirrels hung out from riding his horse around the property and seeing them dart and dash for their holes. We'd drive out in the Jeep and park and wait quietly for what seemed like hours, not saying a word. I not only learned patience, but I also got a lesson in shooting.

Dad could shoot a ground squirrel on the run from a moving Jeep. I had graduated from the single-shot rifle to a Marlin lever action .22 just like the Rifleman on television. I was a good shot, but not as good as with the single shot. Instead of taking my time like I had with the single shot now I just cocked, aimed, and shot at will. Dad let me shoot only at the ground squirrels and the blue jays who were nest robbers. On the few occasions when he caught me shooting blackbirds and sparrows, he'd take the gun away for a few weeks at a time as my punishment.

I sometimes spent the night at the ranch with Dick Jackin, Ray's son, who was about my age. Ray occasionally went to nearby Seminole Hot Springs for what in those days was called "a toot." He sometimes got too drunk to drive home. Dick taught me to drive the Jeep so that I could bring Ray home if Dick wasn't around.

Most Sundays Dad, Nancy, Patti and Ron went to Bel-Air Presbyterian church. They never invited me to join them. Rather than say anything, I sat in front of the television set every Sunday morning and watched football, pretending that I didn't care but feeling left out. Years later when I asked Dad why he hadn't asked me to join them at church, he told me that he hadn't wanted to upset Mom, who was a loyal Catholic, by taking me to Protestant services. I probably wouldn't have gone even if asked because I hated church and I felt God hated me. But if he just would have asked it would have made me feel special and a part of his family.

When I turned fifteen years old, I could legally drive a motor scooter. When I was living with Mom I had always admired the one parked in a driveway at the corner of Camden and Sunset across the street from the famous Beverly Hills Hotel, a place Mom would take Maureen and me on some Sundays just to swim and eat lunch.

Now that I was old enough I went looking for one. It wasn't long before I found a used blue Lambretta that could be bought for around seven hundred dollars. I pestered Dad to get it for me so I could ride out to the ranch on Friday nights and be there to meet him on Saturdays. He bought the scooter, which I promptly painted red. He also promised me a new car if I graduated from high school (at the time it was a good bet for Dad) and five hundred dollars if I didn't smoke or drink until I was twenty-one—the same promise he made to Maureen. I made it to eighteen. One out of two was good for me!

I was a big fan of the Beach Boys, and as we drove out to the ranch, I would listen to their music on a local radio station. Dad would often turn to another station which played "The Swinging Years." "This is *real* music," he would say as he drummed his fingers to the beat of Glenn Miller. I laughed when, many years later, Dad and Nancy came to the rescue of the Beach Boys when they were fired from playing at the July 4th celebration in Washington. I thought that maybe my music finally got through to Dad.

In those days I couldn't wait to get home from Loyola so I could ride my scooter out to the ranch to stay with Dick and Ray. Then I'd wait for Dad, Nancy and the kids to arrive on Saturday. I loved going out to the ranch by myself because it was the one place where I had my own room. The walls were covered with pictures of race horses. Dad proudly hung the framed ribbons I had won for swimming along with my yo-yo patch over my bed. I looked forward to my time alone at the ranch for another good reason: The only girls I knew were at Malibu Lake.

I was curious about sex because all my school years it seemed were spent in Catholic all-boys boarding schools. I was now in my midteens and like all teenagers it was the main topic of conversation at school. I wanted to be like everyone else, and when asked if I had gotten laid I would answer "Yeah," although I was still a virgin. It was not a subject I felt I could discuss with Dad. Anyway, I wanted to be macho like him, and I didn't want him to think I didn't know what it was all about.

Unknown to him, however, I was getting some sex education at the ranch. On the weekends when the family wasn't there, Ray allowed some friends of his, who were photographers for girlie magazines, to shoot cheesecake layouts by the pond or in the woods. Ray had the magazines hidden under his bed and would show Dick and me the photos and regale us with stories about the layouts.

That led me to dingy shops on Hollywood Boulevard where I could rent a camera for two dollars an hour and photograph nude female models, just like the ones I saw at the ranch. I graduated from there to striptease joints where I saw how girls took off their clothes and then to X-rated theaters.

With that limited background of sex information, I went on Saturday nights in Dad's station wagon to Western Avenue, the red-light district of Los Angeles. At first I just cruised and talked with the girls. After months, I finally got up the courage to actually go to bed with one. At last I had something to brag about at school, although I never admitted I had paid for love.

If there was a good side to this, it's that I affirmed my masculinity. I was normal. Straight. The fear of my being a homosexual had finally vanished from my thoughts. But those pictures haunted me every day and I couldn't get them out of my mind. I didn't know how I would explain them. So I kept on reaffirming my masculinity and that cost money. It seemed I couldn't get enough sex to bury those pictures. When I had spent my allowance I began taking money from Dad. It was like a disease I couldn't stop until one day I just said no more. I believe down inside I wanted to get caught doing something awful like buying hookers because I felt as though I had never been punished for what happened with the counsellor.

Nancy told me during the second year I was with them that I would soon be moving out of the living room. Boy, was I glad to hear that! A few weeks later when I came home from school, I saw construction men working on the rear wing of the house. One of the workers told me they were building a new room, and my heart filled with joy; at last I was going to have a room of my own, and I thought that was the greatest thing in the world.

That room under construction was the symbol of my acceptance in the family. I had earned my wings. I had lived with my pain for so long, waiting for something good to happen to me, and now, finally, instead of being sent out I was going to be brought in. Everything was finally going to be all right. Every time I came home during the next five weekends, I walked into that room as it was being completed and pictured in my mind where my belongings would be placed, where the TV would go, which way my new bed would face. I don't think I ever had been so happy. On Sunday night when I returned to school, I knew that the following Friday when I went home for the weekend, I was going to move into my own room and be part of the family.

I'll never forget that Friday when I raced through the big black front door, ran over the black slate foyer, across the zebra skin rug, into the washer-dryer-pantry area and into *my* brand new room. I came face to face with Ron's nurse. "How do you like my new room?" she asked.

My heart sank. They found out, I thought to myself. I was scared as I went to find Nancy. "Where am I going to sleep?" I asked.

"We have moved you onto the day bed in the playroom where the nurse had been sleeping," she said.

I didn't cry, but I went out onto the street by myself; I wanted to be alone. My thoughts were dark; I had counted on that room to make me a member of the family. It was the same old story to me: No one seemed to want or like me. Especially Moms.

When I asked Dad why the nurse got the room and I didn't, he said, "She's here all week and you're only here on weekends."

"I could be here all week too if I were a day student. Nancy wouldn't even have to drive me. I could ride to school with my friends from down the block."

"That's not in the cards," Dad said, ending the conversation.

I was afraid to tell him how I really felt because I was now too insecure about my position in the house.

That night I went into a Hollywood bar where I picked up a prostitute. We got in Dad's station wagon and drove to her home where she took me into her bedroom.

"What do you want?" she asked me.

"I just want you to hold me," I said.

She started to laugh. "That's the most unusual request I've ever had from a John," she said. "You can come back whenever you want for no charge."

Every time I came home from school and saw the nurse in that bedroom it nearly killed me. I was devastated. I felt that if Dad and Nancy didn't want me, I didn't want them either. Why should I care about myself when no one else did? I started self-destructing again.

Regarding the bedroom incident, I don't know whether Dad and Nancy were right or wrong. As a child I needed to feel that I was part of the family. I was always insecure. Subconsciously I felt I was rejected because I was "dirty," although they had no way of knowing that. A room of my own in their home would have meant the world to me and would have gone a long way toward making it my home as well.

I was so upset about not having that room that when Nancy's Lincoln Continental accidentally rolled off the hill in front of our house and was totalled, I laughed and was only sorry she wasn't in it. Then I became angry because the accident meant I couldn't use the station wagon to go out that night on a date. Everything, and I mean everything, had become a personal affront to me.

My relationship with Nancy had begun to deteriorate. I began having the same problems with her as I'd had with my mother. I was convinced she didn't want or like me. To get back at her, I picked fights whenever I could.

It was very easy to get to Nancy. Sometimes when we had an argument I would simply say, "You are not my mom." Although I had left my mother, I threw that up to Nancy anyway, knowing it would hurt her. Naturally, she resented the remark because she believed she had taken me in as a mother would. In two years I had gone from wanting to call her "Mom" to speaking with her only when necessary.

Maureen never lived with Dad and Nancy (weekends and holidays, she stayed with Mom or friends). At that time she hated Nancy and had nicknamed her "Dragon Lady" because she was jealous of Nancy's relationship with Dad, too. To win Maureen as my ally, every time I saw her I'd come up with new reasons why Nancy was Dragon Lady. When Maureen and I were alone together we aired our grievances about Nancy. Maureen shared the same uncomfortable feelings that I had, and we commiserated with each other about our less-than-perfect relations with our parents. I constantly looked for motherly protection, and Maureen was always on my side. Invariably I followed her lead and took her side in family arguments—unless Nancy was against her, in which case I took Nancy's side. This inconsistency on my part must have meant that beneath it all, I still craved Nancy's motherly affection. I was going in circles trying to make friends in the family and all I was making were enemies.

The episode with the new room continued to weigh on my mind. My grades slipped, and I began to act up in school. When I occasionally received a one-day suspension from Loyola, my punishment was to memorize acts from *The Merchant of Venice* before being permitted back into class.

Dad once said to me, "If I live to be a hundred, I'll never understand how you can be in the top percentile on the SAT scores and still be such a terrible student."

I knew why but couldn't find the words to explain it to him.

Chapter VII

"Remember me? I'm your son Mike."

November, 1986. My son has been behaving strangely at home. He is not as talkative as usual, and my wife reports that he is occasionally crying when she picks him up at school. One morning I made it a point to take him to school early and visit with his teacher. "Has Cameron spoken with you?" she asked me. "He has something he would like to share with you."

I sought out Cameron on the playground and asked him to join me on the school steps. I asked him if he wanted to talk. He looked off into the distance and shook his head. Then he started to cry. I put my arm around his shoulders and held him. "Tell me what's troubling you," I said.

He stopped sniffling and looked up into my face. "Dad, am I really the grandson of the President of the United States?"

"Yes," I said. "Why do you ask?"

"Because the kids have been teasing me. They told me that I am not really the President's grandson because you were adopted. They said that your parents must not have liked you very much because they gave you away."

I felt that familiar churning in my gut that I have always experienced whenever anyone mentions the fact that I am adopted. But this time it was worse because it affected my own son, who was so proud to be the President's grandson.

"It's true that I was adopted," I said. "My real mommy and daddy couldn't take care of me, so they gave me to a nice family who could raise me." It was a pat answer, but it was the best I was able to give at the moment. I followed it up with "Look, the family that raised me is really my family. You are the grandson of the President, part of his family just like me. If you weren't, you wouldn't have the Secret Service with you all the time to be certain nothing bad happens to you." He smiled and said, "Thank you, Daddy."

When I left Cameron, he seemed satisfied with my answers. The fact is many adopted children never feel as though they really belong in the family that adopted them. Unfortunately, that insecurity about heritage and roots can even hang over their own children.

Many adoptees seem doomed to wonder who they really are; who were their biological parents? Why did their original parents give them up? Those questions have nagged me almost since the day I found out I was adopted. But I always felt, and was constantly told, that it would be a slap in the face of my adoptive parents if I asked questions about my biological parents. Nevertheless, I was curious and constantly trying to devise a surreptitious method to learn the answers without hurting my parents.

I found that opportunity by accident in 1961 when I was sixteen years old and Nancy got hold of my report card. As usual, it was all bad. She brought me into her bedroom and verbally ripped into me, concluding with "You're not living up to the Reagan name or image, and unless you start shaping up, it would be best for you to change your name and leave the house." She didn't say where I could go.

Nancy had given me the perfect opening to find out about my biological parents. "Fine," I said, "why don't you just tell me the name I was born with so at least when I walk out the door I'll know what name to use."

"Okay, Mr. Reagan," she snapped, "I'll do just that."

At that time Dad and Mom still used the same business manager. To this day I don't know how Nancy managed to get into my mother's file because, as far as I know, it was sealed.

The following week when I came home from school, Nancy told me, "I have the information you requested." I thought she was joking. She proceeded to tell me my given name was John L. Flaugher, and she spelled out my surname. She said that I had been born at Queen of Angels Hospital. My father had been a sergeant in the Army who, while on leave, had had an affair with my mother. Then he went overseas, leaving her pregnant. He never returned. "You are the offspring of that relationship," Nancy said in a cold voice.

"Were my parents married?" I asked in a small voice.

"No," she said.

The other shoe had dropped.

I told Nancy I wanted to talk to Dad when he came home.

"So do I," she said.

I went out of the room thinking, "I am a bastard and I am going to hell." I had just seen the movie *Tom Jones*, which opens with two women denigrating Tom as an illegitimate bastard who would never amount to anything. Without being aware of it, Nancy had rubber-stamped all the fears I'd had for years.

Nancy cornered Dad the moment he came home from a trip for GE. She told him about our argument and that I had asked her to find out my real name, which she had done under duress.

After speaking with her, Dad called me in and said, "I understand you want to talk to me."

"Yes," I said.

He looked hard at me and said, "How could you pressure Nancy into going down and finding out your real name? It was wrong of you, and you should apologize to her."

"Wait a minute," I said. "I want to tell you my side of the story."

"I don't need to hear your side," he said. "I've heard the story. You're wrong. Nancy is right."

In my view Nancy had turned my father against me, and I now had a real excuse to hate her.

A few days later I went to see Mom and Fred Karger whom she had just remarried—this time they had been married inside the church railing because she was Catholic. Maureen, who was home on vacation, was also there.

In the course of the conversation, I casually mentioned my real last name to see if anyone reacted. No one said anything.

Later, Maureen took me aside and asked about the name I had mentioned. "That was my name at birth," I said.

Maureen turned pale. "How did you find that out?"

"Nancy told me."

"How did she know that?" Maureen asked. "Mom doesn't even know your birth name. Those records are sealed."

"I don't know. She told me to get out of the house and this is the name I could leave with because I'm not a credit to the name Reagan." What I didn't tell her was how and why the conversation took place. All I cared about was I had Maureen on my side against Nancy, and in time, with my way of telling the story, I could get almost anyone to sympathize with me.

"Under no circumstances are you to leave that house," Maureen said heatedly, "and don't you dare tell Mom you know your real name or how you found it out."

For years I resented Nancy for telling me the truth about my blood parents. Looking back, I really can't blame her. I had provoked and pushed her to the breaking point. There was no way she could be aware of my private torment.

At the time it surprised me that Nancy wasn't more sympathetic of my problems as an adopted child because her own father had abandoned her a year after she was born as Anne Frances Robbins. Nancy's mother, Edie Luckett, had been a Broadway actress prior to World War I. Alla Nazimova, the famous Russian star, served as godmother when Anne was born in 1921. Edie, whose nickname was De De, went back on the stage using trunks for cradles backstage at various theaters. From the age of two, Anne, who was nicknamed Nancy, was raised by surrogate mothers. A lonely, quiet and thoughtful little girl, she lived for De De's visits. What I didn't know until recently was that Nancy hated her real father and refused ever to see him or have anything to do with him. In 1929, Edie Luckett married Loyal Davis, a distinguished Chicago neurosurgeon. Nancy was fourteen years old when she was adopted by her stepfather. Dr. Davis was a disciplinarian who made Nancy the perfectionist she is today. I have read that no matter what she did to please him, it was never enough. But Nancy soon came to love him. She once told me that it upset her every time people referred to her as the adopted child of Dr. Loyal Davis, because she always thought of him as her father.

Perhaps because she had made such a success out of her situation, she expected no less from me.

Despite all the friction, I didn't move out of the house. I had no place else to go. I had no intention of searching for my biological parents because I was afraid.

My relationship with Nancy was now strained to the point where we spoke to each other only when necessary. We could not exchange two words without conjuring up bitter feelings. I just didn't care anymore about anything. As a result, my schoolwork suffered, and my grades became worse than ever.

A month later, Dad and I had a rare father-son talk as he drove me to school after a weekend at home. Looking back he was distraught as he put his arm around me. "If you can pull your grades up enough to get through high school, I can get you into Eureka." Eureka College was my father's alma mater.

I wanted nothing less at the time than to go to a Christian college, but I didn't want to tell him that. Instead, I said, "If you send me out of state to a coed high school for my last year I promise to get good grades." Ironically, whereas previously I would have done almost anything to live at home and attend a day school, now I was desperate to get as far away as possible.

"It's a deal," Dad said.

Nancy's stepfather, Dr. Davis, knew some people at Judson, a boarding school in Arizona, and he helped get me in there. Although I had to repeat my junior year at Judson, I was happy. There were girls on campus, and I was 420 miles away from Los Angeles. At Loyola, I lived only a few miles from home, and yet was forced to board; so I was resentful. But at Judson, I knew I couldn't go home every night from Arizona. I went out for sports and lettered in football, baseball and basketball. My grades went up, and I made the equivalent of the National Honor Society after my first year. I was on a roll.

As an honor student, I was entitled to live in one of the cottages, which we called "shacks," behind the campus. I moved into a cottage with three roommates and was permitted to spend my study hours there as long as I remained on the honor roll. Most importantly, I was out of the dorm and community shower.

Dad was so pleased with my grades that he asked me what he could get me for Christmas. I told him I wanted a shotgun or a deer rifle so I could go hunting during the season. Ever since Dad had taught me how to use a gun I've loved hunting because it reminded me of my youth with him. When I came home for Christmas, both rifles were under the tree: a beautiful engraved, double-barrel, Winchester shotgun with a gold trigger and a .243 caliber rifle.

The first time I used the rifle I bagged the largest wild pig in the state of Arizona that year. Although it was an ugly beast, Dad had it mounted for me. It replaced the yo-yo patch.

I felt Dad was stingy with my allowance, however, because I got only five dollars a week during my senior year. I soon devised a way to increase my weekly allotment of cash. Thanks to Mom, I was good at cards. There were a lot of kids with money at Judson, so I organized poker parties in my shack and won enough money every week so that I could afford some luxuries such as a movie and dinner with my current girl friend.

Dad and Nancy came to Phoenix every Easter by train (Dad hadn't flown since the war) to visit the Davises and came to see me perform in my first school play, a murder mystery called *The Night of January 16* in which I played the prosecuting attorney. I had been acting out one role or another for most of my life; but this was my first official part as an actor, and I was nervous. After the show, Dad complimented me on my performance, but I doubt he thought I was going to raise the Reagan name to new acting heights. I was so nervous with him and Nancy there that I know I was terrible.

The following year when the family was due back to spend Easter with the Davises, Dad promised to watch me play baseball. I was number one pitcher on the Judson team. I was ecstatic that Dad was coming to see me, but he and Nancy were held up in Los Angeles and couldn't make it in time for the game.

However, Nancy's parents, Loyal and De De, were in the stands. My first time up at bat with two men on base, I heard De De yell, "You better hit a home run, you little sonofabitch."

I had never been much of a hitter and maybe that's why I became a pitcher, but when I realized De De was there, I was so excited that I pounded out my first and last home run.

God, how I loved De De. She was a warm-hearted, generous woman who, I think, knew I was having problems and was always sympathetic to me. When I graduated from high school, she gave me a gold signet ring that I cherish to this day. Sadly, she died recently, and I never told her how much I cared about her. She was, after all, Patti's and Ron's grandmother, and no relation to me. But we had a bond and when she died, for the first time in my life, I cried for a family member other than myself. When Nelle, Dad's mom, passed away in the early sixties, I cried because I thought I was supposed to and people were watching. De De's kindness was contagious and when Nancy sent a piece from her Steuben collection with a note that her mother would have wanted me to have this, I felt a wonderful glow inside.

The Davises lived in a big house in the Biltmore Estates on the edge of a golf course. On that Easter, we hid eggs as always on the fairway for Ron to find. Someone opened the drapes of the large bay window, and there, sitting dead center on the lawn, was a rabbit with an egg next to it. We all looked at each other and laughed. It couldn't have been planned any better. Nancy said, "For the rest of his life Ron will believe in the Easter Bunny."

I was now spending ten weeks each summer at a lovely camp in Northern California, set in acres of meadows with hiking and horseback riding trails galore. I had Rebel with me, and I was happy, comfortable and part of a big family. I had become one of the favorites with the adults there. I learned to hunt with a bow and arrow and to improve my riding skills. In my desire to make points with the camp director, I volunteered for almost every project and was even on the work crew.

During what turned out to be my last summer, however, I felt that the director was taking advantage of me. It wasn't a new feeling; it was an old one that just kept recurring and would keep me unsettled for the rest of my life. One day during an argument, I lost my temper and threw a punch at him. He countered and knocked me down. The end result—I was booted out of camp, put on a plane and sent home.

Luckily, Dad and Nancy were away when I arrived. I realized that I had been wrong, and so I got into Dad's car, intending to drive back to camp and apologize. About one hundred miles en route, I parked by the side of the road to nap. When I awoke I had a change of heart and returned home. I spent the last remaining weeks of summer at the ranch painting fences. I knew that would get me in Dad's good graces and earn me some money.

I returned to school two weeks early in order to get in shape for the football season. My training paid off: I made first string quarterback my senior year. Boy, would Dad be proud.

There are disadvantages as well as advantages to being the offspring of celebrities. In the first place, no one ever believes that you achieve anything on your own. Secondly, even though Judson was a rich kids' school, there were many students even there who said that if it weren't for my parents I wouldn't be at Judson. It was true but I hated to hear it. I became accustomed to kids on opposing teams asking, "Which one is Reagan's kid? Let's beat up on him and find out how tough he is." Even my own teammates often tried to find out just how tough I was. Just as I had in fifth grade, I had to learn to play hurt, because I felt if I didn't, people would think I was the typical sissy son of famous celebrities. These kids always found some way to give my parents credit for anything good I did. Every child of famous parents probably has to go through the same thing. But I played hard and it paid off. During my senior year at Judson, I was named "Player of the Week" by the Scottsdale Press four times out of an eight-game season.

That year, 1963, I led the Judson football team to a state championship, their first and, as far as I know, their last. For that,

I was named "Player of the Year." Jack Stovall, a recruiter from Arizona State, even talked to me about a football scholarship.

At that time Dad was President of the Screen Actors' Guild, and a lot of people were trying to convince him to enter politics. At home during Christmas in 1963, I overheard an argument between him and Nancy. I was in the guest bathroom. They were in the driveway where they often went for private discussions. Since I had never heard them argue before (or since), I tried to hear what was being said.

Nancy was telling Dad that he had been asked to run for Governor of California. She said her stepfather was willing to raise $200,000 in campaign money if Dad agreed to run. Personally, I don't think Dad ever had really strong ambitions to be a politician, but Mommy—his name for Nancy—prodded him. The rest is history and I'm glad.

Although I was not originally on the graduating list because of an indiscretion, one of the faculty members asked if I could prevail on Dad to be the commencement speaker. He hinted that if I was successful I would be allowed to graduate with my class as long as I promised to behave myself in the future. I got his message and asked Dad to speak. He agreed.

On graduation day, prior to his commencement address, Dad was asked to pose for pictures with some of the graduating students. Naturally, I was included in the group selected for the photo. We were all wearing caps and gowns. I was the third or fourth in line. As the others passed in front of him one by one, I heard Dad introduce himself and then ask for the graduate's name. My grin was as wide as a cavern when I came before him.

"My name is Ronald Reagan," Dad said. "What's yours?"

I took off my mortar board. "Remember me?" I said. "I'm your son Mike."

"Oh," said Dad, "I didn't recognize you."

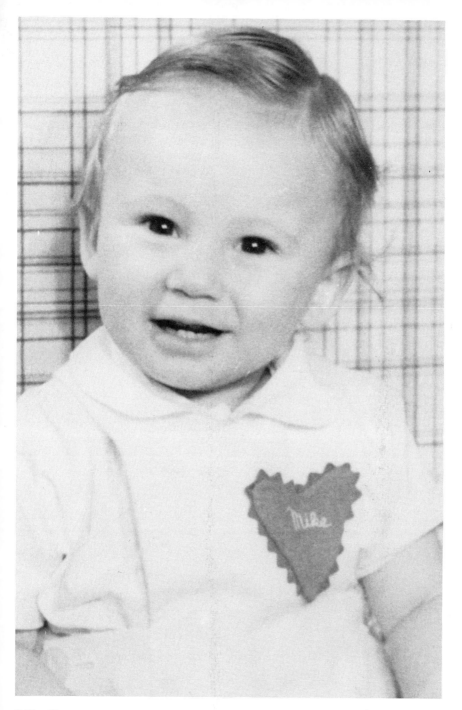

Mike Reagan, age 1
(from the album of Irene Flaugher).

My sister Maureen and me with our parents Jane Wyman and Ronald Reagan (from the album of Irene Flaugher).

Maureen, Mom, and me on Maureen's fifth birthday. (from the album of Irene Flaugher).

With Mom (from the album of Irene Flaugher).

Dad, "Merm," and me at our first house in Truesdale Estates.

Clapping for Dad, Mom, and Maureen.

Family photo: Dad,
Maureen, Mom, and me.

Family photo: Dad, Maureen, Mom, and me.

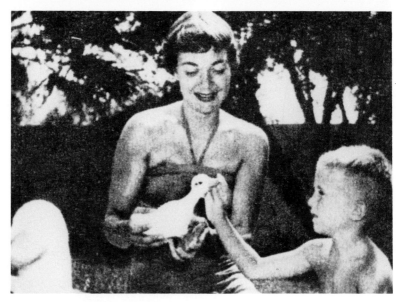

With Mom and the ducks
(from the album of Irene Flaugher).

Me at age 4 with Mom and Maureen.

Me at age 4 with Mom and Maureen
(from the album of Irene Flaugher).

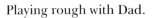
Playing rough with Dad.

Horsing around with Dad.

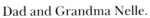
Dad and Grandma Nelle.

Me at age 9, with Mom,
Maureen, and the poodle, Suzette.

Celebrating my 10th birthday
with Mom and the cast and crew
of the Jane Wyman Theater.

Me in the eighth grade at
St. John's Military Academy.

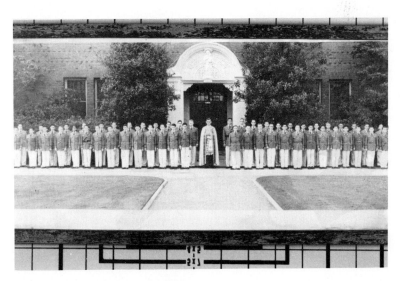

At St. John's Military Academy.

With Dad, Nancy, and Patti
(album of Irene Flaugher).

Big brother Mike with Patti and Ronnie
in the Pacific Palisades house in 1959. I was 14..

Entertaining Ronnie; a rare smile with braces.

Vying with Ronnie for Dad's attention.

Christmas, 1962, with
Nancy, Patti, and Ronnie.

The National Honor Society, 1964.
I am second from the right.

My high school graduation
photo, 1964, from Judson.

With my date Linda Montalban at
the 21st birthday party Mom gave for me at Chasens.

975 wedding photo of Colleen and me with Colleen's father,
dward Sterns, her mother, Eva, Mom, Nancy, Dad, and Ronnie.

Grandma "De De" Davis with usher Vern Mahoney at my wedding, 1975.

Following an evening of charades at Maureen's ("The making of the President").

During the 1976 campaign.

Dad and Nancy during their first
visit with Cameron, 1978.

Who is that nice family waiting
for Ronald Reagan's plane?
At the Detroit convention, 1980.

At the Detroit convention.

Chapter VIII

"I'm in love with a dishwasher."

In May, 1964 I graduated from Judson School as a member of the National Honor Society. Dad, being true to his promise, bought me a brand new Ford Galaxy 500, black with red vinyl interior. All I could think was that all those days Dad let me sit on his lap in the station wagon teaching me to drive had finally paid off and I couldn't wait to go back to my old job as fry cook and dinner chef at the Old Faithful Lodge, which overlooks the awesome superstar geyser in Yellowstone Park, Wyoming, to show it off. Most of the other employees were college kids from all over the country. We were called "Savages." The girls lived in dorms, and the fellows shared quarters in shacks alongside the Firehole River.

Maybe that's why we were called savages. My friends from the previous summer were there and it was a constant party. Several of us would get into my car and blast off to places like The Gusher, a bar in West Yellowstone, where we'd drink beer and then dance to a jukebox until two A.M. I had lots of girl friends, mostly tourists, but I wasn't interested in a serious relationship. For the first time, I was secretly terrified that I might fall in love with someone and later discover that she was my sister.

At this time I began to discover that girls sometimes dated me because of who I was. Frequently, unbeknownst to me, a friend would tell a girl that I was the son of Ronald Reagan and Jane Wyman. The girl would want to go out with me so she could later tell her friends that she had dated a "celebrity." It wasn't great for my ego but because I needed girls around I took advantage of that. More often than not, I made a conquest. Ironically, people seem to think it's wrong for me to benefit from my name, but all right for other people to use me or my name.

At nights, I would lie awake in bed, imagining myself at Arizona State University as a football hero and fantasizing that Dad would be cheering as he watched me play on TV. When summer was over I packed my bags as fast as I could and headed for ASU, a 400-mile drive from the Pacific Palisades.

The campus was beautiful with long sloping lawns. Most important, there were beautiful golden girls in jeans and short skirts blooming everywhere. After years of boarding, primarily at Catholic all-boys schools, this was my idea of paradise, maybe because it was situated next to Paradise Valley.

It already had been arranged for me to live in a dorm on campus, although I hated the notion. Fraternity Pledge Week was in full force when I arrived. While I was registering, a senior introduced himself and invited me to visit the Lambda Chi Alpha fraternity house. He said that if the other members approved me I could move into the frat house at once. He was the first one to approach me, so I agreed because the invitation meant acceptance. But most important it would get me out of the dorm. Naturally I passed inspection because it was a big deal for the frat to pledge the son of Jane Wyman and Ronald Reagan. Although I was somewhat apprehensive, I did feel that living "macho-style" in a fraternity house had its points.

When I called Dad to ask if he would help me out with the finances, he was pleased that I wanted to live in a fraternity house. While at college himself, he had been a member of Tau Kappa Epsilon. He and Nancy agreed to take care of all my expenses. So I moved into the fraternity house but later was dismayed to discover that Lambda Chi Alpha was a Christian fraternity. I just never asked questions. I was in a constant fog and, at this time, didn't know why.

My first assignment in Freshman English class was to write a thousand-word essay about Registration Day. The essay was so good that I received an A+ for my paper, which was read to every other English class at the college. It was then sent to the dean. I never got it back but my professor told me that I was ahead of my class and should take a tougher course. I stayed where I was because I liked the grade but most of all I liked the praise. For the first time I received all the credit. At the end of my first week, I went to find Jack Stovall, the man who had talked to me about a football scholarship while I was at Judson. But he wasn't there and no one in the Athletic Department had heard of him, which surprised me. I needed someone to help push me. Since I was too insecure to hustle for myself, this meant that my dream of being a football hero was shot down. It was probably just as well. Most of the other recruits were coal mining kids from Pennsylvania who looked like bone crushers. I wanted to play, not die. Years later I met Jack, who told me that he had moved north to become a football scout at Oregon State. He also explained that the reason I wasn't offered a football scholarship was because the school executives felt that my parents could afford the tuition and I, therefore, didn't need the financial help. I wish I could have gotten that scholarship.

During the first quarter of my freshman year, my attitude was good, and I did well in class. But I had trouble trying to fit into the Lambda Chi Alpha mold. The fraternity kept a high moral tone, discouraging all forms of high jinks such as drinking and carousing.

After a while I wanted out of the fraternity, so I began to eat my meals elsewhere. Then came a real depression: not only a disheartening feeling of alienation but the greater reality of finding myself in a financial bind. I was dead broke. The money Dad had sent me was gone. As the Christmas holidays approached, I didn't even have ten dollars left for gas so I could drive home to Los Angeles. I didn't know what to do so I called Nancy and told her of my problem. She said, "We've sent you enough money. If you've squandered it, that's your problem. I'm not going to send you more."

In desperation, I called Merm collect. Her advice was to ask Mom for the money. "She'll come through," Merm said. So I called Mom. The next morning a special delivery letter accompanied by her personal check arrived at the dorm. The message was that we would spend Christmas together at Lake Tahoe where she planned to meet some friends.

I will never forget the Christmas of '64. It was the most memorable of my life because it was just Mom and me. I had her full attention, and I relished it. We took the overnight train from Los Angeles to Atherton, California, and then drove in a rental car to Tahoe where some of Mom's friends—including Jim Nabors, singer Kay Starr, her daughter and her wardrobe manager—had rented a house. Kay was performing at Harrah's Club in Tahoe, which provided all the food and beverages including a cook. This was first class and I loved it. After we came off the ski slopes each day, the cook was waiting for us with glasses of hot wine. We were pampered and spoiled. Best of all, Mom and I were getting along great.

We had a wonderful New Year's Eve together at Harrah's singing "Auld Lang Syne." But the moment that meant the most to me came at midnight when I leaned over and kissed Mom and told her how much I loved her. Even though she smiled her approval, I don't think she knew how much I meant it.

Just when it was time for us to leave on New Year's Day, a blinding blizzard started. The others opted to stay for another day or two, but Mom, ever a majority of one, swung the vote. I put snow chains on the tires of our car, and Kay's manager said he would follow us in his convertible. We were the last two cars allowed to leave Tahoe that week, and our drive down the winding, icy mountain road with zero visibility was hairy. On the way, the windshield wipers on the manager's car stopped working. We stopped and I told him, "Ride my car's bumper! I'll use the brakes!"

It was tricky, but we finally made it. When we reached the bottom, Mom looked at me with pride and said, "You can drive me to the moon anytime you want." It was the first praise I ever remember her giving me, and I felt ten feet tall.

Back in Los Angeles, I realized that I didn't have enough gas money for my drive back to Tempe. I didn't want to ask Mom for more money. She had done enough by taking me to Tahoe and showering me with love and gifts. I wasn't about to call Dad and Nancy for help. However, with resourcefulness, I was able to make it back to Tempe by bartering some of my clothing with various gas station attendants along the route. That was probably the beginning of my sales career!

On my return to the frat house, there was talk of Initiation Week. I didn't want to be initiated, so I began to avoid the members, hoping they would ask me to leave. One of my hiding places was an off-campus bar called The Library, which had books painted on the walls. When parents called a frat house or dorm and asked for their child, the person who answered the phone usually said honestly, "He (or she) is at the library."

One night when I was at The Library, a short, thin Italian who was about my age introduced himself as Joe Bonanno, Jr. The name didn't mean a thing to me. He probably befriended me because he knew who I was. I soon learned that his father was a celebrity of sorts, too—a famous Mafioso reputed to be the "boss of bosses." But we had a common bond. We were both the sons of famous fathers. The difference was that where people treated me with respect, everyone treated Joe with hatred and disgust, just because of the difference in our fathers. I don't know what has happened to Joe, but I'm sure it probably turned out bad because he never really had a chance. I liked being in Joe's company because he was the epitome of macho. When we'd go out, people would clear space for us as we walked by. I felt important and tough by just being a part of his retinue.

Then, out of the blue, Dad telephoned me. He said that the FBI had seen my car parked in front of Joe's house and had traced the license plates to me. "I don't want you to see that young man again, he's trouble," Dad said. I didn't know that Dad was considering running for governor of California and my friendship with Joe Jr. might prove to be embarrassing to his campaign, so I got angry. I told Dad that the only time he ever called me was when he thought I did something wrong; he never called when things were going right. I accused him of not ever liking my friends and hung up the phone.

When I relayed the conversation to Joe, we joked about it and decided to go drag racing. We put dump tubes (exhaust pipe extensions) on my Galaxy and went to the Bee Line Dragway, the major drag strip in Phoenix. I entered a race against the hottest driver on the circuit, who had never lost a race. But, as luck would have it, he blew a fuel pump seconds after leaving the starting line, and I won. He was infuriated and challenged me to another go. "No way," I said. "I just retired from drag racing." Just as the discussion was getting ugly, Joe and his friends sauntered over. Their presence cooled the guy down. It was my first and last car race, but I still have the trophy and I always will.

My grades had slipped so badly I was once again at the bottom of my life-long roller coaster ride. One of the school administrators called my parents with a report. Dad and Nancy responded by cutting off my living allowance. "If you want to stay in college," Nancy said to me over the telephone, "you will have to get a job." Since Dad and Nancy would no longer pay for my living arrangements, I moved out of the frat house and went looking for work.

The only employment I could find was at a car wash, but I was fired a week or two later. "It's not that you don't work hard," the owner said. "You're the best man I have. But I want to be fair, and you don't need the job because your parents are rich."

So there I was, unemployed, broke, in trouble with my parents, feeling sorry for myself and with no place to live until some schoolmates said I could move in with them. I stopped going to classes and flunked every one of my courses including English— how stupid!—whereupon, Dad, Nancy and Mom had a rare family conference. The upshot was that they were pulling me out of school. "You can do whatever you want," Nancy and Dad said, "but you can't come back here and live with your mother or us." Her stepfather, Dr. Davis, who lived in nearby Phoenix and had given me the run of his house, now refused to let me come stay with him. Even De De couldn't help.

My options were fast running out. I landed another menial job as a fry cook in a Scottsdale hotel. Once more I was fired. Management had decided to cut back on employees, and I was the first to go because they felt I didn't need the job. Fortunately, I had money enough to drive back to Los Angeles. To save on future gasoline bills, I decided to trade in my Galaxy for a Volkswagen with a sun roof, the kind of car all my friends now drove. It was the car of the mid 60's. I telephoned Dad and asked if he would pay the difference. God, I was gutsy! Dad is (and always was) an easy touch provided I could get past outside interference. I don't know whether or not he talked it over with Nancy, but his business manager took care of the transaction, and I got my VW.

The first thing I did on arriving in Los Angeles was call Merm, who was married to David Sills, a captain in the Marine Corps. Nancy had already spoken with Merm and suggested to her that David contact the Marine recruitment office and have me drafted into the Corps. (Apparently Nancy was not aware that the Marines don't draft recruits.) Merm and David sat me down for a pep talk in their living room. They said unsparingly that I had to get my act together, though both thought my parents were out of line in wanting me to be shipped off to Viet Nam. So David called Nancy and told her that the Marines were filled up.

Merm put me in touch with a friend, David Eyraud, whose father owned Asbury Transportation, a trucking firm in downtown Los Angeles. He arranged for me to work the night shift from five P.M. to one-thirty A.M., loading and unloading heavy freight.

Some friends I'd known for six years from summer camp invited me to stay with them at their home. For good measure, I enrolled in morning courses at L.A. Valley College, doing my best to get back into my family's good graces.

Although I had little time for dating, I got along well with the fifteen-year-old daughter of the family I was living with. Her name was Julie, and she was a cute brunette with dark almond-shaped eyes. We spent hours talking about all sorts of things. One night I jokingly gave her a stock line that I frequently used to tease the young daughters of friends. I gave her a dime and told her to call me when she was eighteen and old enough for me to marry.

"Better make it a quarter," she said. "By then the rates will be up."

I grinned and handed her the quarter. We were like brother and sister.

While I was working on the docks, Dad began his political career with the gubernatorial campaign in California. It worried me so I kept a very low profile, fearful that, somehow, those nude pictures of me taken so many years ago would surface and the press would make an issue of the whole nasty affair. I avoided making any speeches or appearances during his campaign, but I never said why.

The other men on the dock couldn't understand why the son of Ronald Reagan and Jane Wyman was working at manual labor for three dollars an hour. Their assumption, like that of the kids at boarding school, my boss at the car wash and the manager of the hotel, was that I could have anything I wanted because my parents were rich. I never admitted that my parents were refusing to support me because I didn't want to acknowledge what an outsider I really was.

I was trying to fit in somewhere, anywhere. I tried to live the way other people thought I should. Before long I was over my head in debt. It's amazing how easy it was for me to get credit at stores or banks just because of who my parents were. Years later, when people griped to me about Reaganomics, I would joke, "Don't complain to me. I've been living under it all of my life."

With my schedule of school during the day and work at night, I was continually exhausted and developed a duodenal ulcer. The doctor prescribed Maalox, a horrible tasting palliative. I had to sip it every three hours. Taking that was worse than having the ulcer.

One night after leaving work, it all caught up with me and I fell asleep at the wheel of the VW and took out one hundred and fifty feet of fencing on the Golden State Freeway in Los Angeles. My glasses flew off with the windshield, and the left front wheel was welded to a steel fence rod. Luckily I was unhurt, although I was bleeding copiously from a gash in the head.

I identified myself, and the police called an ambulance which took me a local hospital to be checked over. While I was lying on a hospital cot, I was given papers to fill out before the doctor would examine me. I had always gone to a family doctor, and this was the first time I ever had to answer questions about my family history, a history I didn't know. I freaked out because I didn't know any of the answers. I called Mom for information. When she became flustered, I hung up on her. I then called Merm, who calmed me down. I refused to fill out the forms and left the hospital. Later, I went to our family doctor. But my car was totally wrecked. Mom decided that she didn't want me driving a small car anymore, so she bought me a new Oldsmobile, which I proudly showed off at work.

I was offered and took a sit-down job as a dispatcher with another company at the same loading dock. To my dismay, the other dispatcher was gay. I hated going to the office where I was confined with him in a glassed-in room. Every time I turned my back to him he would say, "Ooh, how nice." I couldn't wait to go home every night.

Meanwhile, the family I had been living with moved to another state. I missed them tremendously. However, Dick Jackin, my friend whose father was foreman of Dad's ranch, let me move in with him. Dick was a macho guy, and I ran with him and his friends. One of them was a mechanic named Jack, who loved boat racing and worked on the inboard engines for boat racer Bob Massey. Dick and I sometimes spent Saturdays sitting around and watching Jack prepare Bob's engines for his races, one of which was being held at the Salton Sea just south of Palm Springs.

One Saturday, Bob asked if we would like to go to the race and help refuel the boat during pit stops. That was my first exposure to the world of boat racing. From then on I became fascinated with everything about those terrific, sleek and roaring beauties that seemed so free, nothing holding them back. Wide-open, the drivers gave them full reign as they cut through the waves, spraying fountains of water in their wake. I thought it the best of all possible worlds, and I took to it like nothing before. I was elated; it was me and it could be mine and mine alone.

Dick and I went into partnership and bought a honey of a racing boat with my bank credit. All of a sudden, I wasn't Dick's friend any more. Now I was just a valuable asset, not because of any mechanical know-how on my part but rather for my name, which was now gaining even more luster since my father was campaigning to become governor of California.

I soon discovered that I had a glib tongue which I was able to use to romance some merchants for advertising trade-offs, trailers and tow cars. I was trading on Dad's name, but this tactic opened a lot of doors. Thanks to him, I met people who ordinarily wouldn't have given me the time of day, such as executives from Coca-Cola, our first cash sponsor. Most important, I was able to get us one of the best available motors, a Ford overhead CAM.

In February, 1966, Mom called to say that she wanted to give me a twenty-first birthday party. She intended to invite a few of her friends to her condominium in Santa Monica and asked if that would be agreeable. Of course, I was delighted. A few days later Mom called to say that she didn't want to slight anyone and the guest list had grown; she was going to move the party to a local restaurant. The following week, she called again to tell me that the guest list had expanded even more. Now she was moving the party to the back room at Chasen's, a high-class restaurant favored by celebrities and owned by close friends. Two days before my birthday on March 18th, Mom was on the phone again to say that the party had grown larger still and she had taken over the top floor of Chasen's. Typical of Mom, she wanted everything to be just right, and she also told me I was not to bring my own date. She had arranged for my date to be Ricardo Montalban's daughter Linda. Great, I thought. My twenty-first birthday and I have a blind date!

It was a splendiferous night with lots of gifts. Dad and Nancy, who always sent me a fifty dollar check for birthdays and Christmas, sent me a check for twenty-one dollars. I joked that I liked it better when I was twenty because I got more money than when I was twenty-one.

Everything was going smoothly with the family again until, out of the blue, Patti called me from the Orme School where she had been boarding in the Rocky Mountain country in Arizona. Orme was a nice school where Jimmy Stewart's children went. It also was Judson's arch rival and in 1963, when we won the state championship, we had to beat Orme. So, whenever I got the chance, I rubbed it in.

Patti, who was then fourteen years old, was a trifle pudgy, but she was beautiful with a knockout smile—except when opposing parental discipline—and had Dad's coloring. She used to tease me because she and Dad always got dark tans and I didn't tan as well. In fact, both Ron and Patti resembled Dad while Maureen looked like Mom, especially her pert little nose.

Patti sounded serious when she said, "I have fallen in love with a dishwasher." Since I was twenty-one, she wanted me to drive to Arizona and sign her out of school so she could go away with him.

Patti was completely in earnest, and I didn't know what to do. I feared she would run away from school, but I didn't want to tell

Dad and Nancy because Patti had asked for my confidence. After pondering the problem, I called old-reliable Dave Martin, the family business manager, to ask for advice. I trusted him to do the right thing when he told me to leave it in his hands. Dave promptly located Nancy, who went with Dad to Arizona to pick up Patti and squash the romance. Patti has never forgiven me for betraying her trust and has spoken with me only a few times since.

Chapter IX

"What do you plan to do with your life?"

Dad became Governor of California one minute after midnight, New Year's Day, 1967. He and Nancy were suddenly thrown into the political spotlight, far removed from the klieg-lit stages they once graced as Hollywood personalities. Nancy rose to the occasion and began to cultivate a suitable image. Unfortunately, I don't believe a boat-racer son was consistent with the public portrait of the Reagans that Nancy was trying to paint.

As far as I was concerned, however, boat racing was as legitimate an occupation as acting. I was having fun just like my parents and I never realized that being an actor was work until I became one. It never dawned on me during the time they were away how hard they were working. I thought, like everyone else, they had money and would soon share it with me to make my life easy like theirs. The only time I had ever even been on a film set was when Mom had a tenth birthday party for me on the set of the *Jane Wyman Theater.* (Coincidentally, it is the same set which she uses today for filming *Falcon Crest.*) So a work ethic had not been part of my upbringing.

I became hooked on racing the first time I got behind the wheel of my boat. The speed was exhilarating. Even today, my wife and family do not understand that the most relaxed I ever feel is when I am driving a boat between ninety to one hundred m.p.h.!

I had moved from Dick's house to a swinging-singles apartment complex and began spending so much time racing that I quit my job on the docks. Thanks to that job, however, I am still strong as an ox and can leg press almost a thousand pounds.

Dick and I named our new inboard boat "Fooord" because Ralph Williams' Ford Agency sponsored the engine. We soon began trading off as drivers in races. Unhappily, our personal relationship began to sour because I received all the media attention as the governor's son. Race sponsors used my name to sell events, and this caused friction. Dick was understandably peeved but should have understood. Also, I believe at the end I was a better driver than he was mainly because I wasn't worried about getting killed. My concern was to prove that not only was I a real man but most of all a winner just like Dad.

Every minute I was at the helm of a boat confirmed my manhood. I was having a great time racing all over the country; I'd pick up a girl here and a girl there. And I was beginning to earn respect from the other drivers. I raced with Red Adair, the famous Texas oil-fire fighter, oilman John Meekham, who owned the New Orleans Saints, and astronaut Gordon Cooper. I never won any inboard races, but I always finished as one of the top five or ten racers in the nation.

Because my racing schedule made it impossible to hold down a 9-to-5 position, I worked at a variety of sales jobs to pay my bills. When I wasn't working or racing, I played tennis and lived the life of a playboy, spending every penny I earned. I was doing my best to keep up with what I thought the public would expect from the son of the governor and a film star.

The more I got into debt, the more upset my parents became. In their eyes I was still unstable. They wanted me to have a steady job and a weekly income and were not impressed with my racing exploits. During that period both Mom and Nancy stood back, looked down their noses and asked me, "Where are you going? What do you plan to do with your life?" They were trying to tell me that I was still amounting to nothing. They were right, but I didn't see it that way.

In 1967, Bob Nordskog, the inboard champion, asked me to set up a meeting with my father in Sacramento at which Dad would present him with the Championship blazer. I met Bob, his wife and son Gerry, who was about my age, in the governor's office. When Dad's secretary mistook Gerry for me, it was a smashing blow to my ego.

Dad was cordial as he showed us around his office. During the tour, he pointed to a new red rug on the floor of his cabinet room where he met every morning with the members of his Cabinet, including Mike Deaver and Ed Meese. He explained that the previous governor, Pat Brown, had left behind a torn up rug. Nancy had found some red carpet in storage. Since red is their favorite color, she had it installed in the cabinet room. When the press asked why he chose a red rug, Dad explained with a twinkle in his eye, "Because it hides the blood." We all laughed at the story. In twenty years he hasn't changed much.

Then Dad became serious as he told us that during the transition period he had confronted Governor Brown's budget director to ask about the state's finances. The director looked him in the eye and said, "We are spending a million dollars a day more than we are taking in. Good luck, Governor." With that parting shot, he left the office.

After that I had a few private moments alone with Dad, who used the opportunity to ask me to please be careful with my racing. "You're bound to get hurt sometime," he warned. Unfortunately, he would soon be proven right.

In the spring of 1967, Larry Laurie, press agent for the Outboard World Championship at Lake Havasu, asked me if I would be interested in entering a two-day race. Actually the offer came down through Robert McCullough, the chain saw magnate and Chief Operating Officer of the lake resort community. When I said that I didn't have an outboard boat or engine, Laurie volunteered to cover the entry fee himself if I would get the boat and engine. It was a surefire investment for him, an automatic access to big media coverage if I were involved in the promotion of the race and I knew it.

I prevailed on Rudy Ramos, who had built me a brand new eighteen-foot inboard race boat with a Keith Black 500 c.i. motor, to lend me his boat, which had won the outboard world championship the year before. Another benefactor let me have three Mercury engines. Then I put together the Reagan team: Rudy Ramos, Bill Cooper and myself.

The field of contestants was formidable. It included Craig Breedlove, Pete Foster, Caesar Scotti and Renato Molinari—all outstanding drivers. No one was concerned about our chances of winning. The prevailing attitude was that I was just the governor's son, a kid who had never even entered an outboard competition let alone won a race and was in this one just for the publicity. The skeptics were right. I did want the publicity; I was hoping to impress Dad and Nancy, who these days seemed surrounded only with successful people.

On the night before the race, a Calcutta was held, everyone betting on different boats. Bids for the other racers' boats ranged from two hundred dollars to six hundred dollars. When "The Reagan Special" came up, my stomach churned with excitement. I thought our boat would bring a top bid at least because of Bill and Rudy, but all I heard were some snickers and then dead silence. Finally a man held up his hand and said, "I'll bid thirteen dollars." Someone else laughed and said, "That figures, it's an unlucky boat."

Although we'd previously attracted a lot of press coverage, we were ignored on race day. But we surprised everyone. By the end of the first day—eight full hours of racing over a two and a half mile course—we were tied for first place despite the fact that our boat was falling apart. The hull looked like the bottom of a shoe with the sole coming off.

We were lucky, however, because the favored Mercury team was no longer in contention. Until then, the Mercury people had treated us like country bumpkins, but since we had the only Mercury engines left in the top five, suddenly they swarmed around us asking how they could be of help. They worked on our motors all night while we tried to mold the fiberglass deck back together.

On Sunday as on Saturday, Bill started off as driver. Two hours later, when it was my turn, we had a three-lap lead. Barring an unforeseen accident, there was almost no way my team could lose—that is, if we could only keep the boat together. It was a wreck. I had to hold the dashboard up with my right knee to keep it from falling into the bilge while keeping my foot on the gas pedal at the same time. I drove all out and we won by a lap.

Bill, Rudy and I were the Outboard World Champions of 1967!

I was ecstatic, and most everyone else was dumbfounded. The press went crazy. A man ran up and kissed me on both cheeks. "I love you," he said.

"Who are you?" I asked.

"I'm the guy who bet thirteen bucks on you in the Calcutta, and I just won ten thousand dollars."

The next day the papers reported: "Reagan's Son Wins Outboard Championship." I felt that I had finally done something significant. I was certain that when Dad read about it in the papers he would say, "Doggone it, Mike, you're a world champion. I guess you've finally found your niche," and he, Nancy or Mom would welcome me with open arms because of my success.

I never heard from them. I realized with despair that no matter what I did, it probably wasn't going to be enough to earn the acceptance I so desperately wanted.

That same year I was ranked number five nationally on the speed classic circuit and was named Southern California Marine Association rookie of the year. Although I felt I had earned the title, I suspected it had been given to me only because my father was governor of the state and the Association would get good press coverage before the upcoming Los Angeles Boat Show.

The publicity had an effect, however. Robert McCulloch hired me to introduce the Power Mac-Six chain saw, forerunner of the mini chain saws marketed today. Pictures of me were used in press kits, and I was booked on a sixteen city tour. The company identified me as a conservationist, a relatively new term at the time. On a television show, I was asked what the chain saw and conservation had in common. I was nonplussed for a moment, then finally said, "This chain saw is so easy to use, please don't cut down any more trees than you eat." My line literally brought down the house with laughter, especially when someone shouted, "He's really a chip off the old block."

Hart, Schaffner and Marx, the men's clothing firm, also contracted my services to wear their clothes at store openings and during television appearances. Once more, I began to live up to the public image of the good life on an empty bank account.

But I was still without a public identity. Whenever I went into a bank to cash a check, invariably one of the tellers would ask if I was any relation to Governor Reagan. When I said "yes," the retort would usually be "That's funny, you don't look anything like him."

Such episodes crushed my ego and filled me with rage. I wanted so much to be someone, and I just wasn't making it. One day when I was at the Malibu ranch alone and went to start up the car my mother had bought me, I discovered the battery was dead. My fury was uncontrollable, and I reacted just as I had when the chain was off my bicycle. I got out of the car, slammed the doors back and forth and kicked them until they came off their hinges. Then I went into the garage and found a sledge hammer. Cursing with every blow and blaming the car for all my problems, I busted out the side and rear windows. Then I smashed the headlights and taillights. I stopped my assault on the car only when I was totally exhausted. Dripping with sweat, I sat on the steps of the foreman's house, buried my face in my hands and cried. It was an irrational display of temper, the behavior of a spoiled brat at his worst. It was only years later, after therapy, that I came to realize that I was really trying to destroy my mother. I told Dad that the car had been vandalized and my insurance company paid to have it repaired.

Then in 1968 I received "Greetings" from my local draft board, ordering me to report for a physical. I was afraid of going to Viet Nam and being killed. But I was certain that if I died it would be a hero's death. Dad would be proud of me. But the notion of going into the Army distressed me because I was faced with my old

117

bugaboo: being closeted with a bunch of men in a barracks. I also dreaded being required to fill out a medical history since I still knew nothing about my medical heritage or genealogy.

Mom was no different than any other mother at the time. When she heard there was a chance that I might be inducted, she said, "Over my dead body." She then called her doctor and pleaded with him to write a letter that might keep me out of the draft.

On the morning of my physical, I had a letter from him about my ulcer, which really was acting up; in fact, I was ghostly pale because it was bleeding. While I was standing in the induction center, naked and bent over with a urine bottle in my hand, someone tapped me on the shoulder and asked, "Are you Reagan?" I nodded and was told to report to a private room where there was an army doctor to examine me.

Ironically it wasn't the ulcer or my bad eyes or flat feet that kept me out of the Army. The doctor discovered that I had a pilonidal cyst; it had not bothered me before, although it would later require surgery.

When he told me I was going to be classified 1Y, I asked him jokingly what that meant.

"You know where the Pacific Ocean is, don't you?" he asked. "When the Russians land on the coast, be ready."

I think Dad and Nancy were sorry that I wasn't going off to the army, but Mom was happy as were Merm and David. As for myself, what a celebration! It lasted for days. As I think back it probably could have turned me around.

Soon after that I had the boating accident which Dad had prophesied. During a 250-mile race in Texas with yet another new boat, I crashed and suffered injuries to my back and hips. Within hours I was released from the hospital and back at the race course. But the next day I was so stiff I was unable to walk and could barely crawl to the phone when I heard it ring. It was Dad.

"I heard about your crash from the press," he said. "How're you doing?"

"Fine," I said, as a lightning bolt of pain shot through me.

"I told you that business was dangerous," he said. "There's no future in it."

"I know that, but it's something I really like and enjoy doing."

"I wish you would get into something safer and have a steady job. Why don't you make your hobby your real job and sell boats?"

Later it turned out that Dad had the right idea. But at the time, I thought holding down a steady job was demeaning. To me it was like menial labor. In my mind, because my parents were famous, I'd be a failure if I had to work. Six weeks later I had a new sponsor and was back in the cockpit in a new boat that Rudy Ramos built specially for me.

Chapter X

"When are we getting married?"

One night in 1970, as I was getting ready to go out on a date, the phone rang in my Manhattan Beach apartment. It was Julie. I hadn't spoken with her for months and was surprised to hear her voice. "Hi," she said, "I just turned eighteen. When are we getting married?"

"Oh, no," I thought, she had taken my joke seriously!

My initial dismay quickly faded, however, as the idea of marriage began to appeal to me. If I got married, it would prove to my family once and for all that I could lead the stable life they wanted for me. Both of my parents had been divorced, and at last I had a chance to prove that I was better than them at something, because I would stay married forever. Further, I would be marrying into a family that I loved and had missed since they moved.

A few weeks later, Julie's parents brought her with them to watch me race in Nashville, Tennessee. Julie told me her folks didn't believe I was really in love with her, so I wrote them a letter convincing them that I wanted to marry their daughter—and I really did. The truth is, I did love her, but I didn't know then it was more as a sister than anything else.

I called Dad, Nancy and Mom and excitedly told them about my plan to marry Julie.

I was twenty-six years old and Julie was eighteen and just out of high school when we were married in Hawaii on June 13, 1971. The wedding took place on the lawn at a friend's home just in sight of Haleakala, the widest volcano in the world. Merm and Mom arrived early to help make the arrangements, but Dad and Nancy were conspicuously absent. To my chagrin, they attended Tricia Nixon's wedding in Washington that same day.

That hurt me deeply. As surely as acting had deprived me of my mother, it now seemed clear that politics had deprived me of my father.

Just prior to the wedding, I got a letter from Dad, the first I had ever received from him. It read:

Dear Mike:
Enclosed is the item I mentioned (with which goes a torn up IOU). I could stop here but I won't.

You've heard all the jokes that have been rousted around by all the "unhappy marrieds" and cynics. Now, in case no one has suggested it, there is another viewpoint. You have entered into the most meaningful relationship there is in all human life. It can be whatever you decide to make it.

Some men feel their masculinity can only be proven if they

play out in their own life all the locker-room stories, smugly confident that what a wife doesn't know won't hurt her. The truth is, somehow, way down inside, without her ever finding lipstick on the collar or catching a man in the flimsy excuse of where he was till three A.M., a wife does know, and with that knowing, some of the magic of this relationship disappears. There are more men griping about marriage who kicked the whole thing away themselves than there can ever be wives deserving of blame. There is an old law of physics that you can only get out of a thing as much as you put in it. The man who puts into the marriage only half of what he owns will get that out. Sure, there will be moments when you will see someone or think back on an earlier time and you will be challenged to see if you can still make the grade, but let me tell you how really great is the challenge of proving your masculinity and charm with one woman for the rest of your life. Any man can find a twerp here and there who will go along with cheating, and it doesn't take all that much manhood. It does take quite a man to remain attractive and to be loved by a woman who has heard him snore, seen him unshaven, tended him while he was sick and washed his dirty underwear. Do that and keep her still feeling a warm glow and you will know some very beautiful music. If you truly love a girl, you shouldn't ever want her to feel, when she sees you greet a secretary or a girl you both know, that humiliation of wondering if she was someone who caused you to be late coming home, nor should you want any other woman to be able to meet your wife and know she was smiling behind her eyes as she looked at her, the woman you love, remembering this was the woman you rejected even momentarily for her favors.

Mike, you know better than many what an unhappy home is and what it can do to others. Now you have a chance to

make it come out the way it should. There is no greater
happiness for a man than approaching a door at the end of a
day knowing someone on the other side of that door is waiting for the sound of his footsteps.

Love, Dad.

P.S. You'll never get in trouble if you say "I love you" at
least once a day.

The letter was just like Dad. It was straight from the heart and
full of square, honest, old-fashioned sentiments. I was so touched
when I read it that I cried and then reread it several more times
during our honeymoon.

Julie and I spent our honeymoon visiting various islands
including the island of Kauai, where we saw the location for the
movie *South Pacific.* A few days later we were back in Southern
California in the city of Azusa where I had secured a job working
for a company that manufactured modular homes. Unfortunately, the company went bankrupt just before Christmas, and I
was jobless again. Julie wanted to fly to Mobile, Alabama to see
her parents, but we were too broke.

Things were looking bad. For the first time in my life I turned
to prayer. Julie and I lay in bed every night holding hands and
saying the Lord's Prayer and praying for a miracle. It came in the
form of two plane tickets sent to us by Mom. But I didn't recognize
it as such or even say thanks.

Julie liked Mobile because her parents were there and she
wanted to be close to them. Although I didn't like the city that
much, there was nothing for me back home, so I agreed to settle
there and move in with her family till we found a place of our
own. When we had all been together at camp years before, we'd sit
on the lawn and talk and I'd massage Julie's back while her
mother massaged mine. Now, in Mobile, we spent evenings

watching television, mostly *Hawaii Five-O* because it reminded us of our honeymoon, massaging each other's backs and just being a family. Ironically, I found that more than anything I missed Mom.

I was hired by a real estate company to sell campsite property, a job which sometimes meant I had to be away from home two or three days at a time. Julie worked as a dental assistant to help us with the finances, but because we were apart so much, I prevailed on my boss George to hire Julie as a receptionist-secretary with the company. She loved it and soon began to spend more time with George than with me, although he was married and the father of a couple of children.

George had a radio telephone in his car so he could talk with his other salesmen; he called himself "Number One." Julie sometimes used the phone and, as a joke, began to call herself "Half." Sometimes when we were all at the campsite office, she rode home with him rather than with me. Julie denied they were anything more than just friends, but the suspicion that they were having an affair was driving me crazy. When George sent me out of town on trips, I sometimes would return early and sit in the bushes outside of my apartment, spying and waiting, and hoping my thoughts would not be substantiated. More often than not I would see George bringing her home from dinner, both giggling and happy. Then I would sadly remember our days like that and drive back the one hundred miles or so to where George had sent me, without saying a word.

On March 18, 1972—my twenty-seventh birthday—Mom sent us air tickets to Dallas where we were to meet her and see Merm, who was appearing in a play. While we were there, Julie suggested that we have a child. I thought that was a great idea—not only would a baby add solidity to our marriage, but it would keep Julie at home and away from George. Also, a child would

125

prove to both of my parents that my marriage was solid. I couldn't let it fail.

Two months later, Julie told me that she believed she was pregnant and had arranged to be examined by her doctor. I was ecstatic and was telling everybody. She promised to meet me at the campsite after her appointment to give me the news.

That afternoon I paced anxiously up and down in front of our small trailer-office waiting for the news, praying that everything would be all right with Julie. Then I saw George's car in the distance with Julie in the passenger seat. As she got out of the car, I ran up to hug her but she avoided me. "Yes, I'm pregnant," she said. "And I'm going to leave you."

I felt as though I had been punched in the solar plexus. Tears started to form in my eyes. "Why?" I asked.

"Because you're no fun anymore," she said.

I was devastated. I couldn't believe that our marriage, which I had hoped would gain me my parents' approval, was going down the tubes. Julie had ruined all my plans. I would be a failure in their eyes again. I was so sick I stopped eating and my weight dropped from 180 to 153 pounds within a month.

We didn't have enough money for separate apartments, so we stayed together that month: two close friends who got married and ended up hating each other.

I was determined though to win her back so, on our anniversary, I gave Julie the money to fly to Hawaii for a vacation with her parents and not, coincidentally, to get her away from George. The owner of the company was so upset with the situation that he gave me the money to fly to Hawaii so I could attempt to save our marriage.

Mom and Merm met me in Los Angeles where I changed planes. They were both sympathetic and angry with Julie who, they felt, was probably having an affair with George. I was never more happy to see them even though my tail was between my legs.

126

My meeting with Julie in Hawaii was a disaster. On the day I was to leave for home, I recollected having seen a movie in which a couple was about to break up. The girl was pregnant and her husband said to her, "To stay married would be great, but to stay married just for the baby's sake wouldn't be worth it to the child because the child would grow up in a family with conflict." At the end of the movie, the woman chose to stay with her husband, and everyone lived happily ever after. I repeated that speech to Julie, who told me that when she returned to Mobile she would tell me whether she had reconsidered and wanted to stay married or wanted to go ahead with a divorce. The next day I left for home and waited.

I was on pins and needles the day she was due back. But it was George who picked Julie up at the airport. I was so upset that when I went to sleep that night I dreamt I walked into George's office with a .45 automatic. I pointed it at his head and told him that if he didn't stay away from my wife I would blow his brains out. When I awoke I was bathed in sweat and crying.

Julie's parents didn't know there was a problem until she asked if she could move in with them. Her brother Kyle helped me move her belongings. The night she moved, her father sat us down at the kitchen table and paced up and down. I knew what was coming. Finally, he turned around and lit into both of us. He said we had to stay together and work out our problems. "Marriage isn't easy," he thundered. "It's work, and it's time you both grew up."

When he finished berating us, Julie said, "But, Daddy, I don't love him anymore." She had never said that before.

Julie told me then that she was going ahead with a divorce. "I've thought about what you said to me in Hawaii, and you're right, I don't think it's fair to the child."

While she was gone, I had spoken with Julie's doctor who told me that during the first few months of pregnancy, some women

127

go through an enzyme imbalance. He said that after the child was born, she would probably be back to normal. Hearing this gave me hope. So I told her, "If you can tell me that you want a divorce after the birth of our baby, I'll give it to you." But there was no reason for me to remain in Mobile if Julie didn't want me around.

I packed my Ford Pinto and drove to Florida. I had some racing buddies there who I thought would help get me through my depression. I lay on the beach in the sun for two weeks, playing over scenes from our marriage on closed eyelids, and trying to pinpoint what had gone wrong. I created new scenarios in my mind, torturing myself with visions of Julie and George together now that I was out of the way. I fantasized about how I would react when she finally realized it was all a mistake and asked me to take her back. In those fantasies I wavered from taking her back with welcome arms to punishing her by saying it was too late. Like Clark Gable in *Gone with the Wind,* I would say, "Frankly, my dear, I don't give a damn."

One thing Julie said kept coming back to me: I wasn't fun anymore. I had to do something to change her mind about that. I had met a stewardess in Florida, who happened to have collected postcards from cities all over the world. She gave some to me, and I addressed them to Julie, writing, "Having fun, wish you were here. Love, Mike." The stewardess then took them with her and mailed them from Paris, Rome, London. I thought, "If Julie gets the cards from all over the world telling her I am having fun, she might change her mind and want to join me."

After weeks of moping around, I realized that I either had to pull myself together or commit suicide. I didn't want to face Mom, but I called her to say I was going to drive to Dallas to see friends. I gave her the phone number if she wanted to call. Mom apparently feared I might do something rash and flew to Dallas to meet me. I was a basket case when I saw her. She put her arms around me. "I've gone through a divorce and understand your pain," she said. "I love you, Mike. Whatever happens, you can rely on my support."

She gave me solace and comfort, and very probably saved my life.

I called Merm, who suggested I return to Los Angeles to talk with Dad and Nancy. The visit took place at their home in the Palisades. Nancy sat back during that meeting and let Dad do the talking.

"The best thing you can do is pick yourself up by the bootstraps and continue with your life," Dad said. He told me how much suffering he had gone through when he and Mom were divorced. "I thought I would never get out of the doldrums," he said, "but I was lucky enough to meet Nancy. The same thing will probably happen to you one day. You may not believe it now, but it will."

I accepted his sympathy, but again, I was too involved in my own self-pity to respond to or appreciate his attempt to help me through a difficult time. Only later was I to realize that once again he was right.

The period from June, 1972 to December, 1972 was the worst of my life. It was as though the wrath of God had descended on me. My car was repossessed. I was jobless and without income. And I was heavily in debt. The marriage that I thought would give me stability and respect in my parents' eyes had failed after little more than a year.

I thought then I alone was responsible for my plight, but I chose to blame it on the fact that I was a bastard and therefore doomed to fail just like the character Tom Jones.

I believed that I was not meant to have a home or a future. It seemed to me that nothing I could ever do would work out right. I hated myself and my biological mother, who had abandoned me to what I considered a cruel fate. I hated my adoptive mother for sending me away to school and not taking care of me. I hated my stepmother for revealing that I was illegitimate. And now, just when the woman who I married found out she was going to become a mother, she had left me. It seemed to me that all mothers hated me. All I could think of was that they were all whores.

Chapter XI

"Damn you and the baby!"

It is January, 1987, and for fourteen years rarely has a day passed when I do not think of a boy I have never seen and wonder what he is like and what he is doing now. That boy is from my marriage to Julie. He has never known his biological father, just as I never knew mine. The irony is not lost on me. Perhaps there is truth to that old adage about the sins of the father being visited upon his children.

I wonder, too, what I would say if I were to meet him just as my father probably wouldn't know what to say if he were to meet me. Would I recognize him at once? Is he tall or short? What color is his hair? Does he look like me? Does he know that he is adopted, and if so, does he want to find me, just as I have often thought about finding my real father? There are so many unanswered questions in my mind that I dare not seek to answer.

Cameron and Ashley, my children with Colleen, do not yet know that I was married to another woman before I met their mother and that I have a son by that marriage. I have kept so many secrets for so many years that I am growing weary of the deception, which requires constant vigilance on my part.

I believe the book I am writing is a catharsis for me, but each day that I work on it, I wonder if I am not making a mistake. I have no way of knowing the answer, but for the first time in my life I have decided to be honest in the present in order to live with the past.

I had been racing boats and traveling around the country when I courted Julie. After we were married, I tried to settle down because I thought that's what a married man was supposed to do. Undoubtedly, that had been my undoing. Julie apparently liked the glamorous life, and she saw very little excitement in being married to a campsite salesman. Little wonder that she found my boss more to her taste. At least he was financially substantial and offered a better future.

I thought if I went back into boat racing the glamorous life would return to me. Perhaps Julie would realize that I was still the exciting man she had married. The baby had not yet been born, and I was praying that Julie's doctor was right, that she was just going through a hormone imbalance that was creating emotional problems. I felt more and more sure that when the baby was born she would want me back. Julie knew my background, and I was certain she would not want our child to grow up without its real father as I had done.

I was alone and living in a guest room of my friend Bill Olson's house. I didn't date for a while out of loyalty to Julie, who was always in my thoughts. Bill had just bought a new twenty-seven foot Magnum racing boat and wanted to get back into racing. We refitted the boat with a new engine and new equipment. While in Florida, I had met a wealthy man who was interested in boat racing. Ever the salesman, I convinced him to sponsor us in a California offshore race. After all, I was the governor's son as well as the outboard champion. I could visualize the headlines: "Mike Reagan. Champion Again." Julie would be impressed. As always, I received most of the media attention, and I sent the clippings to Julie as part of my strategy to win her back.

Although our boat was fast, it was too heavy, and we had to quit the race before the time allowed. It was embarrassing. We were the laughingstock of the boating community. I never sent Julie those clippings!

After this fiasco I was so broke that, at Merm's suggestion, I wrapped birthday and other gifts for my parents in newspaper. The family thought I was being original and clever, not realizing that necessity was the mother of invention.

The phone call I had been waiting for since June finally came early in January, 1973. "I've had a baby boy," Julie said. I hung on a thread of anticipation as I waited for her next words. "And I still want the divorce," she said with a note of finality.

The desolation I felt in my gut quickly turned into anger. "Damn you and the baby!" I snapped. "I don't want to see you or him. Ever." Those were probably the very same sentiments, set forth in the same way, that my father expressed to my biological mother; the irony of that was not to occur to me until years later. I felt terrible, however, because I had failed.

I took the only employment I could get: a part-time boat salesman at the Anaheim Boat Show. My years of fast talking paid off.

Before the boat show ended, I had sold twenty-five boats, which made me a hero in my new employer's eyes. I now had a good job and a new apartment, although I didn't have a car. I borrowed one from Bill Olson's mother when I had a date.

Two months later, while I was at the National Boat Mart, two detectives from the District Attorney's office in Santa Ana, California, braced me and said they had a warrant for my arrest. They almost scared me to death. I had no idea what kind of trouble I was in and was relieved when they told me I was to be arrested because I was behind in my child support payments. Then, however, I became furious. I had told Julie that if she didn't want me around to be the father of our child, I had no intention of supporting her or him. So there I was, at the Santa Ana jail in handcuffs where the district attorney explained that a warrant for me had been issued in Alabama. Unless I agreed to sign the divorce petition and pay back child support I would have to go to jail.

I decided to bluff him. "Are you telling me that if I don't sign the petition or pay back child support, you'll put me in jail, give me three meals a day, and I won't have to work for a living? Because, if you are, take me to jail." It was not one of my finer moments.

The DA took me seriously and telephoned Julie's attorney in Alabama, who, it turned out, also represented George in his divorce suit. It was agreed that if I signed the divorce petition and gave up all rights to my son, Julie would forego child support. I signed. My marriage was officially ended, along with my dreams of getting Julie back. Soon after that, Julie and George were married. Later, I learned that George had adopted my son.

In the fall of 1973, Bill's wife Barbara described to me a girl named Colleen Sterns, who worked with her. "I've told Colleen about you," Barbara said. "I think you'd like her."

"Okay," I said, "but I'm already dating eight other girls at the moment. I need another one like I need a hole in the head." The truth was I had started dating other girls strictly for sex and fun.

That's all they were good for. In fact, I had jokingly started with a friend a club that we called "The Never Go Home Alone Club"—and we tried not to.

But Barbara persisted. More for her and Bill than for myself, I allowed them to set up dates for me to meet Colleen—dates which one or the other of us broke three times. Finally it was arranged for us to meet for dinner at the Olsons' home on December 7, 1973, Pearl Harbor Day. I think both of us accepted that date because we were tired of being pestered by Bill and Barbara.

As Bill and I were going out the door to buy some wine that night, Colleen walked in and we were introduced. I liked what I saw. She was a pretty brunette with big brown eyes and a trim figure. I turned my face to her, pointed to my cheek and said, "Kiss me here, please." She started to kiss my cheek, but I turned quickly and kissed her on the mouth. "Works every time," I said. Boy, was I forward.

After dinner, I asked Colleen if she would like to go out for a cocktail. Over drinks she told me that she had just come to L.A. from Kansas City where she worked for the Hertz Rental Car Company at the airport. She was born and raised on a farm in Nebraska and had eleven brothers and sisters. I related to that a little, telling her that both of my parents were mid-Westerners.

She also told me that Barbara had said I was the governor's son, but she had thought Barbara was putting her on. So she had gone to the library and looked up Ronald Reagan. She discovered that he really did have a son named Michael.

After we returned to the Olsons, I gave Colleen my patented line: "Would you like me to take you to my house or would you like me to go to your apartment—or would you like me to take you to your car and you can go home by yourself?" It wasn't the cleverest line in the world, but more often than not, I ended up with another conquest.

"Take me to my car," Colleen said very politely.

135

Her response shook me a bit. She was the first girl I had met who wasn't impressed with my B.S.

"Well," I said jokingly, "if nothing better comes along, perhaps you would like to go out with me next week."

We not only got together the next week but every week thereafter. One night Colleen told me that she would never marry a divorced man and that she was looking for a man who was a homebody, someone who would be a good husband and father. I thought this girl is tough-minded but I didn't let it bother me then that I didn't qualify in any way as the man in her future.

Two weeks before Christmas, I brought Colleen to Maureen's annual tree decorating party. Mom and some of Maureen's friends were on hand to help decorate the tree, which Maureen invariably names Rudolph. Afterward, we all sat in the living room where we sang carols and ate Merm's famous chili. Everyone got along well, but neither Mom nor Maureen paid too much attention to Colleen, most likely because they considered her to be just another of my dates.

At that time Colleen was not aware that I was around forty thousand dollars in debt. Heck, I didn't know; I hadn't opened a bill in so long. My car had been repossessed, my clothing and entertainment bills were staggering and I still owed ten thousand dollars for the race boat that I had crashed in Galveston. I lived on credit, yet I hadn't paid any bills in years and had no intention of paying back any of my debts. Why should I? Everyone was using me or my name. Why should I feel obligated? Although I was making a decent commission as a boat salesman, I spent every cent I earned—and more—keeping up what I thought was my "image" as the son of famous parents on the theory that if I were to get into real financial trouble someone in the family would probably bail me out. The friends I grew up with always got bailed out by their parents; why should I be different?

When the boat company I was working for went bankrupt, I

went to Parker, Arizona, where I started a new business selling burglar alarms for Bill Olson. That venture didn't turn out well. In order to eat, I worked as a laborer, tearing down fences on an Indian reservation in Parker Valley. It was not a job I planned to keep forever, but at least it was work. As with my past jobs, everybody soon discovered that I was the son of the governor of California. Invariably someone would ask why I didn't have my dad get me a job with the government in Sacramento. I explained to them that my dad didn't believe in nepotism and that when he first became governor he vowed he never would give a job to a member of his family. True, I needed help, but I had no intention of asking Dad for it. I thought it would be a sign of weakness. I was always hoping he would see my plight and volunteer to help and, when he didn't, I thought he was just too busy and it made me even angrier.

I missed Colleen and called her almost every night. She arrived for a visit and, much to my chagrin, caught me laboring in the valley. That night she told me, "No man of mine is ever going to toil like that if he wants to be with me. You're coming home." Wow! I thought.

I had finally met a woman who was willing to take control of my life, and I was delighted. But I didn't even own a car, so we went to a Ford dealer in Parker, who I had met while boat racing years before and went dove-hunting with every Labor Day weekend. He was willing to sell me a beautiful, new, blue Ford Ranchero truck—with no money down with one catch—if I could get one of my parents to cosign the loan. That put me in a bind. I already had wasted too much of their money on various extravagances: cars (traded and wrecked), college, and boat racing. I didn't dare call Dad or Nancy, so I had to call Mom for help on this one. Colleen didn't know all the details about my past, so I thought up an excuse to go to a phone alone and worked up the courage to make the call. I explained the situation to Mom, who reminded me of every bad thing I had ever done in my life and then read me the riot act up and down. She ended the diatribe as she always did, by agreeing to cosign the note only if I understood that she would not make one payment. The blue (my favorite color) Ranchero became the first car for which I ever assumed total responsibility. I did that only because I trusted Colleen to figure out how I was going to pay for it without having a job. I had no trust in myself.

Colleen and I drove straight to California and ended up at her apartment in Anaheim. There we had a long, serious talk during which I admitted to her how deeply I was in debt.

"No man of mine is ever going to be in debt," she said. "You're responsible for those bills, and you're going to pay them off."

"What! How? You're crazy," I said.

Colleen was the first person in my life to hold me accountable for my actions, and I was staggered as well as impressed. Here was a girl who was equal in strength to Mom or Nancy. I trusted and needed Colleen and was more than willing to let her take over my problems because I knew that sooner or later there would have come a day of reckoning in my life. I was just trying to put it off forever.

I rented an apartment for myself. Then, because I had a good reputation in the boat industry, I was able to get a good job as a salesman at Mesa Boat Center in Costa Mesa, California. Colleen opened up a joint bank account for us so she could handle my money. She then called my creditors and arranged to pay them off in weekly installments. She told me that she was amazed at how much my creditors liked me. The clothing store where I owed almost eight thousand dollars even told her they were having a sale and invited me to come down and take advantage of it and I hadn't made a payment in four years.

* * *

Dad's last year as governor was 1974. A dinner honoring him was scheduled for August at the Century Plaza Hotel, and I was invited. I thought the dinner would be a good opportunity to show off Dad to Colleen and to introduce him and Nancy to the new woman in my life. They were gracious when they met Colleen, but their reaction to her was guarded. Like Mom, they too were thinking, "Let's not get serious about this girl because it probably won't last." I wonder why they would have thought that.

After dinner, Colleen and I went to Maureen's apartment for cocktails. Maureen, who was twice divorced and had just broken up with her current boyfriend, was going through some difficult times with the men in her life. She asked Colleen, who is very direct and blunt, how she perceived her problems. Colleen told her, "If I was having that much difficulty with men, I would take a hard look at myself and not at the men I was dating."

We all sat in silence for a moment. I remember thinking, "Bravo, Colleen." I had been wanting to tell Maureen that for twenty years. But I was always afraid to speak up to the members of my family. Now here was Colleen, who was able to voice my sentiments exactly, and I was delighted.

When Colleen and I finally got up to go, Maureen found an opportunity to get me alone for a moment. "Michael," she said, "I hope your relationship with this girl isn't going to turn into something serious." I smiled and realized again that at last I had picked the right girl.

Until then, Maureen had been my best friend in and out of the family, and I had always followed where she led. Now, to Maureen's distress, it was Colleen who had control over Michael Reagan. I liked that; I had been out of control for so long that I had given up on myself and couldn't understand why. I would never have admitted it at the time, but Colleen became my

"Nancy" and "Jane." In fact, Mom began to look upon me as a responsible person. She rightfully gave full credit for the transformation to Colleen.

But moms will be moms and nothing proved it more than the time she had an art show in Carmel, California, and had moved there to prepare for it. (Most people aren't aware of it, but Mom is a first-rate painter and has had several successful one-woman shows.) She invited Colleen and me to visit her before the opening.

We drove to Carmel on Highway 1, one of the most scenic roads in California, with the Pacific on one side and beautiful mountains on the other. On the afternoon that we arrived, Mom invited her priest to drop by for cocktails before we went to dinner. Mom introduced me as her son and, to our surprise, Colleen as "Mrs. Michael Reagan." Colleen and I were floored. We thought Mom had jokingly made a mistake, but every place we went together for the next two days, we were introduced as Mr. and Mrs. Reagan. Although Mom had always wanted me to marry a Catholic girl, it was obvious that she had accepted Colleen and, in her own way, was letting me know it was okay to marry the girl.

I hadn't heard from Patti for years, but to my surprise she called me one night on some pretext. I knew by the sound of her voice that she was troubled. Colleen was at my place cooking dinner, and since they had never met, I invited Patti over. Patti told us she had changed her name from Reagan to Davis because, while she was attending classes at the University of Southern California, she had gotten razzed for being Ronald Reagan's daughter. Dad had just left the governor's office, and Patti was now worried about his running for the presidency. She was facing the same identity problems that had always bothered me. Instead of reacting with sympathy and feeling her pain, I retorted flippantly,

"Wasn't your mother, Nancy Davis, the actress in the movie *Donovan's Brain?*"

"Yes," Patti said.

"And didn't Nancy Davis marry Ronald Reagan?"

"Yes."

"And didn't Ronald Reagan become the governor of the state of California?"

Patti nodded.

"It doesn't matter what you do, you're still going to be Ronald Reagan's daughter."

The meeting with Patti ended as a disaster. She had come to her older brother for advice and understanding. Instead of holding her and being sympathetic, I had attacked her and been flippant. She got up and abruptly left the apartment. We were not to speak again for several more years, and then it would be under extremely dramatic circumstances. It was the second time she had confided in me and the second time I had let her down. Maybe if I or someone would have been more understanding then, Patti would be happier now.

Colleen and I got engaged in June, 1975. As an engagement present, Mom gave Colleen a piece of her jewelry that I know was a treasured keepsake. When Mom made *The Glass Menagerie* with Kirk Douglas, he had a brooch designed for her with four emeralds cut in the shape of blue roses. On the back was engraved "Love, Kirk." Mom's gift to Colleen of an object so personal meant a lot to my fiancée. It was important to me, too, because it meant Mom really approved of Colleen. I had finally done something right.

Dad and Nancy also seemed to accept Colleen, and we began to have some fun times together as a family. Once all of us except Patti, who was out of town, got together at Maureen's apartment for dinner. Later, we played charades, using a hat to hold our written assignments. When it was Nancy's turn, she picked out a card with the book title *The Making of the President*. She smiled broadly at her team and pointed at Dad. Then she raised her hands up toward the sky. Maureen, who is probably the most widely read member of the family, was the first one to guess the correct title. We all looked at Dad and he had a wide grin on his face.

Nancy called for a family conference at the house in the Palisades a month prior to my wedding to Colleen. "Since Colleen is going to become a member of the family soon and this is for the family, please bring her," she said. It sounded serious.

Maureen, Colleen and I drove to the house together. On the way, we all agreed that Dad was going to tell us that he had finally made the decision to run for president. Although I was outwardly enthusiastic, I was secretly panicked at the thought. I had kept a low profile when he ran for governor, fearful that the nude pictures of me might surface. But if he ran for president, the press certainly would try to dig up any dirt they could find on him or his family. I was determined to test him that night, to see if the time was right for us to have a private talk so I could test him with my secret. If the circumstances permitted, I wanted at last to tell him about the molestation incident, to put him on guard and to warn him.

When we arrived at the house, Dad was nowhere in sight. I finally located him in his bedroom. I started to make some small talk to test the waters. I knew that I had to speak quickly because family members were always interrupting his conversations by coming in and out of the bedroom.

I started the conversation by saying that I hoped that if he decided to run for president, his campaign would bring the family—by which I meant me—closer. He looked at me quizzically. "But the family is close," he said.

I was pondering how I should best lead into telling him about the pictures when Nancy came into the bedroom and asked what we were talking about. I told her my previous comment, that I hoped Dad's running for president would bring about a rebirth of family closeness.

"I wouldn't count on it," Nancy said. She definitely had something else on her mind.

Her words deflated my purpose, and I dejectedly followed her and Dad out of the bedroom and into the living room where the family conference was about to begin. Nancy sat next to Dad in one of the two chairs facing a large couch where all of us children were seated.

At that time, Ron was not yet in ballet, but he wore his hair long and had a rebellious nature; he, too, had felt the pressure of living up to the Reagan image while Dad was governor. In fact, Dad and Nancy were having difficulties with both their children in school. Patti, still at USC, wanted to become an actress and was politically liberal, which grated on Dad's unshakable conservative values.

Dad, who has a story for every occasion and had just returned from a speaking engagement in Atlanta, Georgia, told us that he had been speaking all around the country. "At every hotel and airport I see 'Reagan for President' placards," he said. "But you know what really gets to me? When I check into a hotel, the bellmen who carry my bags ask me why I don't run for president. 'We need you,' they say. And, as I walk out of my room in the morning, the chambermaids stop me to shake my hand and say they like me and want me to run for president. It doesn't matter where I go; it's always the same. So the grassroots response is out there, and I feel I have a good chance to win if I run for president."

No one said a word for a few moments. I remember thinking that the whole thing was probably set up by Mike Deaver. I was also fearful that my secret finally would be dug up and plastered on the front pages of every newspaper and magazine, but I knew I

143

had to respond enthusiastically because it was expected of me. After a moment, Maureen and I stood up and told Dad we were with him all the way. Ron looked glum. Patti stayed on the couch and started to cry. I think I knew what was going through her mind: For years she had been trying to find her own identity. She'd had enough troubles when he was governor. If Dad won, she would have to live in his shadow for another four years. Similar thoughts were going through my mind.

Undoubtedly, Nancy was hurt because her children weren't enthusiastic. But she had accomplished her goal with the meeting. She had begun orchestrating the appearance of a solid family unit for when Dad announced his candidacy.

After the conference Maureen, Colleen and I stopped for cocktails on our way home. We all began to laugh when Maureen quipped over her drink, "If Dad doesn't make it as president of the United States, he could run and win as president of the Chambermaids' and Bellmen's Union."

Chapter XII

"I love you too, Mommy."

Colleen and I were married on November 7, 1975, at a small chapel in Anaheim, California, across the street from Disneyland. We had planned a small wedding, but once the news got out that Dad was going to be there, the guest list kept growing. It was already rumored that he planned to run for president, so he was a major attraction. All the invitees RSVP'd their acceptances except for Maureen, who said she had a speaking engagement in Washington. Most of Colleen's family from Nebraska flew in, including her parents, who had never been on an airplane before.

Mom arrived in style an hour early in a limousine with Buffum, the new poodle in her life, on her lap. Buffum had a huge gold nugget hanging from his collar and a bow in his hair. Mom was dressed to the nines in a gold lamé dress. I had never seen her so beautiful. The moment she arrived she started to take over and searched out Colleen to ask if she could be of any help.

The ceremony was scheduled for seven P.M., but Dad and Nancy had not arrived by that time. Everyone but me waited patiently and expectantly for them. Patience is not a virtue with me. Finally, at seven-thirty, they arrived. I was taken aback when I saw Ron with them. I had not invited him or Patti because I did not feel that close to them and I felt the feeling was mutual. You could hear a collective gasp as the trio walked in. Dad was resplendent in a dark blue suit, but it was Nancy who got the most attention. She was wearing an elegant green suit with a mink collar. They were seated in the front pew on the opposite side from Mom.

At the conclusion of the ceremony, Colleen and I stood on the steps of the altar for family pictures. Although Colleen's parents had been divorced for twenty years and hadn't seen each other during that time, they stood together. Then the photographer asked for the mother and father of the groom to join the group. Uh oh! I thought. If Dad and Nancy got up, my mother would be upset. If Mom got up, Nancy would be upset. I looked at my parents, who hadn't spoken with each other for years, certain my marriage—only minutes old—was going to cause problems in that first pew. Where was Maureen when I needed her?

You could have heard a pin drop. Nancy was looking at Dad, who continued staring straight ahead. For a moment I thought we were going to need an NFL referee to keep track of the penalty phase of the wedding.

After what seemed like an eternity, Mom stood up, looked directly at Nancy and said, "Nancy, don't worry about a thing. Ron and I have had our pictures taken together before. If you'd like to join us, fine. Now Ron, come on. The photographer's waiting. Let's get our pictures taken."

Dad looked relieved as he escorted Nancy and Ron to the altar to pose for the picture. I was also relieved but at the same time a little annoyed that my stepbrother Ron was included in the picture. Later I would get one without him.

After the photographs were taken, we went to the reception where Dad told me that he had previously sent me a letter regarding his thoughts on marriage. "The sentiments I expressed in that letter still stand," he said. I thought back and remembered the letter and every day of my marriage, like Dad suggested, I have told Colleen I love her and we just celebrated our twelfth anniversary.

Twelve days after Colleen and I were married, Dad announced at the Press Club in Washington, D.C., that he was going to run for president. I was disappointed because I had envisioned that like most candidates, he would have his entire family with him when he announced. But he was accompanied only by Nancy.

After Dad's announcement, a real problem began to brew in the campaign. When Dad was governor, Nancy had begun building the image of a supportive all-American family, but Ron and Patti were not interested in becoming involved in the campaign, while Maureen and I were more than happy to help out. The campaign staff wanted us to keep a low profile, however, because they felt we made Dad look too old; we were, after all, mature adults or would have liked to think so.

The attention Maureen and I received from the press also distressed Nancy but for another reason: We were invariably identified as "the adopted son and the daughter of Ronald Reagan and Jane Wyman," thus reminding Nancy of a marriage that had ended twenty-eight years earlier. Those constant references to a past marriage must have hurt Nancy every time she heard or read them but I didn't understand that then. All I knew was that we felt as though Nancy was pushing us out of the family circle and trying to bring Ron and Patti in.

The cornerstone of Dad's campaign for the Republican nomination in 1976 was those values that he so much cherishes: family, home, moral integrity. That was great for the country, but it scared the hell out of me. There was no way I could live up to that image. I only knew that I felt that I had to protect Dad from the press finding out the truth about me—that I'd had a relationship with a man and there were nude pictures of me. Just as during his campaign for governor, I tortured myself with visions of *those* pictures appearing in publications like the *National Enquirer* or *Penthouse*. They would destroy my father, and I would be responsible for his defeat. Even worse, not only would I lose my father and mother with such a disclosure, I would lose the best friend I've ever had, my wife Colleen. I was scared to death.

So when I was asked to speak on his behalf, I did but stayed mostly in California and rarely spoke out of state. I had never spoken in public until then, and I was shaking in my new shoes and sweating in my new suit. My first few speeches were terrible, but after a while I got the hang of it. I even began to enjoy the attention I was receiving as the candidate's son.

When asked why I thought my father should be president, I invariably answered that I thought he was the most capable man. But there were other unspoken and very personal reasons why I wanted Dad to succeed: I felt that if he did make it to the presidency, it would be partly due to me since I had gone out on the campaign trail to speak for him. Also, if he became president, I anticipated that I would be surrounded with a kind of bubble of protection, that all of his children would become folk heroes like the Kennedy kids, Jack and Steve Ford, and Julie and Tricia Nixon. I felt that with Dad as president, if the pictures did show up, I finally would be forgiven for my past, and the burden I had been carrying would be off my shoulders.

At the same time, however, I feared that if he won I really would lose him. When he was an actor, I felt he was too busy to be an attentive father. When he became governor, he had moved to Sacramento where I saw him only once at his office. I figured that if he were president he would move to Washington, D.C., become the father of the country, and I would lose all contact with him for at least four years.

Dad went into the campaign bucking the odds: he was a Republican running against the incumbent Republican president, Gerald Ford. He did not have the support of many party bigwigs, including New York's Governor Nelson Rockefeller.

I know he was personally devastated when Barry Goldwater, the senator from Arizona who had brought him to the Republican party, turned on him and publicly endorsed Ford. I've never in my life heard Dad say an unkind word about anyone, and he managed to remain mum about his disappointment over Goldwater. But everyone else in our family was livid because Dad had worked so hard to help Goldwater during his campaign. We felt that the least Goldwater could do was support Dad but politics is politics; you have no friends. The one family member who did respond with anger was Nancy's mother, De De. Thank God for De De. She considered the Goldwaters close personal friends and had often opened her house to them. De De called Goldwater on the phone and told him off, saying that he had been to her house for the last time. Dad and Nancy chuckled over De De's forthrightness because, I suspect, they probably would have liked to have told him off in the same way but Dad isn't like that. What he is, despite the family's feelings about whatever matter is at hand, is forgiving.

The schism between the Reagan children seemed to widen with each passing day as Merm and I tried to earn our way to the top. But the staff wouldn't let us stay there. For example, on the night that Dad won the last primary in California, Ron and Patti, who had never made an appearance during the campaign, were invited into Dad's holding room, while Maureen, Colleen and I were told by the staff to sit at a table behind a curtain by the stage and wait. We were incensed. When Patti and Ron came out of the room, Maureen looked at me and said, "Someday I'll get even."

Then the entire family was joined, and we walked out to face a cheering crowd shouting praise for Dad. We stood together on a stage designed to look like a train going to Kansas City and were all introduced. I was so proud to be on that stage with my father that I didn't want the moment to end. If only some of the love those people had for Dad would somehow find its way to me, my problems would be solved. Please love me too, I thought.

We all traveled together on a private jet to Kansas City for the Republican convention. Just after takeoff, Nancy, as is her superstitious custom, rolled an orange down the center aisle. When the orange made it all the way to the rear of the plane, the press applauded, and Nancy giggled like a schoolgirl. Colleen and I had brought a gift for Dad which was presented to him en route. It was a Paducah wood gavel with a brass plate inscribed: "To President Ronald Reagan." Dad delighted us by saying he would cherish it.

Maureen desperately wanted to be a delegate at the convention, but the Reagan campaign people refused to allow it. She was furious. She confronted Dad and told him she had really worked hard for him during the campaign and in fact had been a Republican longer than he had, which is true. "I've earned the right to be a delegate," she said. And she had.

Dad told her that he could choose only one delegate, and he had given that as a gift to Moon (his older brother, Neil) because Moon was getting on in years and probably wouldn't be around for many more conventions. Moon hasn't missed a convention since.

"Why don't you make me an alternate?" Maureen asked.

"I can't do that," Dad said. The subject was closed.

Dad's family and friends sat in a private box behind bullet proof glass at the convention hall. I had never been to a convention before and my spine still tingles at the recollection of the Texas and California delegates shouting, "Viva. Ole! Viva. Ole!!"

On the night before the Republican nominations for president, the Reagan people polled the delegates and discovered that Dad was not going to have enough support to be nominated. The next night Nancy invited the family to dinner in their suite on the top floor of the hotel. Dad was wearing a white dinner jacket and Nancy a formal dress. Dinner was a somber affair with only small talk at the table. No one wanted to broach the subject. Finally, after dinner, Dad invited us into the living room and said he wanted to talk with us. "I know all of you have worked very hard, but I don't have enough delegates to get the nomination," he said. "I'm just not going to get the job done. I'm truly sorry you all have to see this, but I'm glad we are all here together as a family." I believe it was the first time Dad had ever lost anything that he wanted so much, and I could see the hurt in his eyes and hear it in his voice.

Someone asked if he would agree to run for vice-president were President Ford to suggest it. Dad's answer to us was a flat no. Yet, I was certain he would have found it hard to turn down his Commander-in-Chief, knowing the boy scout that Dad is and always will be.

Before we left the suite for the convention floor, Nancy, who was standing by the fireplace, poured champagne for each of us. She toasted Dad and then spoke directly to him, her voice cracking with emotion. I don't remember her words verbatim, but I had the impression that she was trying to take the burden of Dad's loss onto her shoulders and, somehow, accept the blame and pain for his failure. She ended by saying that the support Dad had received indicated that he was loved not only by his family but by many millions of people. She apologized to Dad for pushing him into the first political failure of his life, but she did it because she loved him and no matter what happened they still had each other. I had never before seen Nancy so vulnerable.

She hugged Dad, and I heard him say, "I love you, too, Mommy."

It was a private moment we all shared, and I will never forget it. It was the first time I had ever seen Nancy or Dad puddle up. They embraced as though we were not in the room. Then Nancy looked at us with tear-filled eyes and said, "Dry your eyes, everyone. We are all going to walk into that convention center with our heads up." And, damn it, we did!

Dad remained in his room while the rest of us went to the convention floor. As predicted, Dad lost. We all returned to the suite very dejected but certain that Dad would be offered the vice-presidency; it was no secret that Ford couldn't win without him. When President Ford came into the hotel, Dad went to meet with him alone.

While the meeting was taking place, we all prayed that Dad would accept the vice-presidency, because we thought it was his last chance to serve his country (he was then sixty-five) and we wanted him at least to have that.

When Dad returned from the meeting, we were eagerly anticipating his report that he had been asked to run for vice-president. "He didn't ask me," Dad said. Then, for the first time that day, he grinned. "You know what upsets me most of all about not getting the nomination from the party and then becoming president?" he said. "It's that I really looked forward to representing the American people at the SALT agreements with the Russian Secretary General. I wanted to sit down at a round table and have him tell me through his interpreter everything the United States was going to have to give up to get along with the Russians. I was going to listen to him, and then, at the end, I was going to get up from my chair, walk around the table and whisper in his ear, 'Nyet.' I really am going to miss the fact that I can't say 'nyet' to him." Ten years later in Iceland he got his chance.

The following night, August 18, 1976, Gerald Ford accepted the nomination of his party. Until then, Dad had not been invited to the convention floor, which the Ford people controlled. They didn't want to let Dad speak; it would have been political suicide for Ford because, as speakers, he and Dad are as different as day and night. But after Ford gave his acceptance speech, he surprised everyone by saying, "Come on down, Ron, and bring Nancy." Dad was shocked.

The delegates rose to their feet and began an ovation which seemed to last an hour. The pianist must have played "California, Here I Come" a dozen times. Even Frank Reynolds of ABC News, who had covered the campaign from the beginning, was in tears. People who were already heading for the exits turned and froze as Dad stepped up to the microphone.

Dad is often accused of delivering only prepared speeches, but I know that he was not prepared to say anything on this occasion. His totally extemporaneous speech was probably the best of his political career. I doubt there was a dry eye in the hall when he finished, because most everyone realized that they had nominated the wrong man. Four years later, that speech would still be remembered, and it would help to make him president of the United States.

153

Chapter XIII

"We caught your brother."

After the convention and election, which Ford lost, all of us went back to being somewhat normal, whatever that might have been! For me it was the boat store. We didn't see much of the family during 1977 but one day out of the blue Dad called. I was surprised to hear his voice and even more surprised to hear him say, "Ron has dropped out of Yale after only one semester, and he isn't listening to me or Nancy. He wants to become a ballet dancer. You understand his generation better than I do—what can I do with him?"

I almost said, "Buy him a tutu," but thought better of it. I knew that Ron's choice of a profession did not fit in any way with the

Reagan image; most of the public who supported Dad perceived male ballet dancers as gay. But I was flattered that Dad was seeking my advice about my younger brother and I was kind of glad he was on the hot seat.

We made an appointment to meet in Mike Deaver's newly opened public relations office in Los Angeles where Dad, who was his first client, also had an office and secretary. The first time I had been there was for the grand opening and, of course, Dad was the honored guest. The most touching moment was when Nancy Reynolds, their press secretary, opened up her bag and brought out—all linked together—the keys from every hotel and motel room at which Dad and Nancy had stayed during the campaign. It was nice. This time Dad came into the reception area and brought me to his office furnished simply but elegantly in early-American style.

He sat behind his desk and got right to the point. "You're a lot closer in age to Ron than I am," he said. "Can you tell me why he is so rebellious?"

Dad likes to get to the bottom line quickly in family conversations, so I tried to keep things simple. I took a piece of paper and asked him to draw a line down the center of it.

"Why?" he asked.

"You'll see," I promised. "Write football on one side of the line and baseball on the other," I said.

Dad looked at me quizzically, but he did as I suggested. Meanwhile, I glanced around his office and was disappointed to see the Paducah wood gavel I had given to him on a bottom shelf of a book case, covered with dust. But at least he had it.

"Now write down the number of times you have taken Ron to a football or baseball game." Dad may have thought we were talking about Ron, but I was really talking about me. I knew he had never taken me to a football game, and I was guessing that he had never taken Ron.

156

Dad put his pencil on the paper, hesitated, then looked at me. He was crestfallen. "I took him to one football game, but I don't remember when," he said.

"There's the problem," I said. "You've been just too busy to be a father."

Dad stared at the paper for a moment and then shook his head. "Thanks, Mike," he said.

Our brief session must have affected him because the next day Nancy called me at the boat salesroom. It was as rare for me to get a call from her as it was to get one from Dad, and I knew right away I was in some kind of trouble. "Don't ever talk to your father like that again," she said tersely.

Ron soon moved back home and publicly announced his intention to become a ballet dancer. Some weeks later, when I was visiting with the family at the Palisades, Dad told me that he had called his old friend Gene Kelly and asked him about a good local ballet school Ron could attend. Gene gave him a name and then assured Dad that not all male ballet dancers were gay, a report which obviously pleased Dad.

Soon there were snide hints about Ron's sexuality in the papers. Dad and Nancy have always paid attention to the press; if a story about them is unflattering, they perceive it to be inaccurate or a misquote. But if they read a negative story about someone else, they tend, like most people, to believe the story might be true. Although they were ninety-nine percent certain that Ron wasn't gay, that one percent of lingering doubt must have worried them.

I knew my brother was not gay, but in a mean way, I was glad the press was coming down on him. For once it was Nancy's own child who wasn't reflecting well on Dad. I also realized that if Dad and Nancy were this concerned about Ron's dancing and its effect on their image as good parents, it would break their hearts if they knew what I had done with a man when I was a child. I still did not understand that what had occurred in my childhood was sexual molestation, and wouldn't fully comprehend it for years. I felt that Ronald Reagan's public would have perceived me as a homosexual.

Not long after Ron decided to study ballet at the Stanley Holden Dance Center in Los Angeles, Dad again telephoned me at the boat store. "Nancy and I came back from a trip a little early, and we caught your brother," he said, sounding distressed.

"Caught my brother doing what?" I asked.

"There was a young lady in the house for the weekend," Dad said. "Ron had the cook making breakfast for them in bed and preparing candlelight dinners. And he wasn't using his room; he was using our room and our bed!"

I started to laugh and then realized that Dad was reaching out to me as a member of the younger generation for advice. Dad is a very moral and old-fashioned man and was probably appalled to discover that Ron was having the kind of relationship that in his view should be reserved only for marriage.

Good-news/bad-news jokes were in vogue at the time, so I said, "Well, Dad, there's good news and bad news."

"What do you mean?" Dad asked.

"The bad news is that you came home early and you caught him. The good news is that you found out he isn't gay."

There was a moment of silence on Dad's end of the line. Finally he said, "I hadn't thought of it that way, but you're absolutely right. I guess it is a blessing. Thanks, Mike," and then he paused and said, "I must tell Nancy." He sounded relieved.

1977 was also the year Colleen and I decided to buy a house in order to start a family. Like many people, I wanted to buy the kind of house I had grown up in. I had in mind a two-story Colonial in a nice neighborhood with four bedrooms, a swimming pool, three-car garage and maid's quarters for around fifty thousand dollars. I soon learned that such a house was way beyond our limited budget. I looked at homes with a realtor for a month, but I finally despaired of ever finding anything we could afford, probably because I was not one to make commitments.

So I sent Colleen out to search. Mom and I were getting along great, and since she knew our finances, she said that she would give us one thousand dollars toward the down payment on a house. That was an especially generous gift because, for our first anniversary, Mom had also given us all of her silver.

The way the anniversary gift came about was typical of Mom. We had gone to her apartment to pick her up for dinner. As we were having cocktails, she told me that the reason she never gave me gifts was because she was afraid I would sell the presents and spend the money foolishly. Boy, did she have me pegged. She was probably right, but I was hurt when she said it. No one likes to hear about his bad side.

Then she rehashed for Colleen all the mistakes I had made during my lifetime, ending with a seeming non sequitur: "I guess you want to know what I am giving you for your anniversary." She pointed to a door and told me, "Open up that door, go to the bottom of the stairs and you will find a brown cardboard box which says 'silver' on top. Bring it upstairs." Like a good boy, I did as instructed.

I toted the heavy box up the stairs into the living room. "Now open it," Mom said.

It contained all of her silver. Colleen gasped with pleasure, but I was seething inside because Mom's speech had made me feel so guilty about receiving the gift that I didn't want it. She compounded my guilt by saying, "I doubt you can afford the insurance to protect it, and you probably have no place to put it; so, if you want to, you can go out and sell it."

That was Mom. She could be warm and loving, but she never seemed to miss an opportunity to make me feel guilty about accepting a gift from her. She was equally difficult about gifts she received. Whenever Maureen or I gave her one, Mom invariably included mention of it in her will to make sure that on her death it was given back. It was difficult to buy Mom a gift she would use, so for years, I bought her Taster's Choice coffee because at least I knew she would use that and I wouldn't get it back after her death. At least I don't think so.

When Mom offered us the thousand dollars for the down payment, she attached a minor condition. She insisted that before we make a down payment on a house, she see it first. That was fine with me because, as always, I wanted and needed her approval.

Colleen liked the idea of house hunting with Mom because she missed her own mother, and Mom liked having a daughter to talk with. Colleen finally found the ideal house in a nice suburb of Los Angeles. It was the perfect size for us: two bedrooms and one bath with two orange trees in the backyard you could smell from a block away and a small lawn in front with a red brick wall. It was the kind of house I had always idealized for myself when, as a kid, I watched TV shows about American families. I wasn't sure how Mom would like it, but when she saw the house, she was equally enthusiastic. I was relieved and proud.

Although I was earning a good commission as a boat salesman, we were short forty-five hundred dollars for the down payment, and the escrow had to close in thirty days because the seller had bought a new home. My commissions on sales were not due for two months. I called Dad and told him the problem, explaining that I would be able to repay him in sixty days. Dad agreed to lend me the money for a year. He then called his attorneys, who sent me a check along with a promissory note with a due date one year later. Although I thanked Dad, I was taken aback by the note. I thought, I'm family, not a business associate.

On the day we moved into our new house, Mom was waiting for us with groceries, every bit as excited as we were.

Five months later Colleen became pregnant, and I was euphoric. My child would be the link between me and my parents; he or she would be someone we could all dote on and love together, a terrible burden to put on a baby. But I thought that by giving Dad and Mom their first grandchild, they would finally realize that I had changed, that I was mature and was now accepting responsibility. I also felt that I was giving them a second chance to be real parents.

My euphoria was short-lived, however. Ninety days before the promissory note was due, I received a letter from Dad's attorneys indicating that they hoped my loan would be repaid on time; they did not want to renew it for another year.

Although I had the forty-five hundred dollars in a savings account and had every intention of paying back the loan, the letter read as though it came from a collection agency. I was incensed. When another reminder arrived thirty days later, I was furious. I had considered the loan to be a matter between my father and myself and was enraged that his attorneys were in the middle of it. They didn't trust me because they had no way of knowing that thanks to Colleen I was a changed person and had paid back all my old debts. But my father should have known it. I had even paid off the Ranchero. All my old resentments came into play again. There always seemed to be someone between my father and me.

Thirty days before the note was due, the attorneys started dunning me, which also made Colleen furious. In a fit of pique, I shut myself off from the family. Somehow Nancy smelled out a problem and had Dad call me. As usual, he suggested we get together at his home to talk.

It was pouring rain the night I dropped Colleen off at her designer school downtown and then drove out to the Palisades. It was miserable weather, and I was in a foul mood when I arrived, explaining that I didn't like dealing with attorneys on a personal matter. As always, when Dad is not sure who is right in a dispute, he calls the problem a misunderstanding. He said it again that night and then asked what it was going to take for us all to get along. I saw a chance to blackmail myself into the family—in my mind, nothing else had ever worked and I had never felt like part of the family—so I said that it wasn't just a case of me getting along with him. "I'm tired of trying to get along with you," I said. "If you want to see your grandchild, then you've got to get along with me."

Those were inexcusable words, and as soon as I said them I felt terrible.

Dad looked at me and said, "You don't mean that, do you?"

With that I broke into tears. I apologized to him and Nancy. We all hugged each other. I started to leave, but at the doorway I remembered that Maureen, who knew why I was going to talk to Dad that night, had asked me to mention a similar problem she was having with Dad's attorneys. Her friend Gene Nelson, the song and dance man, had had a stroke. Dad had lent her ten thousand dollars because she wanted it to help Gene rehabilitate himself.

"By the way, Dad," I said, "do you know that your attorneys are also charging Maureen bank interest on the loan you made to her?" Dad was shocked and promised to rectify it immediately (which he did). I left Dad and Nancy mollified and repaid my loan on time.

Everything was great again and soon after our meeting, Nancy invited Colleen and me to come by the house to pick up some needed furnishings for our new home. She brought us into the master bedroom, opened the bottom drawer of a dresser and brought out the receiving blanket her mother had given her when Patti was born, which had also been used for Ron. It was a most meaningful gift. Nancy wanted to start a family tradition and hoped that all the Reagan grandchildren would use the same blanket. She asked only that when Ron got married and had children, Colleen would pass the blanket on so it could stay in the family.

The everpresent Mike Deaver was priming Dad again to reenter presidential politics. Nancy invited Colleen and me to attend a celebrity fund-raising dinner arranged by her old friend Goldie Arthur. Patti and Ron as usual were not going to be there because they hated politics. People frequently made snide remarks about their absence since almost everyone felt they should attend, and I always was there to agree.

As luck would have it, Colleen came down with a migraine headache on the day that the dinner was scheduled. Worse, she started to spot, a bad omen for a woman approaching her delivery date. Colleen's doctor suggested that she go to bed and remain there. We waited until almost the last minute to see if the spotting would stop. When it didn't, I called Nancy and explained the situation to her. It was our first baby and we were concerned and frightened.

"Hang up quickly," Nancy said. "Call Goldie Arthur and tell her you're not going to be at the dinner. We can't have two empty seats right up front."

I called Goldie, but I was heartsick. Nancy hadn't even asked about Colleen's health or how she was feeling. I thought she should have shown more concern for her daughter-in-law than for two empty seats at a table in front. Nancy's only concern seemed to be for Dad and his image.

The publicity about our involvement in Dad's campaign got Maureen and me in trouble with Mom, who resented our involvement with Dad's politics. So Mom, who had been in the habit of reading her will to us once or twice a year, called us over to

163

her apartment and announced that she had deleted us from her will. She said, "You're both so close to *them*, why don't you just have them put you in their will? *He* must be a multimillionaire by now."

When I mentioned that conversation in passing to Dad one day, he shook his head sadly and said, "You and Maureen are not in our will because I thought you were in your mother's."

Chapter XIV

"Whatever you do, protect Nancy."

Our son Cameron was born at 6:42 A.M. on May 30, 1978. I couldn't wait to telephone Dad and Nancy at their home in the Palisades to tell them that they were the grandparents of a healthy boy.

The first thing Nancy asked me was "Have you called Ron?" I hadn't, nor did I intend to, because Ron and I didn't have the kind of relationship that warranted it. But because he was Nancy's pride and joy, I said I would call him with the news.

Then Nancy gave the phone to Dad who offered his congratulations. I told him that if he and Nancy went to the Santa Barbara ranch later that day they might want to stop by the hospital. It was only minutes from the freeway on which they had to travel. "We'll try," he promised. I just knew they would show up—they had to.

Maureen, who I had called earlier, arrived bringing a gift only Merm could bring: a book entitled *How To Raise a Non-sexist Child.* I just laughed.

I had also called Mom, who arrived later carrying flowers and wanting to know all the details: Cameron's weight, length, exact time of birth. Mom offered to pay for a live-in nurse to take care of Colleen for the first two weeks she was home. It was a generous offer, and we accepted it gratefully.

Dad and Nancy sent a plant but did not stop by to visit on their way to the ranch. Even in all my happiness that day, I felt hurt and rejected by this. Of course, they didn't realize that in my mind Cameron was my rebirth—little Mike Reagan born again, spotlessly clean and perfect, everything I had always wanted to be—and I was going to keep him that way. I anticipated that through him I could live my life over again. I felt that I was giving Dad and Nancy a chance to behave as real grandparents. And here they hadn't even stopped in to see their grandson! I thought that Nancy was probably resentful that Dad's first grandchild wasn't also her own, given to her by Ron. Perhaps that's only natural, but as always, I took things in the worst possible way.

But during the first week that Cameron was home, a letter, hand-written by Dad, arrived with a fifty dollar check. The letter dated June 7th, read:

Dear Cameron,

I don't know the arithmetic on compound interest, but I hear it is something sensational if you let it accumulate for say eighteen or twenty years. Then, of course, various and sundry individuals may from time to time throw something

166

in the pot so that one day, when you've come to understand what money is, this will have become a tidy sum. It might even cover the cost of a set of wheels if your parents' and your grandparents' generations have in the meantime done something practical about inflation.

With love,
Your Grandfather and Grandmother Reagan

Dad seemed to always come through. How could I stay mad at him, especially when a week later he called to ask if he and Nancy could come visit. It must have been Nancy who kept him away on the day of Cameron's birth, I thought.

On the July 4th weekend, Colleen's father and her sister Shirley came from Nebraska to visit us. We wanted to take them sightseeing, so we drove to Solvang, a Danish enclave located a few miles from Santa Barbara and Dad's ranch. I had never been to the new ranch because I had never been invited and I disliked intruding on Dad's and Nancy's private time. But I telephoned them prior to our trip to ask if we could all come for a visit so both families could see each other and be with Cameron.

"We won't have time," Nancy said. "Christine Lund and Joseph Benti (prominent Los Angeles newscasters) just broke up. Joseph is heartbroken and has an appointment to talk with your father." Joseph Benti, I thought, what's he to me and Colleen's family? I was tired of all these people being first in line. I didn't think kids should have to make an appointment to see their parents.

I was keenly disappointed and hurt because Colleen comes from a very large family which puts family first before anything else and I considered their refusal to see us as a slap in the face of Colleen and her father who my parents had met only at the wedding.

167

To my surprise, Mom responded to her grandson with endearing enthusiasm. Mom had never raised a baby without outside help and was not up to the nitty-gritty business of being a grandmother, but she tried. When Colleen and I decided to go to Catalina Island with her family for a day, Mom gamely volunteered to babysit for us. She arrived at our house the evening before we left so we could fill her in on the care and feeding of Cameron. She was so cute trying to learn.

I called home when we arrived at Catalina after a two hour ferry ride. Mom answered the phone sounding very frazzled. "Find another grandmother," she declared. "This is crazy. I am ready to run out the door screaming!" We took the next boat back to Los Angeles.

Mom's overwrought reactions worried me enough so that I called her priest and told him I thought something was troubling her and she could use his help.

"I don't feel I can interfere in her life, because it might upset her so much that she will stop giving to the Church," he said.

I was shocked. "Do you mean to tell me that her contributions to the church are more important than her health?"

"That's the way it is," he said. And that's how it ended.

Plans for Dad's reentry into politics became definite in 1979. Mike Deaver, with Nancy's support, had begun regrooming him. This time Dad seemed to have an excellent chance of winning his party's support. President Jimmy Carter was doing a lackluster job, and Dad was proving to be the Republicans' front-runner. His only disadvantage was his age, but that soon became a moot point in the campaign.

The fact is that even today, Dad is in incredible shape for a man of any age. He is a superior horseman, and his idea of a vacation is not to lie around relaxing but to spend time at the Santa Barbara ranch where he invariably gets up at dawn and chops wood before going for a horseback ride.

Dad has told me that his superb physical condition has only a little to do with diet or how much he works out; it's his genes. But I know it's not all genetic. The truth is, Dad constantly works at staying in shape every day of his life. When he traveled, he used to bring with him a small contraption with rollers which he used to exercise.

It seems every time we get together he squeezes my belly appraisingly. Then he demands that I punch his rock-hard stomach. "You've got to stay in shape," he says.

In 1978, Dad went back to Eureka College for a class reunion. He sat on the dais next to a very old and frail man in a wheelchair who knew everything about him. For the life of him, Dad could not remember the man's name. Luckily all attendees were wearing nametags. Dad purposely dropped his napkin to the floor and leaned down to pick it up, using the opportunity to glance at the man's tag. To his dismay it was his college roommate. He said he had never been so embarrassed.

When Dad announced in December, 1979 that he planned to be a candidate for president, Colleen, Maureen and I flew to New York. Maureen, who never forgets, remembered how we had been shunted off at the California Primary Victory Celebration in 1976, and before the evening festivities started, she told Mike Deaver and Lyn Nofziger that she had brought two pair of shoes with her. "One pair," Maureen said, "makes me taller than your candidate (Dad is six feet one inch tall; Maureen is five feet eleven inches tall) and the other pair makes me just a bit shorter. If Michael, Colleen and I are slighted again when the picture is taken, I intend to be taller than your candidate." We weren't slighted and Maureen wore the low heels.

The Reagan "family" was now expanded to include all those people who were important to him: Mike Deaver, Lyn Nofziger and Ed Meese. Everyone seemed to want a piece of Ronald Reagan. It was maddening that I had to go through Mike Deaver or Nancy in order to talk to my own father. It never occurred to me that Nancy had similar problems.

During that Thanksgiving at the ranch, I had to share Dad with all the members of the family, many of whom like me had not seen him during the year and each of whom wanted a piece of his time. Even within the confines of his family, Dad was treated like a god. It was almost impossible to have a one-on-one conversation with him because of his schedule: We had all been told to arrive by five P.M. and be gone by seven P.M.

However, I finally got Dad alone for a moment and told him a joke I had just heard. I asked him how he could tell if there was a Polack at a cockfight.

"I don't know," he said.

"He's the one who brings the duck," I said. "Now, how can you tell if there's an Italian at the fight?"

Again, Dad said he didn't know.

"Because he bets on the duck. Now, how can you tell if the Mafia is at the fight?"

Dad shook his head.

"Because the duck wins," I said.

Dad exploded with laughter. "I'll have to remember that one," he said. He did remember it later but with dire consequences.

The campaign began early for us just after Christmas, 1979. Colleen and I planned to go to Omaha with Cameron, who was going to stay with Colleen's sister there while we went skiing at

Vail, Colorado to celebrate my being named salesman of the year at the boat store. Just as we were leaving home, the phone rang. A man on the end of the line said he was calling from Iowa. "Are you Mike Reagan?" he asked me.

"I am," I said.

"What relation are you to Ronald Reagan?" I laughed outwardly while seething inside.

"I'm his son," I said.

"Then how come I've never heard of you?" he asked.

I was about to hang up the phone when he said, "The Iowa caucuses are coming up and your father hasn't been here yet. We really need a Reagan presence here in Iowa."

I started to refuse the request because Colleen and I had planned this vacation for some time. Then I felt guilty. I wasn't being a good son. Finally it was agreed that the campaign people would pay for our air fare from Iowa to Vail, Colorado; in return, I agreed to spend some time in Iowa.

I ended up speaking for Dad in twenty-five counties over five days. As I went through the state, I realized that John Sears, Dad's campaign manager, was more interested in getting exposure on television for himself than for his candidate.

I called Dad from Iowa and told him that if he were to ask the Iowans who was running for president they would probably say, "John Sears." Dad was silent for a moment and then said, "I'll look into it."

As it turned out, the Iowa caucus saw George Bush taking thirty-three percent of the votes, to Dad's thirty percent. It shook everyone in his camp and made the New Hampshire primary even more important. I was certain that Dad would trounce George Bush for the Republican nomination if only he would fire Sears, and I was determined to work my butt off for him in this campaign. I knew his history as governor as well or better than he did. I had become so adept at speaking on his behalf and giving his answers to questions that people frequently remarked that I was just like him, which was the greatest compliment I could receive. However, by this time, my hair had started to thin, more proof that I wasn't his son. When people remarked about my receding hairline, I had a pat answer. "I let my Dad borrow my hair, and he has promised to give it back to me in his will. In fact, the only thing he is leaving me is his hair. And, in fact, that's all I want."

After speaking in Iowa, I was asked by campaign managers in other states to speak to their constituencies. I was anxious not to offend anyone and for people to know I was loyal to my father, so I accepted each invitation. In that way, I am much like my Dad. Neither of us knows how to say "No," which is one of the reasons why Nancy is such an important buffer for him, and Colleen for me.

The requests for me to speak became so numerous that I finally had to quit my job and devote myself to Dad's campaign. I couldn't be paid for those speeches, and I could ill afford time away from my job; so I made a deal that my wife's air ticket and expenses were to be included in every trip and that a babysitter for Cameron would be provided. We had no intention of leaving our child at home. It would have killed me to leave my son behind and have the same things happen to him as had happened to me. Ultimately, I spent most of 1980 on the road and covered thirty-five states.

Before Maureen and I started with the campaign, Lyn Nofziger briefed us. He told us that Nancy was not happy about our campaigning but we were needed in order to represent a solid family unit because Ron and Patti were not going to campaign. Ron now lived in New York and was with the Joffrey Ballet, while Patti was much more liberal than her father. Although Lyn wanted us to be involved, he asked that we not mention our mother, Jane Wyman; that would remind the electorate that Dad had been divorced, and no man elected president had ever been divorced. His closing words to us were "Under no circumstances are you to make any smart remarks about Nancy. Whatever you do, protect Nancy." He knew our feelings about her at the time and didn't want us to slip up.

While Dad was in New Hampshire campaigning, I received a telephone call at work from Colleen. "Remember that joke about the duck that you told your father at Thanksgiving? Well, he told it to someone on the press bus in New Hampshire, and now it's national news."

The upshot of the incident was that Dad had to go to the American people and apologize for repeating an ethnic joke. I was glad he had forgotten that I had told it to him. Parenthetically, it was the first time I had ever heard my father apologize for anything.

It was also during the New Hampshire primary that, for the first time in my memory, I saw Dad lose his temper. That happened at Nashua High School during a debate scheduled between Dad and George Bush. Originally Dad was scheduled to debate only Bush, who was the party's front-runner because of Iowa. Unknown to Dad, John Sears had called the other five candidates and suggested they show up in Nashua and ask to participate. Dad didn't know about the others until noon of the scheduled debate when Sears brought him a press release announcing the other debaters.

Dad was furious because the Reagan camp was paying for the debate. On his way to the gymnasium that cold February evening, Dad had no idea what was to happen. He met the four other opponents who had decided to come—Anderson, Baker, Crane and Dole—in a classroom in the school and agreed not to debate Bush unless the others could participate.

Bush, who thought it was going to be a one-on-one debate with Dad, spoke first, but the audience turned on him and shouted to

173

let the other candidates speak. J. Herman Pouliot, publisher of the *Nashua Telegraph* and sponsor of the debate, tried to quiet the audience as Dad walked up to the podium.

"Turn Mr. Reagan's microphone off," yelled Jon Breen, editor of the *Nashua Telegraph,* seeking to take control of the gathering.

"I paid for this microphone, and I plan to use it, Mr. Green," Dad snapped angrily, calling the man by the wrong name, the only mistake he made that evening. The sound system was in the hands of the company the Reagan staff had hired, and they weren't about to shut it off without Dad's approval.

After seeing the televised debate which Dad easily won, I called to congratulate him on his speech and the fact that he was so forceful.

"I guess I must have said something right," he said. "When I left the school, there were Bush buttons scattered all over the lawn."

On the day of the primary, Dad telephoned me at home. "I want you to be the first to know," he said. "I am firing John Sears." He then read to me a press release announcing Sears' resignation and the appointment of William Casey as campaign director. Colleen and I were so elated that we toasted Sears' departure with champagne.

Later that night, Dad called again to say that he had won the New Hampshire primary; he had walloped Bush by twenty-seven percentage points; the turning point in the campaign. I was honored to be the first to know.

Once it appeared that Dad was going to win the nomination, I suddenly became everyone's best friend. People I had met casually during the previous campaign called to invite Colleen and me to parties, lunch or dinner and would then try to talk us into some kind of investment on the theory that if my father was going to become president, I would be rich. Actually, the only stock I had ever owned was ninety shares of General Electric which Dad had given me once as a Christmas present when he worked for the corporation.

A man named Rich Carey, whom I had been introduced to during the campaign, came to the boat store. While the salesmen were eating, he pitched us to invest in a gold mine that he intended to take public. Salesmen are invariably the worst suckers, so along with some of the others, Colleen and I bought fifteen hundred shares of stock at around one dollar a share. Without my being aware of it, Carey then parlayed the fact that Ronald Reagan's son was an investor in part of his sales pitch to other potential investors. Ultimately, the gold mine turned out to be only a front for a stock scam. I lost my investment, and the resultant scandal nearly cost me my credibility with the White House.

Colleen and I brought Cameron, who was then two years old, to Detroit with us for the 1980 convention. On the night of Dad's nomination, we all had dinner together as we had in 1976, but this time it was a happy occasion. Afterward, one of Dad's campaign people requested that we leave Cameron behind when we went to the convention floor. Again, it was image: according to him, Dad would look too old if he had a grandson present. Colleen retorted that during dinner Cameron's grandfather asked that he be there. Besides, I was determined that Cameron be present; I wanted my son to be part of the historic event because he might not have another chance.

After Dad won the Republican nomination, Gerald Ford's people pressured him to choose the former president as his running mate. Their feeling, as well as that of several other important Republicans, was that by selecting Ford, Dad would

175

unite the party, a factor Dad took into consideration because the party had been fragmented since 1976. Nevertheless, Dad had yet to make a decision despite the fact that he had seen Dan Rather announce on television that Ford was to be his vice-presidential nominee.

What Rather and the other TV political savants didn't know was that Ford had made it plain that if he was chosen as vice-president he wanted to be on an equal footing with the president. The notion of a co-president caused a furor with Dad's advisers and supporters.

I was in Dad's suite with Colleen and several others of Dad's Kitchen Cabinet, including Holmes Tuttle, Justin Dart, Lyn Nofziger, Mike Deaver and Ed Meese. Tuttle was livid because he thought Dad was going to acquiesce to the pressure and choose Ford. Everyone was shooting opinions at Dad. Only Nancy was silent. I assume she had already spoken her piece in private. She does not forget easily.

Dad leaned against the back of his couch, taking it all in. Finally, he'd had enough. "Stop," he said. "I'll make the decision myself. Call Gerald Ford and tell him he has three minutes to make a decision on my terms."

Three minutes later, Dad looked directly at Ed Meese and said, "George Bush is my man. Get him on the phone."

Dad set a precedent that night by going to the convention floor and squelching the media rumors with his announcement that George Bush was going to be his vice-presidential nominee. There was stunned silence and then thunderous applause.

The following day Dad was scheduled to thank the California delegation. I happened to be wandering around the hotel with Cameron when a mass of people came down a corridor surrounding Dad. They all headed toward us, and Dad said, "Is that my grandson? Let me hold him." At that moment all the TV cameramen turned on their lights. Cameron was so frightened that when I handed him over, he smacked his grandfather on the left cheek.

I was so embarrassed I could have died, but Dad took it in stride and grinned. "Cameron recognizes me better on television where he sees me most often, and he still doesn't know me in person," he said.

The next day we flew with the Bushes to Houston for a rally, followed by lunch with the Bush family before we were to return to Los Angeles. Dad and Nancy sat two rows in front of Colleen, Cameron and me. At one point, I took Cameron to the lavatory. On the way back to our seats, I slowed down by Dad and Nancy, hoping to be noticed. Dad looked up and saw us. "Cameron, come here," he said and held out his arms. He sat Cameron on his foot and began bouncing him up and down and singing to him just as he did me when I was a child. Watching it brought back wonderful memories, happy ones of us playing together.

After about the fifth bounce, Nancy looked at Dad and said, "Not now, Ronnie." Dad immediately stopped and handed Cameron back to me without another word. Why, I thought they were having such fun!

The Bush home was in a lovely suburb of Houston. When we arrived there, George picked Cameron up and promised to show him his grandchildren's toys. He carried Cameron on his shoulders into a playroom where he dumped out all the toys from cupboards for Cameron to play with. I thought then and still do that George Bush is one of the nicest men I have ever met.

Jeb Bush, George's son, told me that after my father won the nomination, the Bush family was dejectedly sitting in their hotel room when Dad's call came. Suddenly their mood changed to one of total jubilation. "My family will never forget what your father did for our father," he said. I knew just how he felt.

*   *   *

My father's recent problems don't surprise me. He has a tendency to rely on and place total trust in the people around him. He delegates authority and puts his trust in his staff though they aren't always honest with him. In September, 1980, Dad's campaign people came to me and asked me to spend the month of October speaking on his behalf. I ended up campaigning for him in nineteen states. One of the last states was Pennsylvania. When I arrived there, I found that all my appearances had been cancelled, even though it was a targeted state. I was so upset that my advance man, Sandy Sanders, suggested I call Dad in Virginia where he was resting. Sandy thought that my father and I were stuck together like glue, and I didn't want him to know that we didn't have that tight a relationship. Sandy insisted, however, because we were two points down in the Pennsylvania polls. Finally, he dialed the phone for me, and I got on it.

"Where are you?" Dad asked me.

"Pennsylvania," I said.

"What are you doing there?"

"Campaigning."

"For who?"

"Who do you think? For you."

"Why are you doing that?" he asked.

"Because I was asked to."

"What about your job?"

"I had to quit it."

I hung up the phone, my eyes tearing up.

"What's wrong?" Sandy asked me.

"He doesn't even know I am out campaigning for him," I said.

"You can't hang up on your father," Sandy said. "You have to call him back. It may not be his fault. Maybe no one told him."

Sandy picked up the phone and got Dad back on the line. "We must have been cut off," Dad said. "What's the problem?"

I told him that I couldn't believe that he was unaware that I was out campaigning for him.

"I'm sorry," Dad said. "No one told me."

When I told him that my appearances had been cancelled, he said, "I'll take care of it."

My appearances were rescheduled. A tracking poll was taken a week after I left Pennsylvania, and we were a point and a half up.

Colleen and I had spent almost a full month on the campaign trail covering nineteen states and taking sixty-six airplane rides. I was satisfied that we had done everything in our power to help Dad win the election.

Chapter XV

"Love, Grandpa."

The family spent election night at Earle and Marion Jorgenson's home in Los Angeles where we intended to watch the results on television. At around five-thirty we were gathered around the three television sets watching the graphs for each state go up—blue for Reagan or red for Carter—when Dad and Nancy arrived. "Have you heard the announcement?" he asked. "I was in the shower when Nancy came in and told me the President was on the phone. 'Can't you tell him I'm taking a shower?' I asked. Nancy said that he had to talk to me right then. So I turned off the shower, wrapped a bath towel around myself and listened to the President congratulating me on winning the election."

181

We were all surprised because no one in the history of presidential politics had ever conceded while voters were still at the polls. Everybody had expected Dad to win by a large margin, but the results were staggering. He carried forty-four of fifty states, receiving more votes than Carter and Anderson combined.

The rest of the evening was an anticlimax for everyone, including Dad, who told us, "It's like getting ready for the big game and the other team doesn't show up." He, too, had anticipated a dramatic night because the most recent polls only showed him to be ten points ahead of Carter.

The following month, Ron was quietly married in New York by a justice of the peace to Doria Palmieri. Doria was a dancer Ron had met some four years earlier at the Stanley Holden School for Dance in Los Angeles. Theirs was a quiet ceremony; no one from the family had been invited to attend, and a Secret Service agent was Ron's best man. Ron's marriage finally put an end to the gossip about his sexual preferences.

That Christmas was the last one we were to spend at Dad's Palisades house, and it was also our first indication of what future press coverage for the family was going to be like. When I arrived with my family at the house on Christmas day, the press was literally hanging from the trees. The grounds were like a zoo.

Dad has always raised cattle at his ranch, and every year just after Thanksgiving all the members of the family get a scroll with a big red ribbon tied around it. On the scroll, Dad doodles either the right or left half of a steer. On the bottom is a note reading: "You are the proud parents of a steer who is now being raised at the ranch. Two weeks from the time you get this, he will have been butchered and wrapped for you to enjoy. Merry Christmas. Dad and Nancy."

A half a steer is a lot of meat, so we finally bought a freezer to store it. Before this Christmas, however, I had told Dad that we were still on the steer from the previous year. "What would you like instead?" he asked. Knowing his taste for fine wine, I suggested some bottles of wine from his cellar. On Christmas day, Colleen and I received two giant wicker baskets of wine, specially bottled for Dad at a California vineyard.

Before lunch, Dad suggested we take a walk outside. He pointed to a house below his on the same driveway that Nancy's car had rolled down years before. The Secret Service had rented the house, which was connected to his by some stairs that came up through the ivy, for fourteen thousand dollars a month. The agents used the stairs to go from one house to the other.

"What do you think it cost to put in those stairs?" Dad asked.

I was unable to make an estimate.

"Well, I just saw the bill for them," Dad said. "GSA (General Services Administration) charged twenty-five hundred dollars to make those steps, and they are charging a thousand dollars more to tear them down. That tells me how much waste there is in government, and I'm going to stop it because Barney (his friend and driver) and I could have done the job for five hundred dollars and had wood left over. This government spends too much money."

Before leaving the house, I took Cameron and Colleen on a tour since it would be our last time there. The rooms were already empty, and I felt a heavy sense of nostalgia. But I didn't show them the maid's room which I had thought was going to be mine.

During inauguration week, I was getting a taste of what most people only dream about. As the president-elect's son, I had a limousine with MIKE on the license plate; traffic came to a standstill as my family and friends were chauffeured from ball to ball and party to party in a motorcade; I had Secret Service agents assigned to protect me and Cameron. The Mike Reagan family basked in the glow of the nation's most illustrious celebrity. And I loved every minute of it. I was important, at last, and safe. Even if my secret was to come out in the open now, I was the Teflon son— nothing could stick to me. My father was president of the U.S.A.

The president-elect's family and retinue were put up at Blair House, the guest house of the president, which is located on Pennsylvania Avenue across from the White House. When Colleen and I were taken on a tour of the magnificent residence, I asked our guide if, after the inauguration, we would stay in Blair House again, because it was so beautiful.

"Oh, no, Mr. Reagan," he said. "After your father is in residence at the White House, you will stay there. If you think it's nice here, wait until you've been across the street. Nobody ever comes back."

I didn't understand that then, but I did a few nights later when I went to the White House for the first time.

On the night before the official inauguration, the weather was a clear but frigid twenty-six degrees. For forty-five minutes, the inauguration spectacular that cost nearly one million dollars was played out before fifteen thousand invited spectators, with millions more watching on television. Laser beams knifed through the sky, linking the Lincoln Memorial with the Washington Monument, the Capitol, the White House and the Jefferson Memorial.

There were so many people in attendance that when Moon, Dad's brother, tried to enter, a guard stopped him.

"I'm the President's brother," Moon said.

"You're the tenth guy that's tried that today," the guard retorted.

Colleen and I were entertaining our son's godparents, the Nygaards, and their daughter Alicia at Blair House when Dad and Nancy came in after the ceremonies. As Dad took off his coat, he shivered from the cold and said he had just come from watching the Mormon Tabernacle Choir singing "God Bless America."

When Alicia asked him how cold it was, he said, "It was the most beautiful music I have ever heard. But it was so cold that when they were singing, I could hear my tears hit the ground."

The most moving event I have ever witnessed took place during the Inaugural Gala at the Capitol Center the following night. Brigadier General Jimmy Stewart wheeled in Omar Bradley, the only living five-star general. After saying a few words, General Stewart then turned the wheelchair around, and both men saluted Dad. There wasn't a dry eye in the house as Dad returned the salute. I think that was probably the first moment when Dad realized he would soon be Commander-in-Chief of our nation. Knowing him, he probably felt he should have been on stage saluting Omar Bradley instead of vice versa.

That night—the last one Dad would spend at Blair House—I noticed a card on his door which read: "President-Elect and Mrs. Reagan." I thought it would be a nice souvenir, so I slipped the card off the door and put it into my pocket.

Tuesday, January 20, 1981—Inauguration Day—dawned blessedly warm. The political omens were equally bright: After four hundred and forty-four days in captivity, it appeared that the fifty-two American hostages held in Iran were about to be released. All of us attended a traditional early-morning service at St. John's Episcopal Church—the church of the presidents—to give thanks.

For the first time in history, at Dad's suggestion, the swearing-in was to take place on the west side of the Capitol. In front of the throng was the Washington Memorial, a simple spire; to one side, the Jefferson monument; beyond the reflecting pool, the Lincoln Memorial; and across the Potomac River, the Arlington National Cemetery, where lay the bodies of American soldiers killed in half a dozen wars.

My family, my brother and his bride, my sisters, Nancy, Dad's relatives and scores of eminent people including Tip O'Neill, Supreme Court justices and prominent Republicans were seated on a banner-draped platform. We faced a hundred thousand people. I waved to the crowd because I wanted everybody to know I was *his* son and I was proud.

There were tears in my eyes as I watched Dad take the oath of office, resting his hand on his mother Nelle's old Bible, so worn with use that it was held together by Scotch tape. It was the first time I remembered seeing it. Then Dad gave a relatively short address. Pointing to the monuments that surrounded him, he said, "Standing here one faces a magnificent vista opening up on this city's special beauty and history. At the end of this open mall are those shrines to the giants on whose shoulders we stand." He ended by saying, "We have every right to dream heroic dreams together. Let us make this a great new beginning."

Afterward, Colleen and I attended a luncheon for Dad at Statuary Hall—so named because every state is represented by a statue—in the Capitol, with members of Congress, Supreme Court justices and special friends in attendance. It was here that Dad officially announced our "prisoners" were on their way home and said it was the greatest inaugural-day present he could receive.

Later, when Dad arrived at the parade, he was accompanied by his military attaché who carried the ever-present black briefcase. As Dad got reports of the release of the captives, he shared them

186

with us. His voice cracked with emotion as he told us that all the American hostages had left Teheran Airport and were on their way by air to Germany. Instead of taking credit for their release, Dad offered the use of Air Force One to Jimmy Carter to go meet them.

Even though the parade, with all its floats and bands, was wonderful, what impressed me most of all was watching General Omar Bradley, who was sitting in his wheelchair off to my dad's right side. As the parade went by I noticed that he never once missed saluting our flag. He was truly a soldier's soldier. I feel honored that I was able to spend some time with him that night, before he passed away.

We then went to the White House for a cocktail reception in the Red Room where the official First Family portrait was to be taken. Maureen, who was engaged to Dennis Revell, a law clerk, came running up to me at Blair House and shouted, "I need your support. I told Nancy that if Dennis isn't in the picture I won't be in it."

"Dennis isn't a member of the family yet," I said.

"As far as I'm concerned he is," Maureen shot back. "And he'd better be in the picture or there will be two of us missing."

"You mean that if Nancy doesn't want him in it, you want me to join you as a holdout."

"That's what I mean."

"No way," I said. "You work this one out on your own." That was the first time in my life that I had ever gone against my sister, but I was determined to have my family included in the portrait as part of history.

Nancy apparently acquiesced because, when the picture was taken, Dennis was in the front row along with Maureen and Nancy's niece and nephew. Dennis did better than I, in the back row holding Cameron in my arms as he mugged for the camera.

(There is a funny sequel to the picture session. After that night,

Nancy called Colleen or me about once a week to ask if I had heard from Maureen and knew anything about her wedding plans. As far as Nancy was concerned, the photo was not "official" until Maureen and Dennis got married.)

After the official photo was taken, Dad and Nancy left to make their appearance at the nine balls scheduled for that night. The rich and famous from California, New York, Illinois, Florida, Pennsylvania—from everywhere—came in by limousine or flew in by private jet to attend the five-hundred-dollar-a-plate dinners. John Jacob Astor's personal train with liveried porters even pulled in from Ohio.

That night Colleen and I hosted the Inaugural Ball for Dad at the Washington Hilton Hotel, the first of his stops. We were waiting for him in the holding room when he came in looking resplendent in white tie and tails. As he stood in front of the mirror fixing his tie, I saw that special sparkle in his eyes. All of a sudden he turned to us and, with a wink, jumped straight up in the air and clicked his heels. "I'm the President of the United States!" he said. I think it was the first time that it really hit him.

The National Christmas Tree had not been turned on that year because of the forty-four Americans who were still being held hostage in Iran. Jimmy Carter had said the tree would only be lit when they returned to American soil. When the hostages reached Germany, Dad turned on the lights to the Christmas tree.

Before returning home to Los Angeles with my family, I told Dad that while he was President there were only two things I would like him to do for me: I wanted Cameron—and me—to fly in Air Force One, and I wanted to have my son turn on the lights on the Christmas tree. Dad said he would keep my requests in mind. "I turned on the tree this year," he said. "Maybe next year one of the freed hostages should turn it on." I couldn't argue with that.

Soon after taking office, Dad wrote a letter on White House stationery to a friend who immediately sold it to a collector for ten thousand dollars. Dad was annoyed, but he realized the worth of his signature and decided that if it was valuable after he was just elected it would appreciate much more in the coming decades.

During the first month of his presidency, he sent a letter to Colleen and me enclosing a letter to Cameron. In his letter to us, he wrote that he was aware that if Cameron ever wanted to sell his letter, he could use the proceeds for his college education.

His handwritten letter to Cameron said that he was in the midst of the final negotiations for the release of the last hostage in Iran, who was a woman most of us had forgotten. "The secretary of state is now coming to my office to tell me whether the offer the United States has made to Iran is accepted," he wrote. The rest is history because the hostage was released. To the best of my knowledge, only Cameron, the secretary of state and a few other select people know of that offer. Dad signed the letter, "Love, Grandpa." The postscript read: "Your grandpa's name is Ronald Reagan, the President of the United States."

Chapter XVI

"Rawhide is not hurt!"

Monday, March 30, 1981—Dad's seventieth day in office—dawned clear and warm in Los Angeles. Over breakfast, Colleen and I had finally come to a decision about a matter which had bothered us for months. I was going to call Dad when I got to the office and ask if we could "sign off" our Secret Service protection. Our disenchantment with the Secret Service began the day they arrived—four to six of them in three shifts—at our house with two motor homes as temporary command posts, which were parked in our driveway for weeks.

That first night, the detail leader told me that the government would provide me with a limousine and two agents who would drive me wherever I needed to go. I thought that was neat. I had visions of a long black limo with me sitting in the back seat like a rock star. The next morning, however, my limo turned out to be an AMC Concord leased from Avis. I said to the agent, "Maybe you don't understand. My father *won* the election." To which he replied, "We know. Just get in the car."

The agents made it clear that they were not chauffeurs— understandable enough—but they soon refused to open Colleen's door even when her arms were filled with packages. As far as they were concerned, she wasn't part of the family. In fact, one day a new agent refused Colleen and Cameron entrance to our home until her identity could be verified. She felt silly standing there with the door key.

I had originally thought it would be gratifying to have the Secret Service with me all the time, but ever since November, 1980, when the agents were assigned to protect Cameron and me, Colleen and I had felt like prisoners in our own home. We couldn't even have private conversations in the car because there were always two agents with us. As Colleen and I talked together, one of the agents apparently took notes on our conversation. For the next forty-eight hours, we were questioned about the matters that we thought we had been discussing privately.

Colleen did not even feel comfortable sunbathing in our backyard because of the surveillance cameras there. One day when she wanted some privacy, she placed a towel over the lens. Seconds later she heard a voice shout, "Get that towel off the lens." On another occasion, an agent who was stationed in the motor home approached Colleen and asked her to put thicker curtains on our bedroom window because he could see through the ones we had. Obviously, we were not to have any privacy and it was nerve-wracking. It felt good to get away and go to friends' homes for dinner but invariably our friends would feel sorry for the agents

he 1981 official inauguration photo.

Cameron and Grandpa,
with Cameron's godfather
Max Nygaard in the background.

*Dear Cameron – Look how tall you are!
It was good to see you.
Love Grandpa.*

With Cameron, before the big race.

Celebrating our victory for the Grace Cup.
Bill Tedford, Jr. is at the far left,
R. Peter Grace the far right; Colleen and
Cameron are beside me.

The Grace Challenge Cup.

The Grace Challenge Cup, Assault on
the Mississippi Victory Dinner.
Peter Grace, Ronald Reagan,
August Busch, me at the podium.

Dear Colleen & Mike – It was wonderful seeing you & Congratulations again – to you Mike for the boat ride & to you Colleen for the coming event. Love D.

With Dad, after Colleen told him
we were expecting our second child.

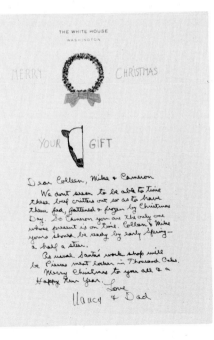

THE WHITE HOUSE
WASHINGTON

MERRY CHRISTMAS

YOUR GIFT

Dear Colleen, Mike & Cameron
We don't seem to be able to time these beef critters out so as to have them fed, fattened & frozen by Christmas Day. So Cameron you are the only one whose present is on time. Colleen & Mike yours should be ready by early Spring – a half a steer.
As usual Santa's work shop will be Pierces meat locker in Thousand Oaks.
Merry Christmas to you all & a Happy New Year. Love
Nancy & Dad

Christmas greetings from the
White House, 1982, with drawings by Dad.

Setting records on the Great Lakes
rare boat (credit: Ed Justis, Jr.).

Cameron and Ashley.

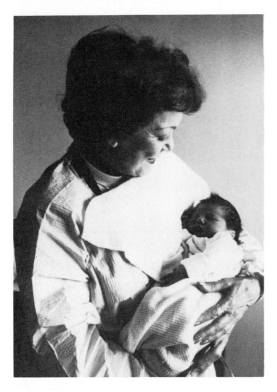

Grandma Jane and Ashley.

Me with the CF kids.

Grandma and Grandpa meet Ashley
for the first time, with Cameron.

Cameron and Dad in the Oval Office.

Ashley and Dad in the Oval Office.

Colleen and me at the 1985 Inauguration.

Grandma Nancy, Colleen, and Ashley
in 1985 at the Century Plaza Hotel.

Grandma Jane and Cameron.

Thanksgiving, 1985. Aunt Bess, Patti,
Patti's husband Paul, Ron with Doria and
Ashley on the floor, Nancy and Cameron,
Dad, Colleen, me, and Moon.

Dad and Cameron building
snowman at the White House.

ameron and Dad showing off their snowman
r the White House photographers.

Dad shows Cameron the ranch.

At the ranch for Ashley's fourth birthday,
April 12th, 1987.

At the ranch.

Nancy's birthday, summer, 1987.

Me, Dad, Cameron, Colleen, Ashley,
Nancy, Ron, Doria, Paul and Patti.

The Flaugher family. Irene—the baby—is at
the far left, seated.

A publicity photo of Betty Arnold,
center, Irene Flaugher's stage name, with
unidentified friends.

With Marge Darlington and my
half-brother Barry Lange.

Irene Flaugher, my natural mother—
the face I waited a lifetime to see.

standing outside in the night air and—you guessed it—they would invite them to eat with us. We just couldn't hide.

As for myself, I was certain that the agency had bugged our house inside. It seemed to me that every time they rang through on the special telephone to contact me, I was either on the commode or in the shower. I also found it a nuisance to notify the agents every time I had to go to the store for a bottle of milk or go to the dry cleaners. Colleen was especially disconcerted when she went to the store with Cameron to buy lingerie and two men accompanied her down the aisles. Hey, George, what do you think she looks better in, pink or black?

Other friends were also intimidated by having agents with us every place we went. One night, while we were in Texas, Colleen and I went out for dinner with some good friends, who drove us in their car followed by the agents. Our host had a glass of wine with dinner. When we went to get in his car at the completion of the meal, an agent firmly suggested that my friend allow him to drive. "You've had some alcohol," the agent said. My friend was so embarrassed, as were we, that it was two years before he had a drink with us again.

I had an idea that Dad would be particularly sympathetic to our problem because, when I had seen him in a Los Angeles hotel on a previous trip, he told me, "The one thing I am going to miss for the rest of my life is the privilege of being alone. You don't know how much I would give to be able to walk out that door and stroll in the street alone as I did when I was a private citizen." I knew how he felt.

That call I was going to make was on my mind during a meeting at Dana Ingall's Profile, a small California aerospace firm where I was employed as vice-president of sales. All of a sudden Agent Mike Luty knocked on the door and came in. "There has been an assassination attempt on your father," he said quietly. "He's all right, and there's nothing to worry about; but I wanted you to know before you heard it on the news."

The other men in the room sat silently looking at me. Someone asked if I wanted to call the White House. "No," I said, "but I would like to be left alone."

I tuned the radio to a local news station in time to hear that Dad was being taken to the hospital. I rushed outside where Mike was sitting. "There's something wrong," I said. "Dad's been hurt. He's going to the hospital."

"He's going there because Jim Brady and some others were shot and he wants to make certain they're all right."

"I'll bet my Dad's been shot, too," I said.

"No, Mike," Luty said firmly. "I've been in touch with the CP (command post). Rawhide is not hurt!" (Rawhide was Dad's code name.)

At that point, Colleen telephoned, her voice laced with fear. "The press is camping out on our front lawn, and the White House is calling."

I hurried home to get more news and to try and call Nancy at the White House. I knew if she was there Dad was all right. But Nancy wasn't there. I was certain then that something was wrong. Meanwhile, the press had descended en masse on our front lawn.

By the time the White House reached me with the news that Dad had in fact been shot in front of the Hilton Hotel and was in a Washington hospital, the Air Force had scrambled a C-140 transport plane which was to bring Colleen, Patti, Maureen, Dennis and me to Washington. We left Cameron with the Prices, good friends from church, who had been with us all afternoon. That one act of friendship in a time of need did more to turn my life toward God than anything before it and I don't think I've said thank you. Our departure was delayed until nighttime, however, because if we were seen rushing to the airport the press would have known that Dad was in serious condition, a condition we weren't made privy to.

I had never been in a C-140 so I wasn't aware that it was usually used for transporting military cargo and had only a few hard seats and no acoustical material. So, I was surprised when an agent gave us blankets, ear plugs and a box lunch. I sat with my arm around Patti's shoulder. I had never seen her so distraught. From time to time, she hugged me for support. We had not really been friendly for years, and it meant a lot to me to know that despite our differences, when there was trouble in the family we were united.

I thought about the ironic fact that I was the only one in the family with Dad's blood type. I know that type O blood is available all over the world, but I envisioned myself being asked to give my father a transfusion. In my fantasy, I saved his life and the country considered me a hero. I relished the thought that at last my blood would flow with his. Then I would truly be his son.

We stayed at the White House and rose early the next morning for breakfast with Nancy Reynolds, the First Lady's press secretary. She told us that although Patti and Ron were at the hospital, we wouldn't be allowed to see Dad until later. This, of course, infuriated Maureen and me. We used the time to go see some of the others who had taken bullets meant for Dad: Timothy McCarthy, the secret service agent who had thrown himself between Dad and the assailant; Officer Thomas Delahanty of the District of Columbia police force; and Presidential Press Director James Brady, who had been shot in the head.

We first saw Officer Delahanty and then went to G.W. University Hospital. Agent McCarthy was in good spirits, although he had been shot in the chest. "I'm going to be the first one out of this hospital," he told me. And he was. (He is now the agent in charge of the First Lady's detail in Washington.)

Jim Brady's wife Sarah was hovering over her husband,

pleading, "Come on, Jim. You can make it." I could almost see the energy going from her body into his. She is the reason he is alive today.

Then we went to where Dad was recovering from surgery. Patti and Ron were already in his room when we arrived, but Maureen and I were told he was too weak to see us, too. When Patti and Ron came out of the room, they walked by us without a word. In fact, we never saw them till the following Thanksgiving.

Maureen and I were fuming, beset by the old jealousy. Maureen whispered to me, "If we're going to get in to see Dad, you're going to have to pull some weight." She knew I could con my way into any place. My problem was conning my way out. I located Dad's doctor, who told me that Dad was awake and was going to have some tests.

"My sister and I have come all the way from California to see our father," I said. "Even if I have to break down the door, we're going in to see him."

The doctor gave me a long hard look. "All right," he said. "You can go in."

Dad was lying in bed, an IV in his arm pumping nutrients into his body, when Colleen, Maureen and I went into his hospital room. The drapes had been nailed shut for security reasons, and the room was insufferably hot because the central air conditioning system had not yet been turned on.

Dad was obviously in pain, but he managed a smile when he saw us. Trying to be lighthearted, I said, "The last time I saw you like this was when you broke your leg."

"I'm told that the parents of this kid who shot me are well off," Dad said, grimacing with pain. "You'd think they would at least buy me a new blue suit." Even while lying in a hospital bed fighting for his life, he was upbeat as always.

We all gave Dad a hug and left the room to find Nancy, who was in an adjoining room crying. She looked pale and fragile. My heart went out to her. It was obvious how much she loved my father, but there was nothing I could say to relieve her anguish. I felt as though I was on the outside looking in.

Some time later, at a family gathering, Dad told us the story of the assassination attempt. He had just finished making a speech to the AFL-CIO at the Hilton Hotel and was about to enter his limousine to return to the White House when a reporter asked him a question. He turned to face the reporter when, suddenly, he heard what sounded like a string of firecrackers going off. He had just enough time to see somebody lying on the ground in a pool of blood (it was Jim Brady). Jerry Parr, head of his Secret Service detail, pushed him—"slammed is a better word," Dad said—hard on the back and into the car where he landed on the differential riser.

"I felt as though I had been struck by a hammer, and there was pain in my left side. I told Jerry, 'You broke my ribs!'"

The limo was headed for the White House when agent Parr pulled Dad erect.

"I coughed," Dad said. "Jerry gave me his white handkerchief, and there was oxygenated blood in it. I thought that I had punctured a lung, which was why I was bleeding. Jerry immediately ordered the car to take me to George Washington Hospital."

I could imagine what was going through Jerry's mind as he sat next to Dad in the car. He must have been thinking, "My God, I have broken the President's rib and punctured his lung, and he's bleeding internally because of me."

Jerry's decision to go directly to the hospital was the difference between my dad living and dying, because after they ripped off

197

his new blue suit, they discovered a bullet had entered underneath his arm.

Up until the time that John W. Hinckley, Jr. attempted to kill my father, I believe all of us had been living in a make-believe world. But the harsh reality that it was all temporal profoundly affected the lives of everyone in the family as well as the nation. My father was the first president in history to survive bullets from an assassin's gun. The experience had a somber influence on him. After his convalescence, he told me that it was only divine intervention that kept him alive. "I am recommitting the rest of my life and this presidency to God."

Ironically, that attempt on his life was to keep Dad from going to church again on a consistent basis. He explained that all those other people had taken bullets meant for him, and he never again intended to put another person in that position. By going to church on a regular basis, he would put all the other parishioners in jeopardy. It worried him that someone might be hurt or even killed because of him.

Nancy began to have sleepless nights and lost weight; she shrank from a size six to a size four. I doubt that she has had a peaceful moment since, especially whenever the man she loves is out of her sight.

The week after the assassination attempt, while Colleen and I were inside our house watching *Dynasty* on television, we heard a commotion outside, and heard Mike Luty shout, "Freeze, you mother, or you're going to die!"

Colleen paled. "You'd better go see what's going on."

I peered through the curtain. "Are you nuts? There are people out there with guns!"

We learned that the man was the neighborhood Peeping Tom who lived a couple of blocks away from us. He had decided to spy on us just at shift change. Half a dozen agents spotted him on the monitor, climbing the fence into our backyard. After being roughly apprehended, he learned that his captors were from the Secret Service. "I've seen you guys on TV," he said. "I could have been killed!" The man hasn't been back to our house since.

Despite our problems with the Secret Service, Colleen and I decided to continue with them in our lives not only because we had the President's only grandchild and we worried about his safety, but also because we were planning a new addition to our family.

Chapter XVII

"We can't have a scandal."

In April, 1981, Maureen and Dennis Revell were married in Beverly Hills, thus making the White House family portrait official and ending all of Nancy's phone calls. Dad and Nancy were unable to make it to the wedding because he was still recuperating from his wounds. But they sent as a gift thirty-six pewter swizzle sticks topped by tiny elephants. People tend to think that because Dad is President, he and Nancy give extravagant gifts. The truth is, that while they can be generous they are also practical. They have never been extravagant; they live within their means despite public perception to the contrary. It was lucky for the newlyweds that Dad wasn't a Democrat.

Not long after the wedding, I received a call from Dennis. "Your sister is upset because you haven't volunteered to help out with her Senate campaign," he said.

I started to laugh. "How can she be angry with me when this is the first time I have heard that she is running for the Senate."

Although I thought Maureen was eminently qualified to be a Senator, I just didn't have the time to campaign for her. Instead, I volunteered to function as a consultant. She wasn't happy about that. She wanted a full, in-the-field effort, like I had given to Dad's campaign. After all, she reasoned, we had a closer relationship, so how could I do any less for her than I'd done for him? She didn't understand it was him I was trying to impress.

Maureen's campaign soon caused problems within the family. Moon endorsed somebody else. I felt he was betting on the wrong candidate, besides betraying Maureen, who had given Dad indefatigable support throughout the years.

Maureen also expected that Mom would come out of her cocoon and make a few appearances on her behalf. Mom agreed, then had second thoughts and declined. That wasn't too much of a surprise because she had always hated politics. When Dad was in politics during the early years of their marriage, she had also refused to get involved.

After Maureen publicly announced, Dad was asked at a press conference if he would endorse her. "No," he said, "and I wish she wouldn't run." The press misconstrued his statement and made an issue of it. Dad didn't mean that he wouldn't vote for Maureen; he meant that as a father he wouldn't wish the trials and tribulations of a campaign on his daughter. Also, he has always made it a practice not to back anybody in a contested primary. Nevertheless, he did make a financial contribution to Maureen's campaign.

If Maureen was upset about not getting Dad's endorsement, I

felt I had every reason to be upset that holiday season as I sat down to watch the White House tree lighting ceremony on TV. A group of kindergarten children were invited to attend. Dad leaned over and picked up a towhead in his arms. "I only wish my grandson Cameron could be here today to celebrate with us," he said. The youngster flicked the switch, and the tree came ablaze with light.

The next day, I called Dad. "Don't you remember the conversation we had? As long as you were going to pick up a youngster, why didn't you let me know and I would have brought Cameron to Washington?"

"You really were serious," Dad said.

"I was."

"Could you have afforded to fly back to Washington?"

"If I didn't have the money, I'd have borrowed it," I said.

Later, I realized that to Dad, the tree was three blocks from the White House, so what was the big deal? And he really didn't think I could afford to fly back to Washington. He had no idea how much remembering his promise would have meant to me.

By the time 1982 rolled around, I couldn't help Maureen, either, because I had to contend with a serious problem. The local district attorney had started to investigate whether I had misused funds given to me during 1979 for gasohol development while there was a nationwide gas shortage. The district attorney also contended that I was illegally manipulating stock in my fledgling company and that I was a partner of Richard Carey in a stock fraud.

I felt that it was a petty vendetta, that the district attorney saw headlines if he could tie me in with a fraud. After all, he was running for office. He even ordered search warrants for my house twice. Each visit was enthusiastically covered by the press, which scented a scandal brewing.

I was beside myself with fear of being indicted by the Grand Jury and a possible prison term. It seemed to me that I was only being singled out because my name was Reagan.

Justin Dart, who was one of Dad's staunchest supporters as well as a personal friend, called me into his office and twisted the knife in my gut when he said, "You're an embarrassment to the Reagan family and the Republican party."

"Do you want to hear what I have to say?" I asked.

"No," he said.

I was sick at heart with the realization that he, and possibly my father, believed I was guilty without even hearing my side of the story. I left his office in despair.

I hired an attorney. The DA responded by also naming him in the indictment. Finally, I found a lawyer who the district attorney's office approved of and who believed in my innocence. But another of Dad's friends, Charles Z. Wick, contacted me to tell me that my new attorney was not good enough. I needed one with real clout. When I protested that my lawyer was convinced of my innocence, Wick said that was all well and good but not enough.

"Your father has just been elected president and we can't have a scandal. You need a top lawyer, and that's all there is to it," Wick said firmly. It was obvious that he, like Dart, was convinced of my guilt. It didn't occur to me that he was only trying to help me. I thought that he only wanted to protect my father. Wick hired the law firm that William French Smith, the attorney general, once worked for when he represented Dad.

It was to be a year later before the matter was finally dropped, but the attorneys ran up a bill of fifty thousand dollars, which they presented to me. I was horrified because they had told me that I would not be expected to pay my legal fees, and in fact, my attorney had done most of the work. When I told Dad about the bill, he said that the matter would probably not have come up were I not his son and he would take care of it. Many times Colleen and I have told him that we felt obligated to repay him and every time he says we are not to worry about it. But I still feel guilty.

No sooner was that mess cleared up than I was involved in another. As vice-president of Dana Ingalls, one of my jobs was to contact purchasing officers at military airbases who might be interested in the parts that we manufactured. After contacting them by phone, I mailed them information on our company with a letter including the paragraph: "I know that with my father's leadership at the White House, this country's armed services are going to be rebuilt and strengthened. We at Dana Ingalls Profile want to be involved in this process."

Using the Freedom of Information Act, *The Oklahoma City Times* printed that excerpt from my letter and accused me of using my father's name to get business. The national press had a field day with the story and came down hard on me.

When Dad was asked in a press conference about the letter, he said, "Michael is aware that he has had made a mistake and shouldn't have written the letter."

When I called to discuss the matter with Dad, he reminded me of the letter he had written on White House stationery to a friend who auctioned it off. His admonition to me was "Don't write any more letters." I haven't.

The irony of the situation was that all of my life, people told me that if they had my name they could make a million dollars. However, more often than not, I found that my name was a hindrance rather than a help in business. For instance, one of my many racing sponsors refused to publicize the fact that my boat used their product because they felt that Democrats would be turned off by it. Many people didn't give me business because they assumed I didn't need the work or the money; after all I was the President's son. Yet I had to earn a living on my own just like anyone else.

By the time I had my business affairs sorted out, Maureen had entered and lost the election. Maureen, who had always campaigned hard for other candidates, found out the hard way that there are no friends in politics. So, feeling betrayed and rejected, she stayed at home on the night that she lost and wouldn't accept phone calls from anyone including me. Some of her personal friends had stuck by her, however, and had rented a room at the Ambassador Hotel that night for what they hoped would be a victory celebration. When I learned that Maureen was too distressed to face her supporters, I went to the Ambassador and, in tears, thanked them on her behalf. Oh, how I love her!

Maureen soon made peace with Dad, but things were never to be the same between her and me. In some way, she felt I was partly responsible for her defeat.

Chapter XVIII

"Get the black out of the boat."

Every time I opened up the front door to go to work there seemed to be newsmen camped on my front lawn. The question most often asked of me was "Why are you using your father's name?" That particular question rankled me so much that I asked one reporter why he was using his father's name.

"That's not the question here," he said.

"But that is the question," I retorted. "I'm proud of my father just as you are of yours, and I have as much right to use my name as you have to use yours."

I rarely turned down interviews or avoided the press because I thought that if I was cooperative the press would like me. I was wrong. They still insisted on referring to me as "the adopted son of Ronald Reagan and Jane Wyman," a label that brought to the surface all the anger I had tried to bury for so many years.

I thought the Secret Service would protect me from the press but was sadly mistaken. They were at my house to protect me from assassins with guns and not assassins with pencils. Cameron was also fair game for the snoopers. It finally got to the point that we couldn't let him play on the front lawn because some idiotic newsman would ask, "Has your father talked with the President recently? Is your father still on the outs with his family?" Cameron knew nothing about our family problems and would run into the house worried and frightened. Colleen and I did our best to reassure him that nothing was wrong. Colleen even wrote a letter to Dad saying that she hoped our rift would not affect his and Nancy's relationship with Cameron. Dad telephoned her and concurred.

Because of the news reports, no one wanted to employ me. They were afraid that the press would investigate their company, hoping to find some impropriety. Dana Ingalls, a small thirty-five employee machine shop, had been made to look like a giant aerospace company in the news reports. The company was almost bankrupted because of the scandal and had lost most of its contracts.

My concern led me to call Richard Allen, former adviser for the National Security Council, who had gone through a similar press lashing when he brought two Japanese journalists for a short interview with Nancy. The journalists gave him a one thousand dollar honorarium for Nancy and two inexpensive Japanese watches for himself. Allen stuck the money in a White House safe without making a formal receipt and went blithely home. The money was discovered some months later after he had moved out of his office. The FBI began an investigation, and the press had a field day at Allen's expense. Allen promptly resigned.

"I know how you feel, Mike," Allen told me. "I quit the government on the morning some idiot from the press nailed my seven-year-old daughter on her way to school and asked what she thought of her father being a *thief.*"

About this time I got a phone call from Joe Alibrandi, an old friend who was president of the Whittaker Corporation, a conglomerate involved in the marine industry. We met at his office where he offered me a job representing Riva, an Italian boat manufacturing company. He also offered me space in his suite of offices where I could hide out from the press. Naturally, the Secret Service accompanied me to the meeting. When we went outside to get in the car, the car was gone. The agent had parked in the wrong zone, and it had been towed away. Did he have egg all over his face! The matter was finally resolved by having Maureen's detail drive from her office to pick us up and bring me home.

Then, at the Los Angeles Boat Show in January, 1982, where I had the Riva on display, my friend Larry Smith, designer of Scarab boats for Wellcraft Marine, asked if I would be interested in driving a boat up the Mississippi River from New Orleans to St. Louis in an attempt to break a decade-old record.

I liked the idea because I needed to change my public image but told him, "The press would probably report, 'President's rich son drives a million dollar boat up the Mississippi.' On top of everything else, I'll be labeled a playboy, and that's not going to do me any good." Although I felt that the press was trying to make me the Billy Carter of the Reagan administration—and succeeding at it—I asked him to give me a couple of weeks to think it over.

However, the idea intrigued me. I had missed racing since quitting in 1971. Although I had been a world champion, I'd never held a world record.

During the interim, I received a phone call from a theatrical agent who had once handled Maureen. He invited me to his office for a talk. He said he had been contracted by a firm asking if he had any clients who might be interested in doing something for the Olympics.

"Since your father is the titular head of the Olympic Committee, you might be interested in making some appearances on his behalf," he said.

There it was again—the very thing I was avoiding at all costs—an invitation to use my father's name. I wanted to get out of his shadow so people would stop asking me, "How's your dad?" I wanted them to ask me how I was. I loved my father, but it had gotten to the point where I knew more about him than I did about myself—which is why I was so good at campaigning for him. It seemed to me I had lived my entire life knowing how my father felt and masking how I felt. The only reason people ever wanted to talk to me was because of him. As far as I was concerned, I was nobody. My only identity was as the adopted son of Ronald Reagan and Jane Wyman. I'd had enough!

I told the agent that I wasn't interested in his proposition. Later, however, I remembered the race I had been asked to do on the Mississippi, so I called the agent back. He put me in touch with Dave Marmel, a fundraiser for the Olympic Committee.

"I don't want to make an appearance on behalf of my father," I told Marmel, "but what do you think of my trying to set a record on the Mississippi? You can coordinate dinners and lunches at the start in New Orleans and in St. Louis where we'll finish, and you can raise money for your committee. We'll put the Olympic logo on the boat, and maybe I can get the vice-president to attend one of the dinners." I knew that George Bush was a racing enthusiast because he owned a boat similar to mine.

Although I was minimally using my father again, at least it was Mike Reagan doing something for the Olympics and not Ronald Reagan. I was orchestrating a scenario to make myself look like a hero, and I didn't care if I died being one.

The Olympic Committee approved the race but said I would

have to guarantee them one hundred thousand dollars in order to put their logo on the boat. I was aghast. I had no idea how to raise the money until I visited St. Louis and saw where the race would end. Just underneath the arch, there was a restaurant housed in a replica of *The Robert E. Lee,* the stern-wheeler which had been one of the first boats to race up the Mississippi in 1872. The restaurant was owned by W.R. Grace Company of New York.

Wow, I thought, we can end the race here and have the reception on *The Robert E. Lee.* So I wrote a letter to W.R. Grace outlining the proposed event and asking if they would be interested in participating. By return mail, I was invited to New York to lay out my plan before a vice-president of the firm.

After I made my presentation, the vice-president asked what I wanted.

"I want you to pledge one hundred dollars a mile from New Orleans to St. Louis," I said. "In exchange for that, you can plan the reception party on your boat, you can have your logo on my Scarab race boat, and most important, we can call the event 'The W.R. Grace Challenge Cup.'"

"Sounds pretty good," the vice-president said. "How many miles is it?"

"One thousand and twenty-seven miles," I said.

"That's $102,700!" he said and turned white. But he picked up a phone and asked his public relations man to join us.

I told the p.r. man the story.

"I think that that's the greatest promotion you're going to get for the money this year," the p.r. man told the vice-president. "I suggest we go for it."

I now had the hundred thousand dollars the Olympic Committee insisted on as my guarantee, so I went after other sponsors. One of them was agreeable, but he had a condition: He wanted a black person in the boat with me.

"Why?" I asked.

"Because you're a Republican and most of our customers are black."

I needed sponsors, so I said I would see what I could do. I made an appointment to meet with Evelyn Ashford, who was the fastest woman runner in the world and an Olympian. She thought it a neat idea.

I called the sponsor back and said I not only had a black person but I had a black woman who was a world champion. I also reported that I had arranged for Vice-President Bush to preside at the kickoff luncheon in New Orleans.

"Next you'll tell me that you'll also have the President there."

That gave me an idea, so I called the White House and, after getting the staff runaround, I hung up and called Dad directly. I told him of my plan and he accepted. I then thought: won't this make me look even better with the sponsor? So, I called him back.

"That's great," he said. "Now get the black out of the boat. We don't need her anymore."

I was furious, and if I had not been such a weakling, I would have turned him down. But I had no intention of disinviting Evelyn. Luckily, she called me to say she had to go to Europe to compete and couldn't make it. I was off the hook.

I then had another problem: Fundraisers usually take a percentage of the monies raised. Thanks to sponsors like W.R. Grace, Evinrude, Budweiser, Justice Brothers, Wellcraft and Descent, I had raised almost four hundred thousand dollars, but if I took a percentage, the press would be on my back saying I was taking money away from the athletes and getting paid for having my father attend an event. I decided not to take a fee from the proceeds but to do the race just to give myself a new identity as a sports hero who raises money for the Olympics.

I had a lot riding on that race. In my view, my future depended on achieving a record. I visualized excited throngs of people at the finish line with music and speeches. Most of all, I looked forward to the Victory Dinner with my dad in attendance.

The race was pure agony. We thundered along most of the distance at night, averaging seventy-five m.p.h. in turbulent water filled with logs and other debris. There was no moon, and the visibility was zero. I was dependent on hand signals from my navigator, who sat glued to a radarscope, while my throttle man controlled the speed. I prayed to God, asking him to let my hands, which were gripped tightly on the wheel, become my eyes.

We knocked sixty-one minutes off the old record and established a new one: twenty-five hours and ten minutes on the one thousand and twenty-seven mile stretch from New Orleans to St. Louis. Some of the agents who had to travel by bus also set a record—for eating Eagle snacks. They were willing to take bullets for Dad, but they were safer in the bus than with me going ninety m.p.h.

Our "Assault on the Mississippi" was a major success. There had been over one thousand attempts to break the record since 1929, but only ten achieved their goal. More importantly, the race ended up being the number one, special event fund raiser the United States Olympic Committee had had to date. The event grossed over one half million dollars.

That night in St. Louis at a Victory Banquet honoring me and August A. Busch, III, chairman of Anheuser-Busch, as Olympic Sportsmen of the Year, Dad called my achievement heroic. But I had been up for forty hours and had fallen asleep in my chair. To my chagrin, I never heard my father give me the praise I had waited all my life to hear from him!

The press reported, "Reagan's Son Establishes Mississippi Record." They didn't even call me Michael Reagan. Each press report still labeled me as the "adopted son." And each time I read that, it took some of the joy away and made me feel like a child again, miserably aware of being illegitimate.

Even though it was my team and I was driving the boat, there were still many people who believed I could not have done it if I were not the son of the President. They were partly right. I was able to put together the sponsors because of Dad. But it took a lot of hard work. And it was I, not my dad, who had the guts to finish the event.

I was still deep in Dad's shadow. I had the feeling that if I were to attempt a world record for a parachute jump, when the chute opened it would have lettered on it: "The Adopted Son of the President of the United States." I wanted to be "Mike Reagan, world champion, man on his own." But no matter where I went or what I did, I couldn't develop my own personal identity. For Dad and Mom it had been easy to overshadow and rise above their parents. Yet, how was I to rise above the Presidency and an Academy Award? I was finding out I couldn't. Then it got worse. Ron was getting publicity as a dancer. When people found out I was the President's son, I was often asked, "Are you the dancer?" That question annoyed me so much that I had a T-shirt made with the legend: I'M NOT THE DANCER. When a news magazine printed a photo of me wearing the shirt, Nancy was quite upset because she thought I was making fun of her son. I guess in a way I was, but I was upset too just at the thought that people mistook me for Ron.

Because of the success of the Mississippi run, Colleen and I formed a company, MCR International (for Michael Colleen Reagan) in order to do fundraising for special events. I liked being a hero, if not to myself and my family then at least to kids. I was still looking for that quick fix—something that would get me instant public recognition on my own.

*   *   *

Colleen, the kids and I drove up to the ranch to spend Thanksgiving with the family. Everything was going well with the family until two weeks before Christmas 1982, when *Newsweek* quoted an unidentified source saying that Nancy considered Maureen and me to be the family screwups. Reading that gave me the same gut-wrenching feeling I'd had when I was a child. I tend to believe the press when somebody says something about me; it's my insecurity speaking.

The story upset Colleen and me so much that when we left the house that night to shop for a Christmas tree we forgot to bring our Sheltie dog Tippy with us. Tippy was a member of the family, and for the seven years since we'd had him, he always went with us for the tree. While we were away, Tippy jumped over our five-foot high wall to look for us and disappeared. We spent most of the night searching for him. The next morning a neighbor told us that he had been run over and killed. We all broke down; it was a very sad Christmas.

Maureen tried to perk us up by inviting my family to her annual tree-trimming party at Christmas time: her way of getting her tree trimmed and having a fun party. While we were trimming Rudolph the tree, we all sang Christmas carols. Cameron, who was sitting on the floor, piped up and asked, "Why don't we sing 'Happy Birthday'?" All the adults turned to him. Someone asked, "Whose birthday is it?" My four-year-old looked up and quietly replied, "It's Jesus' birthday." We all sang "Happy Birthday" to Jesus. I realized then that Colleen and I were raising our son properly.

Chapter XIX

"You are a thief, Mike."

It had all begun innocently enough when, earlier in the month, Cliff Baranowski, the agent in charge of my detail, told me that his supervisors from Washington were coming out for their annual review. I'd had such routine meetings before in which the supervisors asked if I'd had any problems with the detail.

At this meeting we had a big laugh over some recent incidents. One of them involved Cameron at school. He was always accompanied by agents, even in the classroom. The Secret Service is only concerned with counterfeiting and protection, and there is nothing in their training manual concerning five-year-olds with toilet problems.

Most of the children in Cameron's class assumed that the agent in their room was one of the teaching staff. On this day, a youngster approached the agent and asked to be directed to the bathroom. The agent ignored the tyke. "Please, mister, I have to go," the lad said. The agent continued to ignore him until he felt a warm trickle of urine running down the bottom of his pant leg and into his shoes.

The other story concerned the night that the Secret Service drove Colleen and me to the Casa Vega, our favorite Mexican restaurant. When we pulled into the parking area, the Mexican parking attendant came over as always to ask for the keys in order to park the car. The agent who was driving said that he was with the Secret Service and he would park the car. The Mexican youth pointed at a sign reading "Valet Parking." The agent again tried to explain that he was Secret Service and gestured toward all the paraphernalia in the car. The attendant stood his ground, so the agent flashed his badge. When the attendant saw the badge, his eyes grew round as silver dollars, and he turned and ran out of the lot shouting, *"Immigracion. Immigracion."* The agent ran after him shouting, "Secret Service. Secret Service." Finally the agent caught the boy and brought him back to the parking lot where he had the bartender interpret and explain that he was Secret Service and not Immigration. It turned out that the boy was an illegal entrant from El Salvador, which was of no concern to the Secret Service. What made the incident even funnier was that it was the same agent whose shoes had been soiled in Cameron's school.

After some guffawing, the supervisor got down to business. He asked if I had any complaints about the detail assigned to me and Cameron. I assured him that everything was just fine. And it was, or so I thought.

"Are your agents having any problems with us?" I asked.

"No," he said. "Everything is A-OK."

As I soon discovered, everything was not A-OK.

March 18, 1983, my birthday. Jimmy L.C. Miller, head of the Western Protective Division—the West Coast branch of the Secret Service—settled down in a chair in my office, put on his Ben Franklin reading glasses, and with a serious face began reading aloud to me a one-page, typewritten statement. The gist of it was that Secret Service agents are trained policemen and that I was involved with some situations that could be detrimental to the President's reputation as well as to the reputation of my mother. "You have a sickness that can destroy your future in business as well as your family," he said.

I had listened to his recital with pulses pounding and stomach twisting. Now I was almost to the point of throwing up, terrified that somehow the Secret Service had found out the story of my molestation.

"What are you talking about?" I asked fearfully.

"You are a thief, Mike," he said. "We have the evidence; but we know that you don't know what you are doing, and we want to help you."

I didn't know whether to laugh or cry. I knew what I was and I also knew I wasn't a thief. "What am I supposed to have stolen?"

"You wouldn't remember if I told you because you are sick. You are a kleptomaniac," he replied.

At this point, I seriously considered throwing him through the seventh floor window but settled for ordering him out of my office.

The moment the door shut, I telephoned Maureen and told her what Miller had said. "Do you know what's going on?" I asked her, my voice cracking with anxiety.

"No," she said.

Maureen must have heard the hysteria in my voice because she arrived at my office within minutes. "I can't believe it," she said. "There must be some mistake. We have to call Dad."

When we got Dad on the phone, I only had time to tell him that I was being attacked, before I broke down. Maureen took the phone from me and crisply laid the matter out for him. She nodded a few times and finally said, "Yes, I'll take care of it." She hung up the telephone. "Dad has asked me to look into the matter and report back to him," she told me.

I breathed a sigh of relief. Maureen was stronger than dirt. She would sort out the mistake and when she did, whoever was to blame better watch out. I had no idea then, however, that the "mistake" would take almost two years to be sorted out and that it would almost cost me my relationship with Dad let alone the rest of the family.

I didn't hear anything more about the thievery charge for a few weeks. Then, on April 11th, the day before Colleen was to give birth to Ashley, Maureen came into my office and gave me a big hug. I was so excited at the prospect of having another child that I thought that was what Maureen wanted to talk about. I started to tell her the name of the hospital and some of the other details when, suddenly, she interrupted me.

"Michael," she said, "we all have problems from time to time, things we can't even share with our loved ones, especially our spouses. I've had problems in the past, and I am going to give you the name of my psychiatrist. I want you to call him on the phone and make an appointment to see him."

I started to laugh. I thought she was joking and I couldn't believe what I was hearing. "What things do I need to talk to a psychiatrist about?"

"You know," she said.

"But I don't," I said, trying to control myself. "Tell me what it's about."

Maureen insisted that I did know what the problem was. Since we weren't getting anyplace and my mind was on my wife, I finally said, "Give me the number," knowing I'd never call.

"Will you be at the hospital tomorrow when the baby is born?" I asked as she was leaving.

"Who else is going to be there?"

"Some friends and Mom."

"Your mother is going to be there?"

"Yes," I said. "My mother is going to be there and your mother is also going to be there. We do have the same mother."

"I don't know if I want to come."

I started to laugh. Here my sister was telling me that I needed to see a psychiatrist because of something which was a mystery to me, but she was paranoid about seeing her own mother.

"I want you there," I said.

"OK," Maureen said, "I'll be there."

Ashley Marie Reagan was born by cesarian section on schedule. I was in a glassed-in room with Colleen. But I could see the ever-present Secret Service agent, who was outside looking in as he said, "We have an arrival. Raindrop has arrived." (Raindrop was Ashley's code name. Cameron was Rhyme. Colleen and I had always kiddingly assumed that when we had another child it would probably be codenamed Reason.) But it was out of our hands.

Mom, who had already come to the hospital to give Colleen moral support, was soon joined by Maureen. They exchanged only a few words before Mom left to go to the nursery where the nurses let her hold Ashley.

Dad and Nancy sent a beautiful plant. A few days later, when

221

Dad called to congratulate us, he asked if I had taken my sister's advice.

"Why do I need to see a psychiatrist?" I asked.

"Because you have a problem," he said.

"What's the problem?" I asked.

He, too, refused to discuss the matter. I hung up the phone, angry as well as scared. I had been hiding the truth for years, and now I seemed to be losing my family to a lie. This was the one thing in my life that I could not talk my way out of with the family, and ironically, it was the one time I was completely innocent.

I knew that the Secret Service was at the root of my so-called problem, and I was determined to get to the bottom of it because it was driving me, as well as Colleen, mad. One afternoon while I was jogging around the block to let off steam, my detail leader joined me. "For heaven's sake, tell me what's going on," I asked him. He told me that he would deny he had said it but everything started with a report from one of the agents about "the green dress or blouse."

"What green dress or blouse?" I asked.

"The one you got at the kid's store on Colleen's birthday."

Suddenly everything began to fall into place. I recalled the day because it was March 17th, St. Patrick's Day—Colleen's birthday as well as the day before my birthday. Colleen and I had been invited by our friends Bob and Cathy Scullin to Houlihan's Bar in the Valley to celebrate with lunch and green beer.

It was raining and I was miserable with a cold, so I wore my black racing jacket. The Scullins wanted to buy some green T-shirts as birthday gifts for both of us, but there was only one left. I told them to get it for Colleen. It was still raining outside when we left, so I tucked it under my jacket and we headed toward our car. But Colleen, who was in her ninth month of pregnancy, saw a kiddie store and told me she was going there to browse. I went with her for a moment and then returned to our car, took the shirt out from underneath my jacket and casually tossed it on the rear seat and thought nothing of it.

A new agent, who had previously been on Maureen's detail and had been sitting some distance away from us at Houlihan's, apparently never saw the Scullins buy the shirt for Colleen. He only saw me take something from underneath my jacket and toss it on the back seat. He wrote up in his daily report that I had taken a green child's dress or shirt from the children's store.

It would be more than a year later before I was to find out what else I had supposedly shoplifted. In the interim, Maureen's agent-friend also convinced her that I was a kleptomaniac. She, in turn, convinced my father and told him that if anyone ever mentioned my sickness to me I would probably deny it because I was unaware of what I was doing—a frequent symptom of the illness. When I would try to broach the subject of the T-shirt, the only thing the agents, or Maureen, and, ultimately my father, would say was that my memory must be returning and soon it would all come back to me.

I was appalled. The Secret Service had labeled me a thief. These were the same men who had saved my father's life, so no one questioned them. I tried in vain to find out from the President and Maureen what else I was accused of stealing so that I could clear myself. But I was stuck in a Kafkaesque bind.

Finally, I was so incensed that I called my mother for solace and told her what was going on. She responded by reminding me that when I was a child, I had taken money out of her purse—not the answer I was looking for. She was the last person in the family left for me to turn to, and I was at my wit's end.

Despite my problems with the Secret Service, Cameron and I were still under their protective shield. During the fall of 1983, I planned to go to the Genoa Boat Show on business and spend a few weeks on vacation in England with my family and the children's godparents. Whenever a member of the First Family leaves the country, it is the duty of the Secret Service to report to the State Department what countries he or she plans to visit because the police in those countries have to be notified. When the news reached Washington, I received a call from Fred Fields, the White House counsel, who wanted to know: Why was I going? Where was I going? Who was going with me? Did I earn enough money to be able to afford such a trip?

My answer to most of the questions was "It's none of your business." I told him that I was making the trip on my American Express card.

Maureen then called and asked the same questions. The next person I heard from was my father repeating the questions.

Apparently everyone was concerned because there had been a lot of recent press criticism of the Reagan administration expenses. My trip would cost the taxpayers a lot of money because nineteen agents would accompany us. Personally, I thought it madness to have such a retinue protecting us.

Things were getting so bad with the family I sometimes joked that were I taken hostage, my father would undoubtedly refuse to negotiate for me. His long-standing policy—at that time—was to refuse to negotiate for hostages. I remember reading O. Henry's short story entitled "The Ransom of Red Chief" in which a child is kidnapped for ransom and the kidnappers eventually pay to give the child back because he was such a nuisance. I'm sure Dad probably felt that if I was kidnapped, the same situation would likely occur.

The trip was probably the most maddening and frustrating time of my life. We not only had the Secret Service accompanying us, but we picked up local police everywhere we went. The English press reported on how much my vacation was costing

American and British taxpayers—we had a full complement of Scotland Yard detectives for protection while in London. The newspapers made it appear that it was all my fault.

Instead of my family and friends seeing the local sights, we became the sight to see for the locals. Every night before I went to bed, the detail leader asked what time I was planning to get up in the morning, where were we going to have breakfast and what did we plan to do the following day.

The positive side of having agency protection while traveling overseas was that we were on and off planes quickly. We never had to go through Customs, cars were provided and our rooms were often upgraded to suites. Also, our bags were never lost and were waiting for us when we reached our hotel. Not bad perks. Ones I will definitely miss.

Chapter XX

"Are you anybody?"

I was back at the helm of the Wellcraft Scarab again in 1983, this time racing through six-foot swells up Lake Michigan from Chicago and down Lake Huron to Detroit. The twelve-hour six-hundred-five-mile race called "Assault on the Great Lakes" was pure torture for the boat as well as for me, Steve Lyshon, my navigator and Johnny Mann, the throttle man.

The bottom gelcoat of the boat was cracked, and the radar tower had been sheared off. Just about every piece of electronic equipment had stopped functioning. Steve was almost blinded from the knifelike spray. I thought constantly about quitting, but I pushed myself through and beyond the pain barrier, knowing that if I quit, the world press would report it and I would be thought of as a loser. I needed the public to like me.

We finally reached Detroit and were helped off the boat. Before I checked into a hotel and slept for twelve hours straight, I learned we had raised fifty thousand dollars from sponsor pledges and fund raising events. Not a bad day's work!

People magazine asked Cameron after the race if he ever saw his grandfather. "Sure—on TV," Cameron said cheerfully.

Colleen added, "Sometimes I think they should spend more time with Cameron and Ashley and less time with the foster grandparent program." I concurred.

She said that because it seemed that every time we turned on the television Nancy was talking about how wonderful it was to be a grandparent, all the while smiling at some little tyke in her arms. We constantly read stories about how she doted on kids, but as often as Nancy was in Los Angeles on shopping trips and visiting her friends, she never came to see her own grandchildren. Ashley was already a month old and they hadn't seen her.

Colleen and I were very jealous and upset for good reason. Since I couldn't communicate my feelings directly to the people who considered me a kleptomaniac, I used the press to deliver *my* message.

When the magazine appeared on the stands, Dad called me, and he was furious. He felt we were attacking Nancy. He was right, but I felt attacked on the matter of my supposed kleptomania, so I had struck back. It's hard to go up against the President of the United States. On the other hand, I did know his Achilles heel: Nancy.

Three weeks after my run on the Great Lakes, I had my only racing failure. During an attempt to break the record between Miami and New York, my boat quit on me. Although we didn't achieve a record, we raised a large amount of money for the Statue of Liberty Foundation, which had contracted with us to be their first official event.

In October, 1983 I was asked by the Cystic Fibrosis Foundation to help raise funds by attempting a record run down the inside passage between Ketchikan, Alaska and Seattle, Washington.

I had recently been moved by an article excerpted from a book entitled *Alex, the Life of a Child*, written by Frank Deford, a top writer for *Sports Illustrated*. Frank and his wife Carol, like all parents of children with cystic fibrosis, had no idea they were carriers until they found out their child had the disease. Alexandra Carol Deford died in 1980 at the age of eight, and the book her dad wrote about the way she died—and lived—changed the way many people react to the gruesome disease. When I suggested that we dedicate the run to Alex, the CF people were enthusiastic. One of the lines painted on the hull of my boat, just below the names of the crew, read: "In Memory of Alex Deford."

Donations depended on media coverage, so I helped promote the event. I did a series of public service announcements with a little boy named Mark who had CF. At the end of the promotion, which asked for donations, I added: ". . . And how do you know? If we raise enough money, perhaps we can find a cure, and maybe Mark will grow up to be president."

I came in contact with a lot of seven- and eight-year-olds who had CF and, sadly, were soon to die because the disease is a merciless killer. Most of those kids were brave, living their lives to the fullest. They looked happy and, in many instances, were even stronger than their parents. And there I was feeling sorry for myself, sorry because I hadn't been able to spend time with my parents the way I wanted to and blaming people all my life for my problems. Without these kids knowing it, I felt small in comparison to them because they were dying like little men and women while I was dying every day like a child.

229

Prior to our arrival in Ketchikan in June, 1984, it had rained or been overcast for the previous one hundred and forty days. But on the morning of the race, the weather was crisp and clear. A good omen. As part of our publicity plan I had invited Tom Jarriel, who was reporting on the event for ABC's *20/20* program, to be our navigator. If I couldn't be a hero to my dad, maybe I could be one to these kids. I needed someone out there to think I was important.

When we arrived at the boat dock at three-thirty A.M., one of the two bands on the pier began playing the theme from *Rocky*. Bill Dukes, the bartender from the Pioneer Bar—open twenty-four hours a day—which is across from the dock, led about forty people down the ramp wearing "Assault" hats and T-shirts. They were carrying a long chain of folding money taped and stapled together: five thousand dollars they had raised that night at an auction. The group wrapped the money around Frank, who was there with his wife and son. When Bill announced that the money was for Alex, Frank broke into tears as did most everyone else.

As in every race, I brought along my red, felt visor cap, which I considered my good-luck charm. Southland Corporation, owners of the 7-11 stores, was one of our sponsors but, unfortunately, their logo has green lettering. I hated the color green because I thought it brought bad luck to racers and hoped to counter its effect with my red cap.

The seven-hundred-five mile race began at four-thirty A.M. We had some minor problems early in the race with a sticky carburetor, and we broke a propeller; but we kept running. Midway, while running flat out at about ninety m.p.h., we hit a deadhead (a log floating vertically about six inches below the surface) and shattered two lower units on my outboard engines. Thinking we were out of the race, we idled into our last fuel stop on our third motor. Eddie Morenz, crew chief for all my races, was waiting for us with a mechanic from Outboard Marine Corporation whose engines we were running. The mechanic donned a wet suit and dove into the ice-cold water. Somehow or other he managed to fix one of the engines. So, we decided to run the last three hundred and fifty miles of the course on two motors. We could not afford another breakdown, however, because we were out of parts. To be successful, we had to finish in less than fourteen hours.

Johnny Mann, Tom Jarriel and I nosed the Scarab into the Shilsole Bay Marina in Seattle after 13:55:24 hours' elapsed time averaging seventy m.p.h. for the last leg.

The press section was jammed. My son Cameron was there with his godfather Max and the Deford family. Colleen had had surgery for a detached retina and was unable to fly, so it was the first of my races that she had ever missed and I missed her terribly.

At dinner that night, the chairman of UNO, a playing card company, donated an additional fifty thousand dollars to CF, bringing our total to $250,000. Our race was the biggest single fund raiser in CF history. The most moving event of the evening, however, was when thirteen-year-old Kristen Bigos, who had CF, presented me with a trophy. "Thank you, Mike Reagan," she said. "We love you." When I hugged Kristen, I could hear her little bones creak.

Kristen didn't live long enough to celebrate her fourteenth birthday, but her parents have kept her memory alive by forming a committee which sponsors in her name an annual fund raising dinner called, "In Search of the Stars." That dinner now brings in donations of more than three hundred thousand dollars a year for the CF foundation.

The following month we went after the record from Los Angeles to San Francisco. The previous record was eleven hours, but we did it in eight. Once more, the money raised was for the Olympic Committee. By then I had raised almost a million dollars for various charities including the Olympics. My team and

I received special Olympic medals for our efforts. The City of Hope also presented me with the prestigious "Victor Award," considered to be the Academy Award of sports.

Despite the trophies and accolades, the press still referred to me as "the adopted son." In a last ditch effort to establish my own identity, I paid three thousand dollars for the right to run an eighth of a mile carrying the torch in the Olympic relay. I was certain the press would be out in full force to cover the President's son carrying the Olympic torch. But it was just like I had given a party for myself. No one from the press showed up, and none of the spectators knew me. I was just another runner to them. I was proud to run the torch but the worst moment of the relay came when a spectator asked me, "Are you somebody?" I could have cheerfully killed the person. All I had been trying to do was be a somebody.

During that year I refused to go to any family functions and sit across the table from people who thought I was a kleptomaniac. The press soon began to notice that!

The *National Star* called and asked me to contribute to a story they were preparing entitled "Our Mom Nancy." The *Star* story had been approved by the White House to counteract a negative story the *National Enquirer* had recently published. I refused to meet with the reporter, saying that Jane and not Nancy was my mother. The reporter threatened to write that I had declined to give an interview; the inference was that I would be made to look bad. Finally, I agreed to do the interview if the title of the story was changed from "Our Mom Nancy" to "Nancy," so Mom would not be upset. The title was not changed, and Mom was really miffed, as was I, when the article came out.

I was still trying to do a balancing act between my mother and Nancy. If I appeared in a photograph with Dad and Nancy, my mother would get upset. She was already on the outs with Maureen, as I had discovered earlier in the year. I had gotten so tired of being asked about the state of my father's health or other questions pertaining to him that I would occasionally answer, "Everybody knows how my father is; he's on television every night. If you want an up-to-date report on him, call Sam Donaldson. But my mother is Jane Wyman, and I'm proud of her, too. Why don't you ask how she is?"

One day, Maureen telephoned me and said, "Washington and I would appreciate it if you never mentioned your mother again in interviews. Jane Wyman is not and never will be a member of the First Family. *We* would like for you to cease and desist from mentioning her name."

"My mother is also your mother," I said as I hung up the phone.

Until then Maureen had really been a devoted aunt. She often came to our house with presents for the children and even offered to baby-sit for us. Since that conversation, she has never visited the children again.

Chapter XXI

"I love you, Michael."

Prior to the Dallas convention in August, 1984, Dad and Nancy came to Los Angeles for the Olympics and invited Colleen and me to visit them at their hotel to "discuss the problem." I practiced lines beforehand as though I was preparing for a scene in a film. My heart was fluttering from anxiety when we entered their suite. They didn't even offer us a glass of water or a cup of coffee. The emotional atmosphere in that suite was as cold as Siberia. I just knew my life was over.

Dad opened the conversation by saying that everyone in the family was hurt by the way I was acting.

"I couldn't care less," I said. "I hurt when people think I am a thief. Just tell me what I am supposed to have stolen!"

Dad sat still as a statue, but I persisted, trying to get some indication of just what the charges were against me. This cat-and-mouse game went on for more than an hour. Then Dad gave his stock line: "You need help. Even if I told you what the items were, you would deny it because you are a kleptomaniac."

My frustration finally turned into anger. "Let me ask you one more question," I said. "Are you going to take the word of a non-family member over a family member without even giving me a chance for my day in court?" I thought I had him then because he is so loyal to family and friends. But I was wrong.

"Yes, I am," he said.

I was stunned. I had lost my father to a lie and I hoped Jimmy L.C. Miller would catch the next bullet meant for a president.

There was dead silence in the room until Colleen turned to Nancy and asked, "If someone told your husband that he needed a psychiatrist, wouldn't you be angry?"

"No," said Nancy, "I'd send him to one."

Colleen turned to me. "I see no reason for us to stay here any longer," she said and rose from her chair. She took my hand in hers, and we went to the door.

I paused at the doorway to fire one last verbal salvo at Dad. "When you want to put members of the family first again and come up with the list of what I have stolen, then and only then can we be a family." I took Colleen's arm and we walked out.

And that's where things rested until the '84 convention. We didn't intend to go, but we were aware that at such public events, the press always counted heads and makes an issue of it if all family members are not present and accounted for. So we went, if only for the sake of public image.

After one evening's proceedings, Colleen and I were sitting in a Dallas bar having cocktails when someone came over and asked us to move. I asked, "Why?" and was told, "Because Maureen Reagan, the President's daughter, is having a reception for some friends."

When Maureen arrived, I immediately went over to greet her. She turned her back and walked away. We wouldn't talk again until May of 1987.

On the night of Dad's acceptance speech—the last night of the convention—my family had tickets to sit with the family in the First Lady's box. As we squeezed down the aisle past Nancy, I murmured a cold "hello" to her. Maureen, who was standing next to Nancy, stuck out her arm to stop me. She grabbed my shoulder and pushed me into Nancy to give her a kiss. By that time, Maureen had started to build a relationship with Nancy and was even calling her "Mom." I felt that their new relationship probably stemmed from the fact that Maureen had become more and more of a political asset to Dad rather than a liability thanks to her work on the National Committe and the United Nations.

Because we were seated in the First Family's box, press people kept asking me for my name. I had lost weight since 1980 and had shaved my mustache. Instead of glasses, I was wearing contact lenses. When I said, "I'm Michael," no one seemed to believe me.

At the conclusion of the convention, everyone stood up to sing "God Bless America." A photographer snapped pictures of me with my hands on Cameron's shoulders.

After Dad gave his acceptance speech, we went with family and friends to a private reception. Dad picked Cameron up in his arms. "My, how big you've grown," he said and then handed Cameron to Nancy.

While Nancy held Cameron, Dad whispered to me, "Nancy is not happy with the way you have been treating her in the press."

"I'm not happy with the way you and she have been treating me, either," I retorted.

"We'll have to get together and talk," Dad said.

"We just had a talk," I replied. "I meant what I said the last time. I want a list of the items I have stolen."

The next day *The Arizona Republic* printed the picture of Cameron and me on their front page captioned: "White House aide and child." Well, that child—my son—began first grade that September. His first day is one none of us will ever forget. The teacher handed out first grade readers and there, on page 99, was a picture of Cameron's grandpa. Cameron was so excited to have a personalized reader that he told everyone to turn to page 99 so they could see a picture of their grandfathers. To his surprise, everyone had pictures of *his* grandpa. He was so proud! We didn't dare let on there were problems.

A few weeks after my conversation with Dad at the convention, I received a call from Ed Hickey, who worked with Dad. "I've spoken with the President, and I'd like to see you," he said. I agreed to the meeting on the condition that he bring with him a list of the stolen items. "I'll try," he said.

"Don't try," I retorted. "Bring it with you or you won't be allowed in my house."

When Ed came to the house, Colleen and I were waiting for him. A tape recorder and legal pads were spread out on the coffee table. "We won't need that," Ed said. He then read aloud from a sheet of paper a list of the items the Secret Service claimed I had "stolen," beginning with Item #1: the green T-shirt.

Item #2: Agents reported that I had been seen coming off an American Airlines flight in 1982 carrying a mini-bottle of bourbon. Item #3: I had taken some Binaca from a drugstore in Century City without paying for it. Item #4: I had taken an "I Ski Heavenly Valley" pin from a ski shop. Item #5: I had been seen taking a bar of candy from a curio store at the Intercontinental Hotel in London in October 1982.

I didn't know whether to laugh or cry. Those items, worth perhaps fifteen dollars, were what had torn my family asunder for more than a year. But I knew the matter was serious.

"Ed," I said, "that last reference to a candy bar; I'll let Colleen tell you why that isn't in the realm of possibility."

"When Mike was seven years old, he had a strep throat and wanted a piece of chocolate," Colleen said. "Jane told him, 'Mike, if you eat a piece of candy, you're going to choke.' He ate the candy anyway and he did choke. He has never eaten candy since. He even refuses to have it in the house and won't let the children eat it."

All of the other charges were equally ridiculous. A stewardess had given me and some of the other passengers mini-bottles of bourbon. Whenever I flew on an airplane, the agents had me sit next to the window, and they sat between me and the aisle. It would have been impossible for me to reach over them and take a bottle from the stewardesses' tray without them seeing it. "I'm guilty as charged on that one," I said, "but then so is every other passenger who takes with him one of those mini-bottles that he buys or is given on a plane."

I was in a store in Century City when I bought the cigarettes and then remembered I also wanted some Binaca. I paid for the cigarettes and the Binaca and told the clerk I would pick up the mouthspray from a rack myself. The agents who were outside the store looking in thought I had only paid for the cigarettes and then saw me pocket the Binaca.

As the President's son, I was always being souvenired to death. I had flown to Heavenly Valley with some friends for a ski trip. When we arrived at our lodge the advance agent gave us all Heavenly Valley souvenir pins. When we asked how much they cost he said, "Don't worry about it, they are gifts from the owner."

I also told Ed the story behind the green T-shirt. When I finished, he was apologetic. "I believe you," he said.

I breathed a deep sigh of relief. At least somebody believed me. I

239

also offered the names and phone numbers of my friends who were with me on those trips. You see, the agents had always told me and my father I was alone when I took those items. They were, for whatever reason, really covering their tracks.

Ed returned to Washington with my responses to the charges. Three weeks later, he called to say that he had reached a compromise with the Secret Service. They would agree that they had made mistakes on two or three of the charges if I would agree that I stole one or two things. I told him the Secret Service could go to hell.

Colleen and I had not spent many holidays with her family, so we decided to go to Nebraska for Thanksgiving that year. Before leaving, we told Dad and Nancy of our plans. The day before the holiday, while I was watching television with my father-in-law, I saw a news bulletin in which Nancy was quoted as saying I was estranged from the family and wouldn't be at the ranch for Thanksgiving.

Furious, I immediately telephoned Dad and demanded to know why Nancy had said we were estranged and had gone public with our family problems.

"Well, you are estranged, aren't you?" he said angrily. "You have a problem and you need help." That did it.

I called him a few choice words and then said the worst thing I could think of because I wanted to hurt him as I had been hurt. I said, "I wish I had never been adopted by you." I then hung up the phone.

The press soon showed up on my in-laws' front lawn, wanting to know what I thought of the First Lady's charges. Again I responded to an attack with a counterattack and added fuel to the fire. I had just read a news report saying that Nancy had fallen out of bed and bumped her head. I suggested that maybe the bump had temporarily affected Nancy's thought processes.

The publicity Nancy's statement received cost me most of my racing sponsors. They thought that I no longer had a relationship with the White House; that association, after all, had been the major reason people wanted to do business with me.

From then on, I received weekly calls from reporters on some of the tabloid newspapers, asking me for inside gossip about members of the family. They promised me confidentiality as the source of the information and offered to pay me well. At the same time, they promised to be sympathetic to me in their stories.

I refused to talk with them, but I wanted to hurt my family as they had hurt me. Mindful of the money Christina Crawford had received for *Mommie Dearest,* I was tempted to write a book. All of my life I had grown up hearing how great my parents were. No matter what I did or how good I was, people always gave my parents credit. My dad had seemingly never failed at anything. Like many children of famous parents I wanted to show my parents failing at something—and that something was their failure as parents. I wanted to bring him, Nancy and Mom down to a common level and blame my problems on their parenting. After all, if they weren't so famous, I wouldn't be under all this pressure. It's their fault. I wished they were dead.

I contacted an attorney who had publishing contacts in New York. We flew to New York together to meet with some publishers. I found that if I was willing to write a book about my perception of Nancy and Dad, I might get two million dollars in a bank up-front. Dad and Nancy would probably never speak to me again, but they weren't speaking to me anyway.

I had wanted money all of my life because I believed that only by being rich would I be important and maybe I would be important even to them. That money laying on the table was tempting. In

241

addition, I was told that the *Enquirer* had heard about my meetings in New York and had offered to kick in three hundred thousand dollars for the rights to my story.

Colleen and I talked the offers over. Then I called the godparents of our children, Max and Shirley Nygaard who lived in Dallas, and told them what I had in mind. They arrived in California immediately. We talked about the proposed book for days, and I came to realize that although I was willing to hurt Dad by attacking Nancy, I would also be hurting the President of my country. There are two Ronald Reagans, the President and my father. They are separate in my mind, but they are one and the same in the minds of the public.

I also knew deep down inside of me that it would not be a truthful book—it would be an angry book in which I blamed my parents instead of myself for most of my problems. Somewhere along the way, Mom, Nancy and Dad had instilled in me a sense of integrity, and I knew that if I wrote such a book I would never be able to look my parents—or myself—in the eyes again.

But the decision not to write the book didn't resolve my problem. Rarely did a minute go by without my thinking about it. There was no way I could vent the rage which still ate at my insides like a cancer. Instead of busting bikes and cars, it became glasses and doors and even worse, I began to verbally abuse my son Cameron. Then there came a day when I bottomed out in the worst way imaginable. It happened one night when Cameron asked me during a tirade, "Don't you love me, Daddy?"

All my life I felt that if I asked my parents if they loved me, the answer would have been no. If they did, why did they all send me away? So I turned to my son and said the worst thing I ever will say, "No." I suddenly realized what I was doing to him. I fell to my knees crying and asked him to forgive me. I knew then that I had gone too far. I needed help but I didn't know where to turn.

My friends, the Prices, suggested I speak with the pastor of our church. In fact, they even dialed the phone. It was a good idea because I knew that I needed to have someone who my family respected to act as the mediator.

At a meeting with the pastor, I laid out my list of grievances, all of them against Nancy and my mom, who, fairly or not, I made the scapegoats. He asked me if I wanted the matter resolved. "I do," I said, "but I am too angry to handle it myself."

The pastor called Donn Moomaw, Dad's pastor at Bel Air Presbyterian Church in Los Angeles. He in turn contacted Dad. A meeting which the press labeled "the mini-summit" was set for December 28th in Los Angeles. Maureen heard about it and showed up in my pastor's office. He later told me she was checking him out and had told him that she didn't care what I said or if I ever got back with the family again. As far as she was concerned, I was a thief and would always be one. Maureen also told someone in the press that I'd always had a vendetta against the family and I needed help. That statement almost cancelled the meeting. In fact, if it hadn't been for Colleen calling Dad to straighten out Maureen, it never would have been resolved.

Somehow the press got word of the meeting. On the morning it was to take place, the press gathered in front of my house and remained there for the entire day. Newsmen even shouted questions at six-year-old Cameron, who didn't even know there was a problem between me and my family. The press was lying in wait for us when we arrived that afternoon with the pastor and his wife and daughter at the Century Plaza Hotel where Dad and Nancy were staying. As I was going into the hotel, one of the newsmen asked me what I was going to tell my dad. "I'm going to tell him that I love him," I said. That was the best interview I had ever given.

Dad, Nancy and the ever-present White House photographer were waiting for us in the Presidential Suite. Colleen and I were tense, but Dad and Nancy did their best to relax us. They had gifts for Cameron and eighteen-month-old Ashley whom they had never met. Dad was enchanted with his granddaughter. He even lay down on the floor to play with her. Finally, the kids were asked to go into another room to play.

After a few minutes of small talk, the pastor started the meeting off in precisely the right way: He asked us all to pray that we would grow together and learn from this meeting. After the "Amen" he told Dad and Nancy my side of the story. My stomach was churning as he detailed the facts.

Dad and Nancy listened intently, glancing at each other from time to time. There was a long silence when the pastor concluded. Finally, Dad said, "I'm sorry. I guess it's all a misunderstanding."

"Why is it you believe me when the pastor says I am innocent, but when I tell you, you don't accept it?" I asked him.

"Because the Secret Service saved my life, and I trust them more than you because your past history leaves a lot to be desired," he said. Then he asked, "What is it you want from me, Michael?"

"A letter from the Secret Service apologizing and exonerating me from their charges that I am a thief," I said. I had visions of the press using the Freedom of Information Act to pull my files, and I wanted the letter clearing me included in it.

"You'll get it," Dad said. (The promised letter arrived six months later.)

I was not completely mollified. "There's another thing. Maureen still thinks I am a thief."

The pastor told Dad about his meeting with Maureen.

"I'll talk with Maureen," Dad promised. "Is there anything else?" he asked me.

There was something I had wanted him to do for me for years, and this seemed like a good time to request it. "I'd like you to say at your next press conference that you would like the media to stop referring to me as 'the adopted son of the President.'"

244

"Why do you want that?" Dad asked. "You know you are my son as does everyone else."

Like most adoptive parents he didn't understand my feelings about this matter. I couldn't find the words to explain that I was still living with childhood wounds which were reopened every time I read the word "adopted." So I let the matter drop.

At the conclusion of the meeting, I asked Nancy why she had publicly said I was estranged from the family.

She looked at me and said, "I was feeling the pressure, too. I made a mistake in an interview. I'm sorry." That's the first time she had ever apologized, and I knew she meant it.

As we were leaving, I struggled to tell my father that I loved him. Instead I could only say, "You know, you've never told me that you love me."

He looked surprised. Then he said, "Michael, I love you."

Chapter XXII

"We all love each other."

After our problem had been resolved, Nancy invited us to attend Dad's second inauguration. She also issued a statement putting to rest the rumors of family problems. "There are no differences; all is resolved. Everybody loves each other, and this is a wonderful way to start the New Year."

Colleen and I brought our children with us to Washington. Instead of being put up at Blair house, as we were in 1981, we were given a two-room guest suite on the third floor of the White House. On our last visit there, after the assassination attempt, the rooms had been sparsely furnished, and there was little feeling of warmth. Now the quarters had been Nancyized: totally redecorated. Nancy had gone through the old archives and store rooms and selected exquisite pieces from storage. She had also requested and received rare pieces of authentic period furniture from the Washington galleries.

On the night that we arrived, Dad invited us to have dinner in the private dining room in his quarters, a floor below ours. Since we were to dine with the President and the First Lady, I dressed up in a sports coat and slacks. To my surprise, when we all came down, Dad was wearing lounging pajamas and a blue robe. "You could have worn your pajamas," he told me.

"It doesn't seem right to me to have dinner with the President in pajamas," I said.

Dad laughed. "But this is our home."

Dinner was an informal affair with small talk about the upcoming inauguration. We also spoke about the places where we might take the children; on our last visit Cameron had seen the giant pandas at the zoo, and he had not stopped talking about it.

After dinner Dad took us on a tour of the First Family's floor which includes the Lincoln bedroom. The room that he seemed proudest of, however, was the one where he has his exercise equipment and where, he said, I could work out if I so desired.

While we were talking, he grabbed the handle of one of the pulleys of the Universal gym and began to pull it across his chest. "I try to do twenty-five of these with my right arm every day," he said. "Since the assassination attempt, I've put two and a half inches on my chest." I looked at the weights he was so casually manipulating; he was pulling eighty pounds. He then pulled himself up on parallel bars to an L position, which he held for twenty seconds while talking to me, an incredible feat for a man then seventy-four years old.

He brought us to the infamous back stairs at the White House, which led to our apartment on the third floor. Dad reached into the pocket of his robe and took out two envelopes with the Inauguration Seal on them and his picture. "I was having lunch with the postmaster general today," he said. "He told me that if I signed these they might be worth something in the future. So these are for Cameron and Ashley—for their college education."

I asked him how many envelopes he had signed. "These are the only two," he said.

The next day we took Cameron and Ashley to Mount Vernon to see George Washington's home and the site of the original Rose Garden. We thought it important for Cameron to get a taste of the history he would soon be studying in school. As we were driving back to the White House, I decided to give my son a quiz.

"Who was the first president?" I asked him.

"That's a silly question, Dad," he said. "We just came from George Washington's home."

A little later I asked Cameron, "Who is the president now?"

"It's Grandpa," he said.

I then asked him a trick question. "And who was the last president?"

"Grandpa," he replied. A few minutes later Cameron said, "Dad, I have a question for you. Have there been only two presidents?"

That night, before Colleen and I were to go to one of the gala events, we went into the solarium with the kids to watch Dad on television. A White House waiter came in to ask Cameron what he wanted for dinner. "A McDonald's cheeseburger, strawberry shake and a large order of fries," Cameron said. Colleen and I were embarrassed because the White House probably has the best chefs in America, but our son was a typical American six-year-old.

"Just bring him a hot dog," I said.

A half hour later, as we were leaving to go to the event, the waiter appeared carrying a serving tray with a large silver dome.

He lifted the dome off with a flourish revealing a styrofoam container. Inside was precisely what Cameron had ordered from McDonald's.

The next afternoon, Dad telephoned to ask Cameron if he would like to make a snowman with him in the Rose Garden. "Wow!" Cameron said. He was so delighted, he wanted to run down without even a sweater or coat. Dad was waiting for us in the Rose Garden, wearing tan jeans, a leather jacket with fur collar and gloves. The White House staff had already made the base and mid-section of the snowman. Photographers were lined up waiting for Dad and Cameron to make the head and put it in place. They frolicked in the snow making the head while the press snapped pictures. It was the first picture of us as a family taken together since the rift. I remember thinking how sad it was that when Dad wanted to do something fun and private with his grandson, it had to become a media event. He had lost all his privacy. I could only think: was the cost worth the price?

Dorothy, our twenty-one-year-old sitter from Los Angeles, was with us. Dorothy is a Democrat and has a brother, John, suffering from Down's Syndrome. Dad's cuts in certain programs had not benefited her brother, and she was upset about that. I promised Dorothy that I would not tell Dad that she was a Democrat. When he and Cameron were finished building the snowman, I asked Dad to pose for a picture with Dorothy and the kids. While they were posing, I kidded Dorothy, "Don't worry, I won't tell Dad."

Dad asked, "Won't tell me what?"

"I promised not to tell you."

"I'm a Democrat," Dorothy said sheepishly.

Dad put his arm around her and said, "When I was a child, I used to speak as a child, think as a child, reason as a child. When I became a man, I did away with childish things. I think that's First Corinthians 13:11."

Dorothy, who is a strong Christian girl, later told me that she was amazed that the President of the United States would quote biblical scripture to her while standing in the Rose Garden after she had just told him she was a Democrat.

After the photos, Dad took us to the Oval Office. My two-year-old daughter Ashley was especially impressed because she saw a picture of herself on the President's desk—J.F.K.'s original desk, which Jimmy Carter had brought from the Smithsonian Institute. The desk was on risers because Dad is so tall and he had brought the chair he had used when he was governor of California. While we were talking, the door to the Oval Office swung open. A guide with his back to us was explaining that the group was lucky the President was not in the office or they would not be allowed to look in. The visitors suddenly began to snap pictures. The guide turned around and saw Dad waving and smiling. The embarrassed guide apologized and then quickly shut the door. What he didn't realize was that Dad likes people and wouldn't have minded talking to the visitors.

Dad was sworn in for his second four-year term as President on January 20th, the day before his public inauguration, because by law the President must be sworn in on that date, which happened to fall on a Sunday. Chief Justice Warren Burger administered the oath of office on a stairway just outside the Red Room at the White House. The brief and private ceremony was witnessed by about seventy invited guests, including members of the Supreme Court and personal friends.

The weather turned cold, and it was decided to hold the official swearing-in ceremony in the Rotunda rather than outside the Capitol; the first time the ceremony had been held there. In Dad's Inaugural Address, he called on Republicans and Democrats to work together in the months ahead because the nation faced hard decisions that would prove to be a turning point in history. He also reiterated his call for less government spending and a freer economy.

Because of the miserable weather, the Inaugural Day Parade had to be cancelled. One of the traditional features of the parade was school bands from all over the country marching down Pennsylvania Avenue. Dad feared that the youngsters would suffer in the cold but felt badly because he knew they had practiced so long and hard for months for the event. He went to the various places where the youngsters were quartered and personally thanked them for coming to Washington.

That night while we were sipping champagne in the Red Room before getting ready for the official family portrait, Dad saw Dorothy walking with Ashley in the hallway outside. I saw him put down his champagne glass and go to her. Dorothy told me later that she couldn't believe it when she saw him coming. He took her aside and apologized for being so forward in the Rose Garden when he quoted scripture to her. "I shouldn't have done that, and it has bothered me ever since," he said. "You should feel free to be a Democrat or Republican or Independent and vote for whomever you want. I hope you will accept my apology."

"I couldn't believe that he would take time out on the day of his inauguration to talk to me, a baby-sitter, and apologize to me," Dorothy said. "I can no longer believe this man would knowingly hurt anybody. He's wonderful." And she was right.

Chapter XXIII

"You've got to tell . . ."

In 1985 I was forty years old, and I felt that the only identity I had was that which the press had given me. My racing exploits had done little more than make me familiar to some readers of the sports pages and the boating magazines. Most of my sponsors were as interested in my ability to get the President and other top functionaries to attend certain events as they were in my potential to set records and raise money for charity. Unfortunately, the publicity about my recent estrangement from the First Family had cost me much of their support. Although I was on good terms with my father again, I wasn't able to convince potential sponsors of that. One even suggested that he speak with the President personally to check out the status of our relationship.

Luckily, Colleen had put aside money for a rainy day, but not enough for a year. We were soon scraping the bottom of the financial barrel, and I had to sell my racing boat back to my sponsors for a big cash loss in order to get money to survive. I had a family to support, and I was desperate. But I didn't want to go back to selling boats, which would have been extremely awkward. Every time I demonstrated a boat for a potential customer, I had to notify the Secret Service twenty-four hours ahead of time. They would tell the Harbor Master and Coast Guard. When I finally got into the water, I was followed by the Harbor Master as well as the Secret Service. I couldn't put my customers through all that.

One July 4th weekend when my family and I decided to go to Catalina on a friend's yacht, the Secret Service commandeered a hundred-foot Coast Guard cutter to follow us. They anchored off our stern for the entire weekend. Instead of spending a quiet holiday with family and friends, we ended up being the star tourist attraction because everyone wanted to know who the Coast Guard was protecting.

Of course I could have asked the President to sign my family off the Secret Service protection, but Colleen was adamant that it continue. There had been threats from Libyan loyalists after the bombing attack Dad ordered on that nation. The only person killed in that episode was the adopted child of Kadafi, and Colleen was understandably frightened about retaliation against me or our children.

Having grown up with parents who were actors, I always felt an affinity for the entertainment business. However, I had avoided acting as a career option because I was afraid of failure and I didn't want to be compared with my parents. I often thought how much easier my life would have been if they hadn't been such over-achievers.

But one day my agent suggested I take some acting lessons, and I decided it was worth a try. I had to do something.

I enrolled in a class with Rick Walters, who also worked with Kenny Rogers and Priscilla Presley. Unfortunately for both of us, Rick had just hired a publicist. When I went to my third class, the publicist had arranged without my knowledge for *Entertainment Tonight* as well as some of the local news shows and *Time* magazine to cover me.

The pressure on me to perform had always been great, but this time my mouth was dry and my temples pounding. Apparently, the scene was passable because the press reported: "Mike Reagan joins the family business."

As most actors know, it is one thing to study acting, and another to get a job. My agent contacted every show in town, but no one wanted me. Finally I became my own agent. By the end of 1985, I had my own two-hour radio show on Sunday afternoons; I occasionally pinch hit for Michael Jackson on his syndicated radio talk show. I also became a regular guest host on *Mid Morning L.A.*, a local television show. Eventually, I got a job as a reporter on a syndicated show called, *All About Us.*

In 1986 I decided to get a new acting agent. She went down the list of television shows and reported back that the reason I hadn't been hired was that her predecessor had told the casting people that I was a "star name." He had asked for a ridiculous amount of money even though I was unknown as an actor.

"I don't care how much I get paid," I told her. "I just want to work."

One day she told me that the producers of *Capitol*, a daytime soap about hanky-panky in Washington, were interested in having me play a role as a political boss. The pay was scale: around three hundred fifty dollars a day. I knew that what they really wanted was to boost their ratings by having the President's son on the show, but by then, I didn't care. I just wanted work and a chance to prove that I could act.

I was so happy I called Mom who had always had a reputation for knowing her lines and was aptly nicknamed "One Take Wyman." She told me that it was most important for an actor to know his lines and to be on time. Although I had only a few lines on *Capitol*, I studied until I knew my lines cold. On the day I showed up for my scene on time, the press again turned out in full force.

For more than three hours, I did one interview after another. Most of the other professional actors who had been in the business for years were resentful, and with good reason. Here I was, a neophyte, getting all the attention only because of who my father was and not who I was. I didn't care. I wanted people to like me and, because of that, I got used.

After work that night Mom telephoned and asked how I did. "They asked me to come back and do another," I told her proudly.

"One question," she said. "How many takes did you need?"

"One," I said.

"At least you learned something from me," she retorted. "Good luck."

Thanks to the attention I got from *Capitol* I was offered a small role in Sylvester Stallone's film *Over the Top,* which was shooting in Las Vegas. I was scheduled to fly to Las Vegas on a Friday, shoot my scene, and return that night. My scene was delayed, and I was panicked; I am nervous when I am away from my family for more than a day at a time. Also, I had made a promise to be home, and I had never broken a promise to my kids. So I called Colleen and, after much talking, we decided I should stay the night. As luck would have it, we could not finish the scene, so the producer asked me to stay over again. Although it was my first film and I really wanted to work with Stallone, I decided to return to Los Angeles.

At the moment I was telling the executive producer of my decision, Stallone and his then wife were leaving the hotel. The producer looked at me. "Why don't you tell Mr. Stallone that you are going to quit his movie," he said testily.

With tears in my eyes, I flashed on my future in films being ruined by my decision to leave, but I had no intention of telling my children that a film was more important to me than they were; I had always felt that movies had taken my parents away from me. I went to Stallone and told him that I appreciated a chance to be in his movie, but I was leaving because I had promised my children that I would be home. "If I break that promise now on my first film, by my tenth movie I won't care if I have a family anymore."

Stallone turned from me and told the executive producer, "I like this man and I like what he stands for; and if I were him, I'd do the same thing." Stallone then told me, "Go home to your kids. Tell them I care about them and that I care about you, and when I do my next movie, I want you in it."

I felt thirty feet tall when I got on the plane for Los Angeles. I knew I had done the right thing.

Soon after that I landed a featured role in the movie *Cyclone,* with Heather Thomas. It wasn't much of a film, but I received good reviews for the three scenes I had with Tim Conway, Jr.

My agent began calling the casting people at *Falcon Crest* to ask if they would allow me to read for them. She was told that they couldn't hire me without Mom's okay because she was the boss as well as the star. But no one dared to ask her about me. Finally, I called Mom myself. "Your casting people have said they would like to have me on your show, but no one is willing to ask you if it's all right. Will you please tell them it's OK to hire me."

"I'd love to," she said.

257

Soon after that my agent called me and, to my surprise, said, "Miss Jane Wyman has requested your presence on her set. The producers will see you and tell you what part you will be playing."

I went to the studio and was given a script. Then I was told when to report on the set. I was euphoric. I had wanted to be near Mom all during my life, but it had seemed to me that her work had always kept us apart. It had always bothered me that, even though she drove past our house every day to and from work, she never stopped to see me or the kids. I truly missed her and now, in the twilight of her career, I would have a chance to be a part of her life, and I relished the opportunity. In truth, I would have taken a job as a grip or carpenter just to be close to her.

Some of the air was let out my balloon when Mom called me that night. "I've opened the door for you," she said. "But when you come on the set, you are to keep your mouth shut. I don't want to hear who your father is or what he does. If I see one line of publicity about your being on the show or you give one interview touting your father, you'll be fired. This is my show, not Ronald Reagan's. Understand?"

I understood. I was still in the middle, between her and Dad. It had been more than three decades since they were divorced, but the antagonism was still there. I was fearful that I would be fired before I got started.

When I arrived on the set, Mom greeted me with open arms. She introduced me to most everyone and then went off to makeup and wardrobe, but when it was time for me to play my scene as concierge of her spa, she stood in a corner of the set. I knew she was watching to be certain I knew my lines. My stomach was in knots, but I needed only one take. I was signed for more of Mom's shows but always with the same admonition that I never give an interview or mention my father's name.

The exposure I got on *Falcon Crest* had an effect. I began to receive calls from various organizations and groups asking me to speak on a variety of topics. I found it difficult to say no even though I felt that people were using me. I was always chasing rainbows so I was not in a position to have a full-time manager, but I prevailed anyway on Mike Emery, a highly respected Los Angeles business lawyer who also manages people such as Chuck Norris, to take me on as a client. He agreed to act as a buffer and screen any employment offers I received. I had proved I was incapable of doing it.

The first thing Mike asked me to do was bring him a list of the things I was working on. I brought him a list of around fifteen projects which included the book offer I had discarded a couple of years previously. Mike asked me about the book and why I had turned it down.

"Because I did some soul searching," I said. "The only reason children of famous parents write negative books about their successful parents is to show that their parents are failures in at least one department—as parents. Many of those children, because they were never held accountable, go on drugs or get into trouble just to show that their parents are really not perfect and to get attention.

"The public believes that the person they see on the screen is the same person at home, and they like to read that it just isn't so, that public heroes have feet of clay. But my father is probably the only celebrity I know who is exactly the same person off screen as on. The public image of him is that he's damn near perfect, which has always been one of my hangups: I've tried to be like him, but I've never made it. It just wouldn't be fair for me to blame him for my failure."

There are so many nice things he does that no one ever sees or hears about, like the time he called my friend, Joe Bruno. Joe had just been diagnosed as having lung cancer. I went to visit him in the hospital. Joe was so gray and emaciated, but all he could talk

259

about was the President. Dad had just been operated on for colon cancer, and Joe told me to tell my dad he was praying for him. That really touched me so much that when I got home, I called my father and, in tears, told him the story. Dad asked me for Joe's phone number and, when we hung up, he called him. The doctors say it added weeks to his life because Joe had talked to his President.

"Then why don't you consider writing a positive book?" Mike suggested. "You won't get as much money from a publisher, but your story might be of interest to the public."

"Let me think it over," I said.

While I was talking about the book with Colleen, I received a call from Mark Itkin, an agent at the William Morris Agency. He had set up a meeting for me with Ralph Andrews, the producer of a new game show called *Lingo*, who was interested in having me host the show. I didn't know it then, but the producer was meeting me only as a favor to Mark. An hour after the meeting, Mark called me to say that contracts were being drawn up. I was hired! The pilot film was made the day before Thanksgiving.

Meanwhile, I had finally decided to write the book. Mike put me in touch with a writer. I soon discovered that although I wanted to write a positive book it was almost impossible; I was still nursing too many hurts and still blaming my parents and everyone else for my problems. I viewed everything that had happened to me negatively and was convinced that had I not been adopted by Ronald Reagan and Jane Wyman my life would have been different—not necessarily better but certainly different.

Through the course of the interviews with the writer, I realized that I was not being honest and never had been; I was still trying to hide the one secret that I thought would hurt me and my parents. Only if I was truthful could I also be fair to my parents. But the thought of baring my soul and my secret scared me. I still wasn't ready to be honest, not with myself or anyone else.

One afternoon my friend Bob Neill told me, "If you're going to write a book, you have to admit to the reader why you act and sometimes overreact to things that happen to you, or you're not being honest." Little did Bob know the path he was sending me down.

Soon after that discussion, Colleen and I dropped the children off at their school. We then went to a restaurant for breakfast. My mind was on the book outline and my darkest childhood memory. I was sullenly studying the menu when Colleen asked me what was troubling me.

"Nothing," I said. "I was just thinking."

"Do you want to tell me about it?"

"No, not right now. Maybe in a day or so."

As a child I had feared that my parents would kick me out of the family if they knew what I had done. Now I feared Colleen might leave me if she knew the only secret I had kept from her.

On November 6, 1986, the day before our eleventh wedding anniversary, I had coffee with Colleen in our kitchen. The confusion of my memories welled up within me, and despite myself I began to cry.

"Do you want to talk about it now?" Colleen asked.

"Yes, but I don't know where to start or what to say."

Colleen led me by the hand into the den. We sat on the couch, and she held my hand and started asking me questions. We played a cat-and-mouse game for a few minutes until she finally asked, "Did something bad happen to you when you were a child?"

"Yes," I whispered.

"When?"

"When I was very young."

"Were you molested, Michael?" she asked.

I broke down then and, with my head buried in her shoulders, sobbed out the story of the molestation and those pictures.

261

Colleen was the first person that I had ever told about that childhood experience.

Colleen pulled me into her arms and hugged me tight. "I love you, Michael, no matter what. What you've told me happened a long time ago. That was in the past and it's over."

"It's never been over," I said. "I have lived with that memory every day since then. All this time I've felt dirty."

Although Colleen didn't completely understand why I was so troubled, she was sympathetic as she tried to soothe my pain. Later, I asked her if she thought I should include the molestation story in my book.

"You've got to," she said. "There's no way you can write your life story without it because it explains so much of your behavior. Also, it has to be told in order to help other people."

I hadn't dealt well with the molestation incident during my lifetime, and if I was going to face it, I needed help. I learned that free therapy was available in Los Angeles for victims of child molestation. After my first few weeks in therapy, I came to realize that what had happened to me was not so unusual; thousands of children file reports on molestation each year but many more thousands live with the secret as I had. The majority of adults who have been sexually abused or molested as children and have never revealed it are doomed to live with their secret and its subsequent pain and anguish.

The story of my childhood misadventure was included in the book outline, although my parents were still unaware of it. I had yet to find the courage to tell them. I figured when I was finished writing the book, I would let them read it and answer questions later.

Chapter XXIV

"Nancy and I support you one hundred percent."

Palm Sunday, 1987 was the first day of the rest of my life. That was the day that Dad and Nancy had invited Colleen, the kids and me to celebrate Ashley's fourth birthday at the Santa Barbara ranch with them.

A few weeks prior to our visit, Colleen received a message from one of the Secret Service agents saying that the First Lady was trying to reach her. After days of trying to make contact with each other, Colleen and Nancy finally spoke. Nancy, who was preparing the menu for the birthday party, wanted to know if the kids liked hot dogs. Colleen and I had a big laugh over that. Nancy was able to plan dinners for the heads of state from around the world, but obviously, it had been a long time since she'd entertained children as guests.

Dad and Nancy were not aware that I was in therapy at the time, trying to deal with my bitter feelings about Mom and them. One day while in the therapist's office, it finally struck me as I was backtracking my life. All of a sudden I buried my face in my hands and broke into tears, not only for myself but for all the people I had unwittingly hurt. "If I had only told someone about the molestation when it happened, I wouldn't have lost thirty-five years of my life," I said, but then, as now, children don't know what it is that is happening to them.

"What happened to you shouldn't have happened to anyone," the therapist said. "But it doesn't make the things you've done since then right. People who were molested aren't lined up in front of my door to come in for therapy because many are still afraid of having to face themselves. At least you now are facing it and can restart your life. Think of those who never will."

I knew then that I had to tell Dad and Nancy about the molestation, but I also knew it wasn't going to be easy. On that Palm Sunday, as the three of us were out by the horse corral while the kids were walking around the pond with Colleen, I knew the moment for confession was at hand. I felt as though I was drowning. I started to stammer and then I burst into tears. I couldn't talk. I felt as though my guts were being ripped out of my body. I was shaking.

Nancy put her arms around me and began to rub the back of my neck just as she had when I was a child on the way to the ranch. But I couldn't look at her or Dad.

"Tell us," she said softly.

With my head bowed, I regurgitated the secret I had kept hidden for all those years. "I was molested by a camp counsellor," I blurted out.

"What?" asked Dad in a shocked voice.

"He was molested, honey," Nancy said.

"By who?" Dad asked.

"By a counsellor at day camp," Nancy repeated patiently.

"Who was the guy?" Dad demanded. "I'll find him and kick his butt."

"Let Mike get it out of his system, honey," Nancy told Dad firmly.

There was almost no stopping me once I started. For an hour, perhaps more, I explosively and compulsively spilled out a condensed version of all the scars of my childhood. Occasionally, I had to wipe tears from my face on a handkerchief Dad took from his hip pocket.

Bile began to rise in my stomach. Some would spill out; the rest I would swallow. I came close to vomiting more than once. Like Linda Blair, who played the demon-possessed girl in *The Exorcist,* I felt as though I was spewing green slime from my mouth.

Nancy occasionally interrupted to ask pertinent questions: How old were you? What was the name of the camp? How many days a week were you there? For how long a period of time did the molestation go on? Each question brought out more information from me.

I couldn't bring myself to look at Dad. All I could do was stare at his belt buckle. Despite my anguish and theirs, I knew that I was holding something back, that they wouldn't understand the whole story until I shared what I considered to be the worst part. I led into that by telling them that the man took nude pictures of me and made me develop them and that I always feared that those pictures would make Mom and Dad mad at me.

Dad moved closer to me. I looked up at him then for the first time and said, "Dad, he orally copulated me. He took me in his mouth." Having said that, I almost dropped to the ground with exhaustion. I felt Dad's strong arm around me.

"Why didn't you tell me about this when it happened?" he asked.

"Because I was afraid you would stop liking me."

"You should have known better," he said quietly. He was right but, as a child, I didn't know.

I finished my story only when there was nothing left unsaid, no more pain left in me. Exhausted and limp, I put my head down. Nancy hugged me again. Dad, who was at my side, put his arms around me, too.

We all embraced and went to join Colleen and the children. Nancy took me aside for a moment and said, "It would make us all feel better if we knew there were some positive things about your father in the book." I smiled: Nancy, the consummate protector.

"There are good things about Dad in the book," I said. "What I'm happy about is that there are also good things to write about you." Nancy looked stunned, but she understood what I was saying.

When we were at our car saying good-bye, Nancy hugged me again. "The hardest thing was to get it out of your system," she said. "From this point on, it will be easier." She and Dad then hugged Colleen and the children. Colleen and I later agreed that it felt like the first real hug they had given either of us in years.

That day was the first time I had ever been totally honest with Nancy and Dad. It was a major breakthrough in our relationship, and especially important for me because I had also confronted myself for the first time.

Two days later, I left for Washington D.C. with my family to spend Easter week sight-seeing and to attend the Easter egg hunt on the White House lawn. Dad had told me that much as he wanted to be at the Easter festivities he felt that if he were there, the forty thousand or more people who show up for the annual event would have to be screened through metal detectors, and he didn't feel that was fair to them.

That week in Washington was the first time that I didn't feel as though I were an impostor. Immediately after we returned home, I called Dad, who was back at the White House, to thank him for arranging everything for us. I also told him how much it meant to Colleen and me for him and Nancy to listen to my story.

"Nancy and I have had a lot of time to talk over what you told us, and I want you to know that it was almost as hard on us to hear those things as it was for you to tell them to us. To think that you have been living with all that for thirty-five years pains me."

"Then you're not upset that I am writing a book," I said.

"On the contrary," he said firmly. "Nancy and I support you one hundred percent, and we hope that your book will be of benefit to other children."

I felt as though a load had been lifted from my shoulders.

The following week I received word that some of the CBS "O' and O's" had picked up *Lingo,* the game show for which I had done the pilot. We would be on the air five days a week across the board, starting in September, 1987. It seemed as if everything was headed in the right direction.

Then, the first week in May, I learned that a gossip columnist for a sleazy publication had somehow gained access to the outline for my book and intended to publish the story of my molestation. That meant the national press would undoubtedly pick up the story. My worst fears were about to be realized.

I immediately called Nancy to warn her. I told her that Dale Olson, my publicist, had advised me not to make any comment, to say only, "Read the book."

"I don't think that's good enough for us," Nancy said. "I feel that your father and I should make a stronger statement (probably because Nancy is National Chairperson of Child Help U.S.A., an organization that deals with abused children). We are going to say that we support your book and that we hope that your tragic story will be of help to other children." She also said that she

267

would tell the other Reagan children about the molestation so they would not be surprised.

The next day Maureen called me to tell me she loved me and understood why I had never told her. She also told me she now knew why I hated green because the haze that comes off developing fluids is green, a color I had seen that frightful day.

It was the first time since Dad had become president that the White House had ever made a public statement in support of anything I had done, and I was elated. But I knew I still had to tell my mother about the upcoming story, too.

I was apprehensive as I dialed the phone. When Mom answered, I was shaking all over as I tried to think of a way to break through that outer layer of her character. All I could say was "Mom, I really have to talk with you sometime within the next two days at your convenience." I told her I'd meet her anywhere, at anytime.

Mom repeated what she had told me before. "I'm busy. You can tell me anything you want over the phone."

"Mom, this is something I can't say on the phone."

"Well, that's just what you're going to have to do," she said.

Telling Dad and Nancy had been difficult. Telling Mom was almost impossible. I took a deep breath and thought, it was now or never. "Mom, I was sexually molested by a camp counsellor when I was seven years old."

"What did you say?"

I repeated it. There was silence on her end of the line. Finally, she said, "I guess I have to believe you because you are telling me." She paused a moment. "I assume you already told your father and Nancy. What do they think about that in Washington?"

"They're supportive of me and my book."

"Well, that shows how good their judgment is," she retorted.

There was another long silence. Mom finally said, "Michael, we do need to talk. Can you come to the studio or meet me at my home?"

"Just tell me when," I said.

"I'll be in touch," Mom said and hung up. A few days later she called Colleen and cancelled Mother's Day with me and the kids.

When the article broke in May, 1987, it was, as I had feared and anticipated, excerpted from the magazine by press and broadcast media. That was bad enough, but the *National Enquirer* had a picture of my family and me on their front cover with a headline: "Family Feud Over Tell-All Book by President's Son." The subhead read: "Outraged Nancy Bans Michael Reagan From The White House." Even though I had admitted the molestation to my family, I was not strong enough to handle the devastating stories in the press.

I have kept a daily journal from time to time, and my entries for the period tell what I went through.

5.14.87—Reliving molestation through *Enquirer* article and CBS news report. The article tells how I got kicked out of the family for telling I was molested, which is why I never told my parents in the first place. Other molested kids reading this will fear that if they tell what happened to them they, too, will be kicked out of their families.

5.18.87—More calls about that *Enquirer* article. I keep having to defend myself because it is false. Even while in Nebraska visiting Colleen's family, people asked me about the article. I've been embarrassed to walk into a grocery store all week. When I do, I want to hide.

Received a nice positive letter yesterday from a woman with a twelve-year-old adopted son who had been molested by his father. I feel the weight of these kids.

5.20.87—*Enquirer* finally off the counters, thank God. I didn't want to go out at all during the week for fear someone would recognize me. Everything has been so positive recently, but now

I'm back in a negative mode. I thought about killing myself today. Why doesn't Mom love me?

5.22.87—Jim H. called today. He is spokesman for one of my sponsors, and he told me that because of the *Enquirer* article, his people don't feel they want to sponsor me again. How mean, punishing me for that article.

6.3.87—All my anger has come back during these past two weeks. It's like I've been caught in the act and I can't explain myself. I've been taking my anger out on my family. I pray that it isn't true that abused children tend to grow up to be abusers themselves. I realize that I can no longer deal with my inner anger alone. The only place I can put it is on the shoulders of Christ. Please God, give me strength to heal my anger.

The following week, I got the surprise of my life when Nancy called and asked if she could visit. Nancy had never visited our home in Sherman Oaks before and I was excited that she was coming by to see Colleen, me and the kids. She stayed for two hours and we talked about the article and the book. But what meant the most was the picture she brought of Dad and Nelle Reagan. Until then, I had never had a picture of my grandmother, the one who started us all in church. I don't know if I said it then, but thank you, Nancy, for that day.

Epilogue

I make no apologies for presenting what is undoubtedly a one-sided view of my life. After all, it is my story. I have told it the way I recall it, just as a person in analysis usually recalls only the pains and traumas of childhood and has difficulty recalling the good times. Given a choice of seeing an event from the eyes of another person or my own myopic perception, I invariably weighed the scales in favor of my predilection for seeing most everything that happened to me as punishment.

By virtue of therapy and the soul-searching necessary to write this book, I realized that I had to discard my crutches if ever I was to become a whole person. But that meant I had to start at the beginning with the circumstances of my birth. I never tried to find my birth mother because I was afraid that anything I found out would only confirm my worst suspicions. And I had convinced myself that my adoptive parents would be upset if I tried to find my birth parents, a not unreasonable fear on the part of many adopted children.

When I finally decided to learn about my heritage, as much for myself as for my children who also need to know their roots, I contacted Annette Baran, author and expert on adoption. With her help I composed a letter which I sent to Mom.

The letter read:

Dear Mom:

I know how you feel about unexpected surprises, and I want to spare you; therefore this letter.

All the years of my growing up, I have been very aware of how you feel about the past, ancestors, relatives, family, prying questions, etc. I know the degree of your sensitivity and desire for privacy, and I have tried to respect the importance of that in your life. I want you to trust that I would never violate or try to invade that area.

My needs, however, are very different from yours, and I am asking you to try to understand the reasons why I now feel the importance of finding my roots. As you know, this past year I have been involved with writing my book. During this time, I have become more and more aware of how much I need to search for my birth parents so that I may be able to answer a great many questions for myself and my children. These questions have nothing to do with my love and devotion to you as my mother. Instead, they are concerned with other issues: medical, ethnic, cultural, etc. I am not asking you to help me unless you want to. If you wish to share information with me from my adoption file, I would be extremely grateful, but otherwise I can find the information by diligent searching. That is not important. What is important is that you try to understand why I am trying to find out the facts of my background, and realize that it is for my needs and has nothing to do with my lasting love for you.

Mom was predictably silent. I could only assume that she was still dealing with her own ghosts of the past. I had not heard from her since I told her on the phone that I had been molested. Three weeks later, I sent a copy of the letter with a note to Dad. He responded immediately by putting me in touch with a member of Governor Deukmejian's staff who suggested I write directly to the Department of Social Services in Sacramento.

Once I started the search for my birth mother, an incredible series of events occurred almost simultaneously. My letter to Sacramento brought an immediate response: a six-page, single-spaced report dated September 28, 1987. The report contained a synopsis of a social worker's interview with my birth mother on May 3, 1945, a few weeks after I was born.

My birth mother, who was not identified by name, told the social worker that she was born in Kentucky of "an American mixture." She was one of ten children with seven brothers and two sisters and was raised as a Protestant. According to the social worker, my mother was five feet three inches tall, weighed one hundred fifteen pounds and was attractive. She told the social worker that everyone in her family played musical instruments and sang. She had an alto voice and sang in the church choir in her home town. She also played the piano and the saxophone. She had been married for five years and was divorced. At the time of my birth, she was twenty-eight years old and was working as a waitress and actress in Hollywood.

She described my father as being her age and from Kentucky or Ohio. He had been raised as a Catholic and was of German-

American parentage. A college graduate with a major in psychology, he was a cadet in the U.S. Army Air Corps where he was also a swimming and boxing instructor. My mother described him as being six feet one inch tall and extremely handsome with green eyes and light brown hair.

The story of my birth parents' romance is contained in one brief paragraph right out of a romance novel or soap opera. "According to your birth mother, your birth father was married at the time of your birth. She stated that he had plans of divorcing his wife and marrying your birth mother. However, he was sent overseas before he could obtain the divorce and marry your birth mother." When I read this, I thought how little men's lines to women have changed over the years.

There was also information about the health of both of my birth parents as well as their parents. My mother told the social worker that she was "strong as an ox" and her parents were in good health and in their seventies. My paternal grandfather was dead (cause unknown), but my paternal grandmother was alive. Those facts put to rest one of my major fears about my heritage—I had inherited good genes if not a full head of hair.

What caused my heart to sing, however, was a full page of the adoption report describing the *Circumstances of Placement*. I quote it in its entirety: "Your birth mother told the social worker that she wanted to keep you. However, she stated that it would have been impossible to raise you out of wedlock in her hometown. Therefore, she made the decision to place you in an adoptive home. According to your birth mother, the members of her family had no knowledge of her pregnancy or your birth. The social worker noted that your birth mother had a genuine attachment for you.

"Your birth mother stated that your birth father knew that she was pregnant. She told the social worker that he paid for her transportation to California, and he paid for her medical and hospital expenses. Additionally, he approved of the plan to place you in an adoptive home.

"When the social worker inquired about the arrangement of your placement, she stated that she heard your adoptive parents were looking for a child. At first your birth mother did not want to know the identity of the adoptive parents. However, the social worker informed her that the nature of the independent adoption program was to place her child with someone she knew. Therefore, your adoptive parents were revealed to your birth mother when she signed the consent to adopt form.

"Your birth mother stated that your adoptive mother came to the hospital to meet her. Your birth mother told the social worker that she talked to your adoptive mother awhile. Your birth mother told the social worker that a major portion of the conversation was centered around your birth mother's and birth father's backgrounds and his physical characteristics. According to your birth mother, she liked your adoptive mother and was happy to let her take you home. Your birth mother told the social worker that she recognized your adoptive mother but kept the information to herself."

I can imagine the scene between the two women in a tension-filled room: my birth mother, her heart fluttering with fear and intimidated by the beautiful actress sitting opposite her, trying to make a good impression and praying that Jane would adopt her son and give him the good home she could never provide; Jane, in charge as always, calmly asking questions about the backgrounds of my mother and father, nodding approvingly at the happy coincidences: my birth father was tall, handsome and a champion swimmer like Dad. Both birth parents came of good solid American stock and were a Protestant-Catholic mix as were Dad's parents.

When the brief interview ended, I suspect that the women tearfully embraced, each shedding tears for different reasons. My birth mother was giving up her child while Jane was getting the son she could not have herself but so much wanted for her husband's sake.

I had always been told that I had been adopted through an agency so my mother would never know the identity of the birth parents. It was typical of Mom not to admit that she had met my birth mother. Perhaps she felt it would have made me less her son.

My adoption papers were finalized on November 29, 1945, seven months after I was brought home by the Kaplans.

When I put the report down, I felt a strange sense of calm. For the first time in my life, I realized that my birth mother loved me. I don't mean that Mom and Dad didn't love me, but the day I read the social worker's report was the first day that I *felt* loved. Until then, I had thought my birth mother didn't want me and had just given me away. I wasn't aware of the pain that she had suffered by putting me up for adoption. Looking back, I now realize that there was nothing Mom and Dad could have done to get me to believe that they loved me—no matter what they gave to me or did for me—because I wouldn't accept it. Without being aware of it, theirs was not the love I wanted or needed. I was searching for my birth mother's love.

I read and reread the six-page report, committing sections of it to memory. It was the closest I had ever gotten to my real mother. All of my life I had been filled with anger at her for giving me up. In my mind she was little better than a whore because she'd had sex out of wedlock. That interview which took place forty-two years ago proved that my birth mother didn't want to give me up until she met and approved of the woman who was going to raise her child.

I was suddenly aware that the book I was writing was actually for my birth mother, to give her an account of what had happened to me since the day she put me up for adoption. I wanted to say,

"Look, Mom, this is what happened to me because you gave me away. I was hurting all my life, I was molested, I never thought that my adoptive parents loved me and I didn't love them. It was all your fault."

I wanted to let my birth mother know where I was and who I am. Now that was no longer necessary. She had known about me and my whereabouts all of my life. She had probably lived with the pain of having given me up every day of her life. At the same time, she must have been happy that she had made the right decision because her child became the son of the President of the United States. Every time she saw me on television or read about me, however, it must have been difficult for her not to admit to anyone that I was her son.

Now, instead of hating her and wanting to ask her why she gave me up, I wanted to say simply, "Mom, I missed you" and to hear her reply, "No more than I missed you." God, how I missed the mother I never knew.

Until I read the adoption report, I had always felt that I had an emptiness in my heart. That emptiness has finally been filled. The sense of calm and joy stayed with me for the rest of that week as I prepared to go to Vancouver, Canada where my game show, *Lingo*, was to be taped.

It was in Vancouver on October 6, 1987 that a most uncanny series of events unfolded, which again proves to me that God moves in mysterious ways. That day of taping had been particularly traumatic for me. The show's producer learned that one of our contestants was born of a wartime love affair. She had just found out that her real father lived in Australia. She had come on the show, hoping to win one of the trips we give away or to win enough money to pay for her trip to Australia to meet her father for the first time.

The producer and I talked it over. He told me that whether the contestant won or lost I was to tell her on the air that we knew why she was on the show and that we at *Lingo* would send her on an all-expenses-paid trip to Australia to meet her father.

She did win the game and a trip. As we moved to the bonus round area of the show, my thoughts were still on the information I had received from Sacramento. It was then that I told her what we planned to do. We both cried over her joy at the news that we were sponsoring her trip. I envied her. At least she had found her father!

In my hotel room that night, I was unable to fall asleep. I never before called my answering machine in Los Angeles for messages at midnight, but on this night I did. There was one message. "Mike, this is Margie," a female voice said. "I was a bridesmaid at your wedding to Julie. If you want some information about your birth family, call me back." She left a telephone number in Orange County, California.

I tossed and turned for the rest of that night, my mind a turmoil of thoughts and speculations. Promptly at nine A.M. the following morning, I telephoned Margie, who said, "While I was on a business trip to Ohio recently, I met a young man who says he is your half brother. His name is Barry, and I think he's telling the truth. On his mother's death bed a year and a half ago, she told him that he had a half brother. It is you."

I gasped aloud at the news. My mother was dead.

"Are you all right?" Margie asked.

"I'm fine," I said, but as a Reagan I was accustomed to people wanting to use me for their own reasons, so I was cautious. "What else did he tell you?"

"His mother said that the reason she had never told him before about you was that she was afraid that if he knew about you he would think badly of her.

"At first Barry didn't believe her. Then he remembered that all during his mother's life she had kept scrapbooks on the Reagan family. He always thought that his mother, who had been an actress in Hollywood, had had an affair with Ronald Reagan. But when he went through the scrapbooks, he found that you were included in all the pictures and stories.

"He didn't know whether or not you were looking for your family or how you would react if he contacted you. He had the information, but he didn't know what to do with it until he met me. When I happened to mention that I knew you, he turned white and asked if I would relay the information to you. Do you want me to follow up on it?"

I sat on my bed in total shock. My mind and heart were racing as I went to the dresser drawer where I kept the adoption report and scanned it. My mouth was dry as I told Margie hoarsely that I had a few questions to relay to Barry which would quickly determine the validity of his story. "Ask him if he knows the color of my mother's eyes. Where was she born? How many members were in her family? How old was she when I was born?" I also asked the key question which only Barry might be able to answer: "And what was my birth name?"

My heart was pounding so much that I went to a nearby gym to work out. I wanted to calm down before Margie called back. She was on the phone again within the hour. We went down the list of questions. Barry's answers tallied with every detail in the social worker's report except for one. When I asked for my mother's name, Margie said, "Her acting name in Hollywood was Betty Arnold."

That name meant nothing to me, so I asked Margie if Barry knew my mother's maiden name.

"Irene Flaugher." She pronounced it as in flower.

"Spell it," I said.

Margie spelled it out for me as had Nancy on that long ago day. My heart pounded as I asked my last question:

"Does Barry know my birth name?"

279

"John," she said.

"Tell Barry he has found his brother."

Everything had happened too fast for us to feel ready to talk directly, so we hid behind Margie, who acted as liaison. I learned that Barry, an only child, was seven years my junior. He didn't have any information about my father, but we have an aunt and two uncles in Florida who are in their eighties and who supposedly know the entire story. Barry said that I looked just like my Uncle Jim. That news staggered and delighted me. I looked like my mother's side of the family! To an adoptee who had no roots and identity, it's terribly important to find out that you look like a blood relative.

The most important thing of all to me, however, was the fact that my mother's last thoughts were of me! All of my life I had fantasized that maybe when Dad or Jane were on their death beds they would think of me. In my fantasies about dying in a boat crash, I visualized my parents standing over my grave and saying, "Mike died a hero." Those fantasies were the only way I could have felt love. Now I learned that even though my mother had given me up for adoption forty-two years ago she never forgot me just as I never forgot her.

Margie arranged for Barry and me to meet privately at a friend's house in California away from the prying eyes of the press, which would undoubtedly have made a circus of the son of the President having a first meeting with his half brother.

On the day we were to meet, I was filled with a sense of trepidation, my mind filled with troubling thoughts: Would I like Barry? Would he like me? What kind of guy is he? Would he look like me? I arrived early for our meeting and paced the floor anxiously. When the doorbell rang, I hesitated to go to the door, still fearful that I had made a mistake in arranging the meeting. Barry's face was ashen color when our eyes met. Suddenly he was in my arms and we hugged. All my fears disappeared. This was my brother, no doubt about it.

Barry is my height with the same body-build even to the slouched shoulders. Except for the fact that his eyes are blue and mine are brown, we have the same facial features and coloration even in our hair—but he has more.

Within minutes we were talking like old friends. There was an instant bond between us. We shared information about our mother. He told me what he knew, and I gave him the report I had received from the state. He had brought with him family scrapbooks as well as the scrapbook our mother had kept of me. I pored over those pictures. As a matter of fact, most of the early pictures included in this book are from that scrapbook.

Together we called our mother's older sister, Aunt Margaret, in Florida. She said that my mother would have been hurt to read that I had been molested. I was glad that her death on December 26, 1985 had at least spared her that.

During our conversation, I told Barry that I was going to go to church that night and then have dinner with some friends.

"Cholesterol," Barry said. "Watch your cholesterol."

"What do you mean?" I asked.

"Every person in our family who has died before seventy years of age, including our mother, has had a heart attack due to high cholesterol. If you make it past seventy, you may live forever."

Interestingly, although I am in good shape because I work out three days a week, my biggest problem has always been my high cholesterol level.

We went for a drive together, and I showed him the house on Beverly Glen Boulevard where I grew up. I told him about the Freibergs who lived next door.

"Are you talking about Fred Freiberg who used to manage the Bullocks store in the Valley?" he asked.

"Yes," I said.

"I used to work for him," Barry said. We discovered that Barry, who had once worked as a writer for the show *Happy Days*, had lived in Sherman Oaks less than a mile from my house. For more than a year we had lived less than a mile from each other! Another coincidence: He has been married for eleven years, and I have been married for the same length of time. He has a seven-year-old son and my son Cameron is nine. He had married a Barbara, while Colleen and I were introduced by a Barbara.

We sat outside the house talking for about fifteen minutes as I took him verbally through it, telling him about the laundry chute, pointing out Maureen's bedroom and mine, and the tree I climbed down when Mom sent me to my room. But I never told him about the bad things, only the good. It was as though I had been cleansed of the cruel memories. It was the first time in my life that I had ever shown off the house proudly.

Barry told me that our mother Irene had been extremely proud of the fact that my adoptive father had gone on to become president. And whenever I was on television, Irene would pull up a chair and insist on quiet while she stared at the set. "I never understood why until she died," Barry said. "If mother had any inkling that you wanted to meet her, I am sure she would have been on the next plane to California."

Not only had I found a brother, but I found roots, more than I could ever have imagined. Barry showed me a yellowed copy of a news story about my maternal great-grandmother's death in 1938 at the age of ninety-one. At that time, this remarkable woman had fifty-seven grandchildren, one hundred and one great-grandchildren and six great-great-grandchildren.

I think that Barry may have been even more affected by our meeting than I was. I always knew that I had a mother someplace, but until recently, he never knew that he had a brother. He told me of nights that he played with the other kids in his neighborhood

282

and his mother called him to come home for dinner. He went home to his parents, and although he loved them, he was always jealous because most of his friends had brothers and sisters and he was an only child. He told me that he was elated to discover he had a brother, but what was more important to him, his son had an uncle. That simple statement made me feel great; I was wanted as part of a family.

Before we parted company that night, I asked Barry where our mother was buried. He told me the gravesite was in Ohio. "Let's visit her together so she can finally be with her boys," I said. Barry agreed.

At the doorway, Barry and I embraced. I somehow felt closer to him then than I have ever felt to Maureen, Patti or Ron, Jr. It's not their fault. It's just that Barry and I share someone special, the same mother.

Although my mother is dead, the umbilical cord that joined us was never completely severed. Perhaps it's just as well that we never met during her lifetime. This way I will always remember her as a frightened twenty-eight-year-old girl who wanted the best for her baby. There are no warts on that image. I now have only an image of love. I hope that when my mother died at the age of sixty-nine she had found peace.

When an adoptee says he doesn't think anybody in his adoptive family truly loves him, I now know that's because adopted children are usually insecure. You can give a child to another family, but that doesn't necessarily make him or her a part of it. My parents did their best to make me feel loved, but I needed to know who I really was in order to accept their love. Maybe now that I have found myself it will be easier for me to accept the love that my parents have been trying to give me for all these years.

One of my ghosts has been exorcised, but I still have another to

283

deal with. Some time ago, Bob Likes, my Bible study teacher, told the class, "Never let someone else determine your attitude for the rest of the day." As he said those words, I realized that my molester had determined much of my attitude since I was seven years old. At that time I was not ready to confront the past. Only after I had found my mother did I feel capable of putting that last ghost to rest.

Of course I remember the counsellor's first name, but I have forgotten his surname. The day camp's files do not go back to 1953, so I have been stymied in my search for him. I know that by now he is probably in his late sixties and very probably a grandfather. Statistics indicate that many sexual abuses are committed by men of that age, so I am still trying to find his last name in order to enter it in a computerized list of child sex abusers.

For years I have thought about what I would say and do were we to meet each other again. For a long time I imagined that in such a confrontation, I would thrash him. Now I suspect that I would probably tell him that I feel sorry for him and that I was praying for him and suggest he seek help so that he doesn't continue to hurt young children.

For the first time in my life I am trying to function without my crutches, standing on my own two feet. I still wobble occasionally, all too willing to blame some aberration of behavior or flash of anger on the past. Then I realize that if I am truly to be my own man I must forget about the past and live in the present.

The timing is fortunate. Dad will soon be out of office. After my father became president, people constantly asked me what I planned to do when he was out of office. In their view, everything I had done was based on my being his son. To some extent, that was true. But I have already started to try and drive a straight line path to my future, and I look forward to being completely on my own.

The nicest thing to happen to me in years took place recently in Vancouver. A lady in the studio audience came up to me after a show and asked for an autograph. She glanced at my signature. "You spell your last name the same way as the President," she said. "Are you related to him by any chance?" "Yes," I said proudly, and then I kissed her on the cheek. She had made my day.

The future looks bright. *Lingo* is already in several markets and is being hailed as one of the upcoming new daytime shows. My manager, Mike Emery, calls me daily with offers for acting roles and speaking engagements.

I have a new-found confidence in myself. This book has been a difficult one to write, and I am proud of having made it through the sometimes harrowing memories. I hope that my story will help other adoptees and their parents with their problems. As a result of some of the advance publicity I have received, I have been asked to talk to youngsters who have been abused and molested. It's hard to understand the problems of these children unless you have walked in these kid's shoes as I have. I have also spoken about the problems of the adoptee with many parents of adopted children. What I see in my own parents is that they tend to blame themselves: But it was nobody's fault.

I am currently trying to start an organization that will counsel the parents of molested children just as Alanon counsels the families of alcoholics. The children have a common bond. The parents need to know their children are dying a little bit inside every day and they can help bring them back to life. Maybe that is my ministry. Perhaps that's what God had in mind for me during all those trying years.

A few months ago, Dave Miller, the new pastor of our church, gave a sermon on anger, using James 1:19, 20 from the Bible as a reference. I listened as he spoke of anger ruling your life and the effect it could have. I knew it was time for anger to stop ruling me and, now that I am ridding myself of the constant anger that plagued me for most of my life, I have found an inner peace that I never had before. I am relating better to my own children. I relish being with them during their childhood. I have also started to try and build a new relationship with Dad and Nancy in preparation for the day when he will no longer be the father to the nation but just a father and grandfather. Although I still haven't spoken with Mom, I hope that she will come to realize that I love her more than ever.

I realize now that all during my childhood I never told my parents that I loved them and I never appreciated the love that they gave to me. However, the most important thing I have learned from examining my life is that if we children are to survive we must first learn to forgive our parents and hopefully our parents will also forgive us.

Thanks, Mom and Dad!
Love,
Mike